DRAMATHERAPY FOR BORDERLINE PERSONALITY DISORDER

Dramatherapy for Borderline Personality Disorder: Empowering and Nurturing People Through Creativity demonstrates how dramatherapy can empower those individuals struggling to live with borderline personality disorder (BPD), and help them embrace and control the emotional inner chaos they experience.

Based on current research into the aetiology, symptoms and co-morbid disorders associated with BPD (and emotionally unstable personality disorder), this book demonstrates the effectiveness of dramatherapy for individuals and groups on specialist personality disorder wards and in mixed diagnosis rehabilitation units. It also reveals a creative approach for making dramatherapy work in harmony with approaches such as dialectical behaviour therapy and cognitive behaviour therapy.

Aimed at those working with service users, and utilising a range of case studies and clinical vignettes, *Dramatherapy for Borderline Personality Disorder* provides insight into the potential of dramatherapy, which will be welcomed by mental health professionals.

Nicky Morris is an HCPC registered dramatherapist and BADth member, who has worked in NHS and private mental health services for thirteen years, predominantly with women diagnosed with BPD.

Dramatherapy: Approaches, Relationships, Critical Ideas
Series Editor: Dr Anna Seymour

This series brings together leading practitioners and researchers in the field of dramatherapy to explore the practices, thinking and evidence base for dramatherapy.

Each volume focuses on a particular aspect of dramatherapy practice, its application with a specific client group, an exploration of a particular methodology or approach or the relationship between dramatherapy and related field(s) of practice, all informed by ongoing critical analysis of existing and emergent theoretical ideas.

This series will be essential reading for trainee dramatherapists, arts practitioners and academic researchers engaged in multidisciplinary enquiry.

In this series:

Dramatherapy and Autism
Edited by Deborah Haythorne and Anna Seymour

Dramatherapy for Borderline Personality Disorder
Empowering and Nurturing People Through Creativity
Nicky Morris

For more information about this series, please visit: www.routledge.com/mentalhealth/series/DRAMA

DRAMATHERAPY FOR BORDERLINE PERSONALITY DISORDER

Empowering and Nurturing People Through Creativity

Nicky Morris

Routledge
Taylor & Francis Group

LONDON AND NEW YORK

First published 2018
by Routledge
2 Park Square, Milton Park, Abingdon, Oxon OX14 4RN

and by Routledge
711 Third Avenue, New York, NY 10017

Routledge is an imprint of the Taylor & Francis Group, an informa business

British Library Cataloguing-in-Publication Data
A catalogue record for this book is available from the British Library

Library of Congress Cataloging-in-Publication Data
Names: Morris, Nicky, author.
Title: Dramatherapy for borderline personality disorder : empowering and
    nurturing people through creativity / Nicky Morris.
Other titles: Dramatherapy (Series)
Description: Abingdon, Oxon ; New York, NY : Routledge, 2018. |
    Series: Dramatherapy | Includes bibliographical references and index.
Identifiers: LCCN 2018002571 | ISBN 9781138285903 (hardback : alk.
    paper) | ISBN 9781138285910 (pbk. : alk. paper) |
    ISBN 9781315210926 (ebk) | ISBN 9781351811132 (epub) |
    ISBN 9781351811125 (mobipocket)
Subjects: MESH: Psychodrama | Borderline Personality Disorder—therapy
Classification: LCC RC489.P7 | NLM WM 430.5.P8 |
    DDC 616.89/1523—dc23
LC record available at https://lccn.loc.gov/2018002571

ISBN: 978-1-138-28590-3 (hbk)
ISBN: 978-1-138-28591-0 (pbk)
ISBN: 978-1-315-21092-6 (ebk)

Typeset in Bembo
by Apex CoVantage, LLC

Dedicated to the memory of my late mother, Sandra Jean Marks, who encouraged my creativity and inspired me to become the person I am.

CONTENTS

ACKNOWLEDGEMENTS

This book was inspired by the experience of working creatively with hundreds of women, struggling with internal demons and predominantly diagnosed with borderline personality disorder. During the past few years, whilst working towards the formation of this book, many of these women have been very supportive and were keen for their creative work, feedback and dramatherapy experiences to be included. Regarding more specific examples, numerous clients gave written consent. Their identities remain confidential throughout the text and they have all received pseudonyms, with no reference made to any locations or identifiable data.

There are ten colleagues I would like to thank for their contributions. Each took the time to complete detailed questionnaires and the first three offered further support and feedback: Georgia Ntzimani (occupational therapist), Preeti Gour (ward doctor) and Kevin Healy (ward consultant and medical director). Also, Margaret Gyasiaddo (social worker), Kosi Nojaduka (ward manager), Maria Bermeo (health care assistant and DBT therapist), Menat Abdoun (registered mental health nurse), Julie Johnson (assistant psychologist), Dina Vara (occupational therapist) and Sherlyne Howell (unit manager).

I would also like to thank the thirteen dramatherapists (from across the UK) who responded to my request for research participants and completed detailed questionnaires. Many also answered further questions: Ruth Beesley, Alison Gilmore, Catherine Goodwin, Claire Powis, Debra Colkett, Gillian Downie, Holly Dwyer Hall, Jo Noble, Kairo Maynard, Katie Richardson, Marta Paglioni, Ryan Campinho and one dramatherapist who chose to remain anonymous.

I would not have been able to write this book without the support and guidance of Anna Seymour (the series editor), Kate McCormack (my clinical supervisor of the past fifteen years), the team at Routledge and those who originally tutored me at Roehampton University. I would also like to thank the many individuals who have given me love and support throughout this process: my friends and family, particularly my loving husband, Simon, and our two beautiful daughters, Lucy and Ella.

FOREWORD

It is a privilege to write the foreword to this much-needed book.

There is no 'cure' for borderline personality disorder and for years it was not considered treatable. This has been challenged in recent years and now NHS Choices (website), The Department of Health and National Institute for Health and Care Excellence guidelines recommend the implementation of arts therapies, including dramatherapy for BPD.

In this book Nicky Morris, a dramatherapist and expert in this field, recounts her work with this population of clients. Her ability to have enduring compassion and empathy for this often maligned group of people needed to be written about. As Nicky writes in the introduction to this book, "They have suffered enough and this is a crucial part of the motivation for writing this book".

The book is the first of its kind to explore the use of dramatherapy in assisting those with BPD to find solace, to understand themselves further, and to find elements of peace and some meaning in their lives through creative expression. The clients' pain is often expressed through maladjusted behaviour, including at times life-threatening self-harm. This pain that is so bonded with self means that change requires a new identity, which can be uniquely explored through dramatherapy to alter and incorporate new ways of being. Dramatherapy offers the possibility of finding meaning where the tussle between life and death is paramount, particularly through the exploration of story and myth. Self-harm, so often at the core of this disorder, has many reasons and effects but brutally reveals and communicates the pain and distress of the person. Nicky cites Kellogg and Young describing the life of a person with BPD as "a kind of inner theater in which the forces of cruelty, rage, submission, and self-numbing each take their turn on the stage". Dramatherapy offers a space through the medium of drama and theatre to try out other ways of managing the trauma.

Other therapies used in the treatment of BPD are documented, together with the history of dramatherapy. The huge and very real impact on practitioners working with this client group and ways to manage the anxiety and maintain hope in the face of adversity are discussed. Self-harm and challenges to relationships through fear and mistrust can be very difficult for the therapist to withstand and Nicky writes of the struggle of practitioners working with these people who have 'experienced such depth of emotional pain' – how such valiant efforts can be met with recurring symptoms and subsequent lack of hope. Nicky does not shy away from exploring the grief so many of these clients have felt and feel and the reality of death in a population of people where one of ten completes suicide.

This book beautifully tells the story of Nicky's work with these traumatised people and gives voice to those with BPD, incorporating poems and words from service users. This enormously important book is written by a dramatherapist, poet, actor and mother who meets her clients with her uniqueness as a human being and most of all her love.

Kate McCormack
Senior Dramatherapist at The Bethlem Royal Hospital

PART 1

Definitions, history, theory and treatment options

1

INTRODUCTION

Colliding emotions
Held within a creative vessel
Identity fused with pain
Disentangle
See oneself through new eyes
—*N. Morris, 2016*

This book demonstrates the positive impact of dramatherapy on individuals with borderline personality disorder (BPD), enabling them to gain new perspectives and to distinguish between their emotional pain and core selves. Historically spurned by the health care system, this client group presents a significant challenge to mental health services and effective interventions are vital. Dramatherapy has the capacity to embrace and contain the inner turmoil they often experience, described by Kellogg and Young as "a kind of inner theater in which the forces of cruelty, rage, submission, and self-numbing each take their turn on the stage" (2006, p. 447). For thirteen years, I have facilitated safe and stimulating dramatherapy sessions, in which clients are able to explore their inner selves, express themselves freely and interact playfully – a process that enables positive transformation.

I do not work in isolation and it is the combined effort of many individuals across various disciplines (as well as supportive friends or family) which genuinely helps people towards recovery. This includes RMNs (registered mental health nurses), HCAs (health care assistants), OTs (occupational therapists), OTAs (occupational therapy assistants), ward doctors, consultant psychiatrists, psychologists, clinical managers and social workers. Working within a multidisciplinary team has its challenges, however, and it is vital that colleagues support one another, take care of their own mental and physical health needs and fully utilise supervision. As Holloway and Seebohm acknowledge:

Our workplace can often feel difficult, competitive and isolating. But we do not want to lose sight of the possibility of restoring, maintaining or finding more creative, collaborative and relational ways of working, which are implicit in the roots of our profession, and find their potential expression in the theatrical notion of 'ensemble'.

(2011, p. 5)

This is the first dramatherapy book to focus predominantly on BPD and is intended for clinicians, service managers, commissioners and students. It will demonstrate the effectiveness of dramatherapy for individuals and groups on specialist personality disorder wards and in mixed-diagnosis rehabilitation units. It will reveal how dramatherapy also works in harmony with approaches such as DBT (dialectical behaviour therapy), CBT (cognitive behaviour therapy) and OT (occupational therapy), as well as treatment models such as MBT (mentalisation-based therapy), TFP (transference-focused psychotherapy) and ST (schema therapy).

Although women with BPD are at the centre of this book, the plight of men is also considered. Whilst their methods of self-harm and levels of emotional distress are thought to be similar, men with BPD have distinctly different personality traits, co-morbidities and use of treatment (Sansone and Sansone, 2011, p. 16). In support of the evidence base, many examples of personal practice will be described and analysed. Research questionnaires completed by ten colleagues from various disciplines and thirteen dramatherapists working across the UK will also be examined and shared. Poetry and song lyrics feature throughout the book, mostly written by service users and a couple of my own reflective pieces. As Motion suggests, poetry is "a fundamental requirement of the human spirit" (2009).

Battling stigma

At the age of 68, Dr Marsha Linehan – who developed DBT for people diagnosed with BPD – shared for the first time that she had experienced severe mental health problems since her teens and had been hospitalised at the age of 17 for extreme social withdrawal. Following her interview with Linehan, Carey (a journalist with the *New York Times*) reflected that "the enduring stigma of mental illness teaches people with such a diagnosis to think of themselves as victims, snuffing out the one thing that can motivate them to find treatment: hope" (2011, part 1, p. 1). Linehan's decision to share her story publicly was part of her fight against stigma regarding mental health problems.

Mental health charities across the UK, the US and other parts of the world continue their efforts to reduce stigma by promoting positive mental health awareness. Despite a general improvement, however, people with BPD continue to face prejudice and are often confronted with a lack of empathy and understanding (Gunn and Potter, 2015, p. 113). Historically, they were labelled as treatment-resistant and manipulative. In his review on the development of the diagnosis, Gunderson (professor of psychiatry and pioneer of BPD research and treatment) identified the following as a recurring theme: "the persistence of borderline personality disorder as a suspect category largely neglected by psychiatric institutions, comprising a group of patients few clinicians want to treat" (2009, p. 530). Preconceptions about people with BPD will be challenged in this book and the causes of the disorder explored in depth.

The National Institute for Health and Care Excellence (NICE) states that "People with borderline personality disorder should not be excluded from any health or social care service because of their diagnosis or because they have self-harmed" (2009, p. 11). I have worked with several clients who have been treated with disdain by hospital staff, however, when attending accident and emergency services in the UK, after severely self-harming. Some were accused of misusing valuable resources and others refused treatment. Mental health nurses and health care assistants escorting these clients were also accused of not doing their jobs properly. Self-harm can be severe, even life-threatening. Individuals who feel driven to commit such dangerous acts against themselves need compassion and care, not rejection and judgement. NICE also reminds professionals offering services to clients with BPD that many will have experienced "rejection, abuse and trauma, and encountered stigma often associated with self-harm and borderline personality disorder" (2009, p. 12). They have suffered enough and this is a crucial part of the motivation for writing this book.

In 2017, brothers Harry, Prince of Wales, and William, Duke of Cambridge – together with the Duchess of Cambridge – launched a campaign to raise the profile of mental health in the UK, joining the fight against stigma. For the first time, they spoke publicly about the impact of the loss of their mother, Princess Diana, who had suffered from mental health problems and tragically died in 1997. On their website, they reflect that "Too often, people feel afraid to admit that they are struggling with their mental health. This fear of prejudice and judgement stops people from getting help and can destroy families and end lives" (Heads Together, 2017).

Personal motivation

In my early twenties, I lost my mother to cancer, four weeks before my wedding day. This loss had a significant impact on my mental health and I felt unable to continue with my acting career. With support, I found the courage to pursue a new vocation and trained to become a dramatherapist. I also became a mother, which brought new challenges as well as joy. dramatherapy then helped to reignite my spirit and gave meaning back to my life. Since qualifying from Roehampton University in 2005, I have worked in adult mental health units across South East England, in both the public and private sectors.

At the age of 8, I began to write poetry and songs to express how I was feeling, particularly when I was experiencing difficult emotions and thoughts. As an adult, I have transferred this skill into my professional work as a dramatherapist, putting the words of the people I work with to music. I concur with Andrew Motion's belief that "poetry is as natural and necessary as breathing" (2009). Encouraged by service user Sandra, I wrote a poetic song about my own experience and the words of the chorus are pertinent to this book:

> I am no saviour, I have no cures
> Just a woman, once a child,
> With no answers, I am blind

The final three words (I am blind) symbolise the helplessness that may be felt when working with people who have experienced such depths of emotional pain. Whilst impassioned to help them, our efforts may at times feel somewhat futile. This is where regular clinical supervision and a supportive multidisciplinary team are essential in helping clinicians to remain grounded and hopeful.

Summary of chapters

Following this introduction, Chapters 2 and 3 focus on defining BPD and exploring recommended treatments, including dramatherapy.

Chapter 2 offers a comprehensive description of BPD – also known as emotionally unstable personality disorder (EUPD) – including a historical perspective, diagnostic criteria and co-morbid conditions. It begins with the history of the diagnosis, summarising how it developed and was first acknowledged in psychiatry. The impacts of mental health problems on the UK's population are then shared, highlighting the percentage of mental health service users with BPD. The diagnostic process and the most recent definitions offered by the American Psychiatric Association (APA, 2013a, 2013b) and the World Health Organization (WHO, 2016) are also described and symptoms and co-morbid disorders identified.

Chapter 3 describes a wide array of psychological and psychosocial treatments relevant to people with BPD. These are crucial, as there is no medical cure for the disorder, only psychiatric medicines that may relieve some of the symptoms associated with co-morbid disorders. The 2009 NICE guideline on the treatment and management of people with BPD offers a comprehensive account of several interventions. Some are more highly recommended than others, based on the strength of their evidence base. There is also helpful information on the NHS Choices website (2017) and in a detailed handbook commissioned by the UK's Department of Health (Bolton et al., 2014).

Chapter 4 presents the rationale for selecting dramatherapy as a key intervention for the BPD client group. Specific reference is made to the 2015 Quality Standard from NICE (QS88) and a definition and brief history of dramatherapy are given. The methods used by thirteen dramatherapists with experience of working in the field are revealed alongside the approach I have developed and refined for women with BPD: a person-centred, transpersonal approach, influenced by Jung (1968) and Rowan (1990), comprising dramatic rituals, projective techniques and play. With the potential to support both male and female clients with BPD, dramatherapy is explored in relation to attachment and trauma, and the importance of evaluation and evidence is discussed.

Part 2 includes Chapters 5 through 8. The first two focus on the clinical practice of dramatherapy in two different settings with the client group, including many clinical vignettes. The penultimate chapter explores existential issues concerning grief and the client group's ambivalence towards life and death: self-harm versus self-preservation. In the final chapter, belief, hope and courage are presented as the antithesis to this and the role of dramatherapy is illuminated.

Chapter 5 is a response to working with women on a Tier 4 secure ward for women diagnosed with BPD and co-morbid conditions. Recurring themes are highlighted and six styles of intervention described, supported by session vignettes and samples of creative work. A detailed case study of a client's one-to-one dramatherapy journey follows, explored in relation to schema therapy (Kellogg and Young, 2006), Rowan's subpersonality work (1990) and several Jungian concepts: integrating internal aspects, the shadow and individuation (Jung, 1968). Finally, feedback from colleagues and clients is shared.

Chapter 6 describes the work on a secure step-down unit for women with severe and enduring mental health difficulties, predominantly BPD and paranoid schizophrenia. We also have service users with bipolar disorder and schizo-affective disorder, as well as those with co-morbid disorders, such as PTSD (post-traumatic stress disorder), anorexia nervosa and drug or alcohol dependency. Freedom, choice and acceptance are themes that often arise, and the dramatherapy group provides service users with a space in which to safely voice their frustrations and celebrate their individuality. A selection of session vignettes, key themes and interventions is shared in this chapter, together with creative pieces, to illustrate the vitality of the work generated. The issue of stigma and mental health is explored in relation to the use of drama and songs born in the therapy space and then performed for service users, hospital staff and close friends and family. Finally, three colleagues from different professions share their thoughts about dramatherapy, demonstrating how the intervention may be perceived and can work in relation to a multidisciplinary approach.

Chapter 7 introduces grief as an enduring theme that arises on both conscious and unconscious levels within dramatherapy sessions. The client group's ambivalence about life and death is also prominent, as many express their emotional pain through severe acts of self-harm, which place their lives in jeopardy. Case and session vignettes are used to highlight how the therapeutic process supports clients struggling to cope with issues around death. Many struggle with suicidal thoughts; some have survived suicide attempts and others have friends or family members who have committed suicide or died from natural causes. As Yalom explains, whilst self-awareness makes us human, it also reveals our mortality, and "Our existence is forever shadowed by the knowledge that we will grow, blossom, and, inevitably, diminish and die" (2008, p. 1). The emotional pain experienced by clients, whether in response to their past or present, may also have a considerable impact on those working with them. This issue is explored in relation to personal practice and research, including feedback from colleagues and dramatherapists. The complexity of the therapeutic relationship is then considered with regards to attachment and rejection, hope and futility, transference and countertransference.

Chapter 8 demonstrates that with belief, hope and courage, individuals can find new meaning in their lives – the antithesis to the ambivalence towards life and death described in Chapter 7. Dramatherapy plays a vital role in this process, encouraging clients to see themselves differently and to tolerate and safely express powerful emotions. The importance of other interventions and support is also stressed with regards to recovery. An individual's first hurdle may be finding the courage to leave the familiarity of emotional and physical suffering, which could throw them into a temporary state of loss and confusion, their identity having fused with their pain. In this fragile state, dramatherapy can safely support them, providing a creative space in which they will be empowered and nurtured.

References

APA (2013a) Borderline Personality Disorder, Diagnostic Criteria. *Diagnostic and Statistical Manual of Mental Disorders, Fifth Edition (DSM-5)*, 301(83), pp. 663–666. Arlington, VA: American Psychiatric Association.

APA (2013b) Alternative DSM-5 Model for Personality Disorders. *Diagnostic and Statistical Manual of Mental Disorders, Fifth Edition (DSM-5)*, pp. 761–783. Arlington, VA: American Psychiatric Association.

Bolton, W., Lovell, K., Morgan, L. and Wood, H. (2014) *Meeting the Challenge, Making a Difference: Working Effectively to Support People with Personality Disorder in the Community* [Online]. Commissioned by the UK's Department of Health (DH). PDF available from: http://repository.tavistockandportman.ac.uk/864/1/Heather_Wood_-_MeetingTheChallenge.pdf [Accessed: 01.10.17].

Cambridge, Duke and Duchess and Wales, Prince Henry (2017) About Us [Online]. *Heads Together*. Available from: www.headstogether.org.uk/about-heads-together/ [Accessed: 23.04.17].

Carey, B. (2011) Expert on Mental Illness Reveals Her Own Fight [Online]. *The New York Times*. Available from: www.nytimes.com/2011/06/23/health/23lives.html?_r=0 [Accessed: 07.12.16].

Gunderson, J. (2009, May) Borderline Personality Disorder: Ontogeny of a Diagnosis. *American Journal of Psychiatry*, 166(50), pp. 530–539.

Gunn, J. and Potter, B. (2015) *Borderline Personality Disorder: New Perspectives on a Stigmatizing and Overused Diagnosis*. US and England: Praeger.

Holloway, P. and Seebohm, H. (2011) When Worlds Elide: Culture, Dialogue and Identity in Multi-Professional Settings. *Dramatherapy*, 33(1), pp. 4–15.

Jung, C. G. (1968) *The Archetypes and the Collective Unconscious*. Second edition. Kindle edition. Volume 9, Part 1 of Series (2014) Sir Read, H., Fordham, M. and Adler, G. (eds.) *The Collected Works of C. G. Jung*. Translated by R.F.C. Hull. Abingdon, UK: Routledge.

Kellogg, S. and Young, J. (2006) Schema Therapy for Borderline Personality Disorder. *Journal of Clinical Psychology*, 62(4), pp. 445–458. Wiley Periodicals. Available from: www.interscience.wiley.com

Motion, A. (2009) Yet Once More, Oh Ye Laurels: Andrew Motion Will Be the First Poet Laureate to Retire: As He Prepares to Stand Down, He Looks Back on the Pleasures and

Pitfalls of His Tenure [Online]. *The Guardian*. Available from: www.theguardian.com/books/2009/mar/21/andrew-motion-poet-laureate [Accessed: 12.11.17].

NHS Choices (2017) Treatment, Borderline Personality Disorder [Online]. Available from: www.nhs.uk/Conditions/Borderline-personality-disorder/Pages/Treatment.aspx [Accessed: 20.01.17].

NICE (2009) *Borderline Personality Disorder: Treatment and Management: National Clinical Practice Guideline 78* [Online]. National Institute for Health and Care Excellence. Developed by the National Collaborating Centre for Mental Health. UK: The British Psychological Society and The Royal College of Psychiatrists. [Reproduced with Permission of the Licensor through PLSclear]. PDF available from: www.nice.org.uk/guidance/cg78/evidence [Accessed: 10.10.17].

NICE (2015) *Personality Disorders: Borderline and Antisocial: Quality Standard 88* [Online]. National Institute for Health and Care Excellence. PDF available from: www.nice.org.uk/guidance/qs88 [Accessed: 21.06.17].

Rowan, J. (1990) *Subpersonalities: The People Inside Us*. London: Routledge.

Sansone, R. A. and Sansone, L. A. (2011, May) Gender Patterns in Borderline Personality Disorder. *Journal Innovations in Clinical Neuroscience*, 8(5), pp. 16–20.

WHO (2016) F60.3 Emotionally Unstable Personality Disorder [Online]. *ICD-10 Version: 2016*. Available from: http://apps.who.int/classifications/icd10/browse/2016/en#/F60.3 [Accessed: 08.10.16].

Yalom, I. (2008) *Staring at the Sun: Overcoming the Dread of Death*. Kindle edition. London: Hachette Digital, Little Brown Book Group.

2

BPD

A complex and emotional mental health disorder

> You think you know me?
> You think you can categorise me into one of your boxes?
> BPD, OCD, anorexia? I am none of these things.
> Now don't think I'm saying I don't struggle with the symptoms, I do.
> But I am simply so much more.
> I am the sister, daughter, friend;
> I am my love of animals and the hours I can read, lost in stories I can only wish were my life;
> I am my pure enjoyment of walking in the woods and running;
> I am my need for adrenaline and my impulsivity.
> —*Leona, 2016*

Encouraging clients to explore and acknowledge the different parts of themselves is key to the dramatherapy process. As well as recognising the impact of their past experiences, clients are encouraged to explore who they are and who they would like to be, through a diverse range of creative methods. Individuals with BPD often have a limited perception of themselves. This may be reinforced if they spend considerable time as inpatients on mental health units, where one's identity can fuse with being a service user with a diagnosis. People often struggle between the desire to leave hospital and the fear of living freely. This connects to the relapses frequently experienced close to discharge or when service users become informal patients when a section is removed (under the Mental Health Act). Within dramatherapy sessions, clients are offered the opportunity to transcend the limits of their diagnosis, self-perception and inpatient status.

Each week, the clients I work with on a secure ward for women with BPD continue to explore the themes that arise in the dramatherapy group on the following day. During a reflective session, they are invited to express themselves through images and words. The opening poem is client Leona's response to the theme in one of these groups: *there's more to me than what you can see*. With an undertone of anger and passion, she declares that despite her challenging symptoms, she is so much more than something that can be categorised within a diagnostic manual. As Bateman and Krawitz reflect, mental health diagnoses "can potentially include a failure to recognize the uniqueness and humanity of the person with the condition" (2013, p. 5). Nevertheless, understanding the complexity of BPD remains vital when working with the client group and this chapter offers a comprehensive description – from historical, diagnostic and current perspectives – whilst remembering the human beings at the heart of the matter.

BPD historical overview

As well as understanding current perspectives and statistics, it is helpful to explore the roots of the BPD diagnosis, which can be traced back over thousands of years (Crocq, 2013; Ritschel and Kilpela, 2014). Although psychiatry did not emerge as a medical science until the end of the eighteenth century (Crocq, 2013, p. 149) there are accounts of people suffering from mental health problems (similar to BPD) centuries earlier. For example Greek philosopher Hippocrates wrote about patients with intense anger, melancholia and substantial mood vacillation in 400 BC – resembling symptoms of the conditions we now refer to as BPD and Bipolar Disorder (Ritschel and Kilpela, 2014, p. 1).

Gender issues

Whilst this book focuses on women – as they are the source of my clinical material (and much of what is available) – I have endeavoured to balance this by considering men with BPD wherever possible. Research has revealed that the disorder may be equally present in both sexes (Grant et al., 2008, p. 1) and NICE suggests that the lower number of men with BPD in clinical settings and studies is due to their general reluctance to seek help and therefore diagnosis and treatment (NICE, 2009b, p. 20). This could also account for the higher suicide rate in men, who remain "three times more likely to die by suicide than women" (HMG/DH, 2017, p. 9).

Men's reluctance to seek professional help with mental and emotional difficulties could also be viewed as an adverse effect of the persisting assumption that they should be stronger, in body and mind, than women. Similarly, Hamilton et al. suggest that the 3:1 ratio of women to men receiving the diagnoses may reflect the way that women are perceived by society (2015, p. 441). Women have been portrayed as physically, mentally and spiritually inferior to men in many literary sources spanning the past 4,000 years (Taylor, 2010, Chapter 9; Gunn and Potter, 2015, Chapter 2). In relation to this, Gun and Potter connect misogynistic roots to the criteria for BPD in the current *Diagnostic and Statistical Manual of Mental Disorders* (*DSM-5*). They propose it gives the impression of a dangerous and chaotic woman "more like a feral creature than a human person" (2015, p. 7). Elements of these archaic views about men and women linger on in modern society and gender expectations can therefore have a negative impact on both men and women regarding the diagnosis of BPD (and other mental health disorders). It should also be noted that both men and women with mental illness have endured fear, misjudgement and maltreatment within societies and cultures across the world for many centuries (Hinshaw, 2006, p. 55).

BPD defined as a psychiatric condition

Pinel is thought to be the first physician to classify a personality disorder as a psychiatric condition. He described 'manie sans delire' (mania) in 1801 – states of agitation without delusion (Crocq, 2013, p. 149) and 'borderline insanity' was defined by Hughes, an American psychiatrist, in 1884 (Ritschel and Kilpela, 2014, p. 1). Kraepelin introduced seven types of 'psychopathic personalities' in 1915, naming the first 'The Excitable', which has features of BPD (Crocq, 2013, p. 151). Defining ten psychopathic personality types in 1923, Schneider summarised them as people whose personality traits caused them or society to suffer (Crocq, 2013, p. 151). Whilst these historic terms and concepts relate to people now diagnosed with BPD, psychiatry, followed by psychoanalysis and psychotherapy, has evolved, with a considerable shift in attitudes and language. We now perceive the problematic personality traits of people with BPD as maladaptive coping mechanisms, borne from personal suffering. This will be explained later in the chapter.

Stern introduced the term 'borderline' into psychiatry in 1938, to describe patients he believed were on the border between psychosis and neurosis (Senol, 2016). In the 1940s, Knight then added an ego-psychology perspective on borderline disorder, suggesting that impaired 'ego-functions' – the processes used to address thoughts, feelings and responses to life – resulted in 'borderline states' (Friedel, 2004, pp. 53–54). The term 'borderline personality organisation' was used by Kernberg in the 1960s to describe a level of personality bound between sicker patients with psychotic personality organisation and healthier patients with neurotic personality organisation (Gunderson, 2009, p. 530). His ideas helped to move the diagnosis away from the psychotic spectrum, towards our current understanding of personality disorders.

World War II also had a significant impact on the development of psychiatric classification, due to the extensive mental health problems endured by soldiers, documented by the Veterans Administration (APA, 2016). Influenced by this, the World Health Organization (WHO) included a section for mental disorders for the first time in its sixth edition of the *International Classification of Disease* (*ICD-6*) in 1948 (APA, 2016). In response to these developments, the American Psychiatric Association (APA) then established its first edition of the *DSM* (*Diagnostic and Statistical Manual of Mental Disorders*) in 1952 – a modified version of the *ICD-6* and the first official manual of mental disorders that focused on clinical rather than administrative use (APA, 2016).

The *ICD-6* included ten categories for psychoses and psychoneuroses and seven for disorders of character, behaviour and intelligence. Within these, there were eight types of 'pathological personalities' and an 'immature personality' with six elements, the first of which was 'emotional instability' (WHO, 1948). This links to our current understanding that the personality development in people with BPD and EUPD is often hindered by childhood or adolescent trauma. Personality disorders were then included in the eighth revision of the *ICD* (WHO) in 1965, and in 1968, Grinker, Werble and Drye published a book describing 'the borderline syndrome'. Gunderson and Singer then published an academic paper entitled 'Defining Borderline Patients' in 1975, which led to the development of assessment criteria. In the same year, borderline personality disorder was included in the ninth revision of the *ICD*, as one of twelve personality disorders categorised (WHO, 1975). Borderline personality disorder was then included in the *DSM-III* (APA, 1980) and remained within the *DSM-IV* (APA, 2000) and current *DSM-5* (APA, 2013a).

The *ICD-10*, published in 1990, included eight specific personality disorders, of which one was emotionally unstable personality disorder (EUPD) with two sub-types: impulsive and borderline (WHO, 2016d). Linehan then introduced a specific form of psychotherapy for people with BPD in 1991, named DBT (dialectical behaviour therapy), and Bateman and Fonagy established MBT (mentalisation-based treatment) in 1999 (2013).

BPD in the twenty-first century

The diagnosis of personality disorders remains a highly contentious area. Gunderson reflects that BPD is regarded as "a suspect category largely neglected by psychiatric institutions, comprising a group of patients few clinicians want to treat" (2009, p. 530). Historically, it was considered a chronic and untreatable disorder. There has been a significant change in attitudes and practice over the past twenty years, however, and Sperry observes "an increasing consensus among clinicians that many patients can be helped with current treatment interventions, even those meeting DSM-5 criteria for Borderline Personality Disorder" (2016, l.300–301).

The prognosis for BPD (and EUPD) has improved significantly, as our understanding of the condition has developed in line with more effective treatment options. Gunderson reports that until 1980, less than 15 research papers had been published on the disorder, and during the following decade, over 275 were written (2009, p. 532). This increase demonstrates the influence of WHO's *ICD* and the APA's *DSM*, as BPD entered the *ICD-9* in 1975 and the *DSM-III* in 1980 – giving the diagnosis sufficient credibility to secure funding for research.

In 2003, the National Institute for Mental Health in England (NIMH-E) published *Personality Disorder: No Longer a Diagnosis of Exclusion* – a policy outlining the development of services for people with personality disorder. NICE then published a clinical guidance in 2009, *Borderline Personality Disorder: Recognition and Management* (2009a), followed by a quality standard to improve the treatment and management of both antisocial and borderline personality disorder, in 2015. The latter was a response to the UK Department of Health's publication *No Health Without Mental Health: A Cross-Government Mental Health Outcomes Strategy for People of All Ages* (HMG/DH, 2011).

The US House of Representatives unanimously passed a resolution in 2008 naming May Borderline Personality Disorder Awareness Month. They did this to increase public awareness and to encourage further research and funding for BPD, due to its prevalence, severity and high public costs (Gunderson, 2009, p. 530).

Current statistics

The Mental Health Foundation UK has published statistics on the impact that mental health problems have on tens of millions of people each year. It also highlights the financial impact of mental illness on health services, estimating a yearly cost of £70 to £100 billion (2015, p. 1). One in four adults and one in ten children are estimated to have a mental health problem every year, only a quarter of whom receive ongoing treatment (2015, p. 1). Concerned about public funding for mental health services, Mind (a leading mental health charity in England and Wales) sent every local authority in England a freedom of information request in 2015 to identify how much of their public health budget was used for mental health services the previous year. The results showed an average expenditure of just 1% and nine authorities admitted they had spent nothing (Mind, 2015, p. 1). An independent mental health task force then formed, chaired by the chief executive of Mind and commissioned by NHS England, to develop a strategy to improve mental health services:

> For far too long, people of all ages with mental health problems have been stigmatised and marginalised, all too often experiencing an NHS that treats their minds and bodies separately. Mental health services have been underfunded for decades, and too many people have received no help at all, leading to hundreds of thousands of lives put on hold or ruined, and thousands of tragic and unnecessary deaths.
>
> *Farmer and Dyer (2016, p. 3)*

NHS England has made a commitment to transform mental health services, by investing more than a billion pounds a year by 2020/21 (2016a). It published an implementation plan (2016b) that described how it would deliver the *Five-Year Forward View for Mental Health*, created by the Independent Mental Health Taskforce (2016). The taskforce made twenty-four recommendations, the fourteenth of which said that NHS England should invest more money to increase access to psychological therapies for people with psychosis, bipolar disorder and personality disorder (2016, p. 33). BPD is considered the most common and complex of the personality disorders and therefore presents a significant challenge to mental health services worldwide. Co-morbidity plays a big role in this, with 98% of those diagnosed having at least one co-morbid mental illness within their lifetime (Bender et al., 2001, p. 296).

The largest and most recent epidemiological study of the general population in the US revealed a 5.9% lifetime prevalence of BPD (several per cent higher than in older studies) and the difference between men and women proved negligible (Grant et al., 2008, p. 1). Whilst many men meet the criteria for BPD, their numbers are significantly lower within clinical settings and studies, as they remain less likely to seek help and therefore diagnosis and treatment (NICE, 2009b, p. 20). Whilst it is thought there is little difference between their methods of self-harm and levels of emotional distress, men and women with BPD have distinctly different personality traits, co-morbidities and use of treatment (Sansone and Sansone, 2011, p. 16). Grant et al. also revealed an extensive overlap with mental and physical disability, especially among women (2008, p. 8). In the UK, research suggests that over 50% of psychiatric service users have a personality disorder, of which BPD is the most prevalent within non-forensic settings (NICE, 2009b, p. 20). In the US, it was estimated that 20% of all psychiatric inpatients and 15% of all outpatients have BPD, of whom 75% are female (Gunderson, 2011, p. 3).

BPD has potentially devastating consequences, with 60% to 70% of those diagnosed attempting suicide within their lifetime (Oldham, 2006, p. 20) and up to 10% successfully ending their own lives (Gunderson, 2011, p. 3). Personality disorders are thought to be present in over 30% of individuals who die by suicide, 40% of those who make suicide attempts and 50% of psychiatric outpatients who die by suicide (Oldham, 2006, p. 20). Within the criminal justice system in the UK, personality disorders are also prevalent and equally diagnosed in men and women. They are thought to affect 60%–70% of prisoners and 50% of offenders in probation services (NHS England and NOMS, 2015, p. i). Men are mostly diagnosed with antisocial personality disorder and women with BPD. Both must be carefully assessed regarding risk to themselves and others: "whilst women are more likely to self-harm, men are more likely to commit suicide" (NHS England and NOMS, 2015, p. 9).

The criminal justice system has taken significant steps towards meeting the needs of offenders diagnosed with PD, as research has shown that their types of offences often link to their mental health problems. After a public consultation in 2011, "New services, which aim to form a pathway of care, are now available in the community and prisons jointly, led and delivered by clinical and criminal justice staff" (NHS England and NOMS, 2015, p. i). Staff within the criminal justice system are now encouraged to consider biological features, genetic inheritance, social and cultural factors, and the consequence of insecure attachments and trauma when managing offenders diagnosed with PD, understanding the impact that childhood experiences can have on adult behaviour and relationships (2015, p. ii). For some offenders, incarceration may provide their first experience of the containment they lacked in childhood (Seebohm, 2011, p. 121), and through interventions such as dramatherapy, positive containment and attachment can be fostered.

Grant and colleagues reveal a significant decline in BPD symptoms from the age of 44 (2008, p. 8) and Gunderson and colleagues report that over a ten-year course of BPD, despite the persistence of impaired social functioning, there were high rates of remission and low rates of relapse (2011b, p. 3). Zanarini's ten-year study of individuals with BPD revealed similar results, with 50.3% of the 290 participants making a full recovery after ten years (2006, p. 42) and 93% experiencing remission (p. 52).

Diagnosis

Diagnosis is a challenging process that requires a sensitive and skilful clinician. Whilst the initial impact of a BPD or EUPD diagnosis may be negative, it has the potential to help individuals access recommended therapies and specialist services. As Bateman and Krawitz advise, "Avoiding making a diagnosis to avoid clinician and client negativity is now inappropriate given the positive, natural course of the disorder and the availability of effective treatment" (2013, p. 4). The criteria for BPD and EUPD described in the current *DSM-5* and *ICD-10* respectively play a significant role in the diagnostic process, alongside several standardised interviews. Approaching each person with integrity, empathy and patience is paramount to their recovery, however, and diagnosis should be considered a helpful tool, rather than a means to define a person.

BPD in the DSM-5

The APA published the *DSM-5* in 2013. Prior to this, there was much debate about the section on personality disorders and they are no longer diagnosed on a separate axis. Personality ranges from healthy to disordered across a continuum; thus personality disorders (PD) are complex to diagnose via a categorical method. Although a dedicated PD work group spent several years developing a dimensional model of diagnosis, the Board of Directors rejected it, considering it "too complex for clinical practice" (APA, 2013c, p. 2). In response, they created a hybrid dimensional-categorical model, included in Section III (Emerging Measures and Models), named the "Alternative DSM-5 Model for Personality Disorders" (APA, 2013b, p. 761).

In Section II of the *DSM-5*, BPD is described as "A pervasive pattern of instability of interpersonal relationships, self-image, and affects, and marked impulsivity, beginning by early adulthood and present in a variety of contexts" (APA, 2013a, p. 663). The diagnostic criteria remain similar to how they appeared in the *DSM-1V* – indicated by five or more of the following: (1) frantic efforts to avoid real or imagined abandonment; (2) a pattern of unstable and intense interpersonal relationships, characterized by alternating between extremes of idealisation and devaluation; (3) identity disturbance: markedly and persistently unstable self-image or sense of self; (4) impulsivity in at least two areas that are potentially self-damaging, such as spending, sex, substance abuse, reckless driving and binge eating; (5) recurrent suicidal behaviour, gestures or threats, or self-mutilating behaviour; (6) affective instability due to a marked reactivity of mood (e.g. intense episodic dysphoria, irritability or anxiety usually lasting a few hours and only rarely more than a few days); (7) chronic feelings of emptiness; (8) inappropriate, intense anger or difficulty controlling anger (e.g. frequent displays of temper, constant anger, recurrent physical fights); (9) transient, stress-related paranoid ideation or severe dissociative symptoms (APA, 2013a, p. 663).

In contrast to this, through the Alternative *DSM-5* Model, personality disorders are assessed via two criteria: the level of impairment in personality functioning and an evaluation of pathological personality traits (APA, 2013b, p. 762). Only six of the ten specific personality disorders from Section II are included in Section III: antisocial, avoidant, borderline, narcissistic, obsessive-compulsive and schizotypal. The dimensional approach allows for a trait specified diagnosis of personality disorder to be made, however, if PD is thought to be present but does not meet the criteria for one of the six specified conditions (APA, 2013b, p. 761). For a diagnosis of BPD, there must be at least a moderate impairment in personality functioning revealed in two or more of the following four areas: (1) identity; (2) self-direction; (3) empathy; (4) intimacy. Four or more of the following seven pathological personality traits must also be identified (at least one of which must be impulsivity, risk-taking or hostility): (1) emotional lability; (2) anxiousness; (3) separation insecurity; (4) depressivity; (5) impulsivity; (6) risk-taking; (7) hostility (APA, 2013b, pp. 766–767).

The APA decided to include both strategies in the *DSM-5*, to encourage clinicians to consider each of them and "to preserve continuity with current clinical practice, while also introducing a new approach that aims to address numerous shortcomings of the current approach to personality disorders" (APA, 2013b, p. 761). It seems that through endorsing both methods, the APA has allowed clinicians more flexibility, enabling them to adjust their approach to diagnosis to meet the needs of each service user.

EUPD in the ICD-10

EUPD (emotionally unstable personality disorder) is one of the ten 'specific personality disorders' included in the tenth revision of the *ICD* and has two types, impulsive and borderline (WHO, 2016d). Personality disorders (specified, mixed and unspecified), plus enduring personality changes, are said to "represent extreme or significant deviations from the way in which the average individual in a given culture perceives, thinks, feels and, particularly, relates to others" (WHO, 2016b). The ten 'specific personality disorders' are not thought to link directly to any disease, damage, brain injury or other psychiatric disorder, and are said to manifest after childhood or adolescence, continuing through adulthood. They are described as severe, affecting several areas of the personality and usually accompanied by extreme distress and social difficulties (WHO, 2016c). EUPD is described within the *ICD-10* as follows:

> A definite tendency to act impulsively and without consideration of the consequences; the mood is unpredictable and capricious. There is a liability to outbursts of emotion and an incapacity to control the behavioural explosions. There is a tendency to quarrelsome behaviour and to conflicts with others, especially when impulsive acts are thwarted or censored. Two types may be

distinguished: the impulsive type, characterized predominantly by emotional instability and lack of impulse control, and the borderline type, characterized in addition by disturbances in self-image, aims, and internal preferences, by chronic feelings of emptiness, by intense and unstable interpersonal relationships, and by a tendency to self-destructive behaviour, including suicide gestures and attempts.

WHO (2016d)

WHO began working on the *ICD-11* in 2007 and released a draft copy for its member states to review at a conference in Tokyo in October 2016. Its plan is to begin implementation of the eleventh revision in 2018 (WHO, 2016a). The new version proposes a radical change to the section on personality disorders, employing a dimensional approach to diagnosis, which "abolishes all type-specific categories of personality disorder apart from the main one, the presence of personality disorder itself" (Tyrer et al., 2015, p. 721). Thus EUPD (and every other subtype) would be removed. Tyrer et al. explain that this approach would allow an easier, rapid assessment of personality, through which "a clinician should be able first to identify the presence or absence of personality disorder, then its degree of severity, and, if relevant, its domain trait features" (2015, p. 723).

The anticipation is that a less complex method will allow more people to be diagnosed and then access the help needed. My concern, however, is that diagnosis should not be rushed and the removal of PD subtypes (which have emerged after many years of research) will have an impact on the interventions developed to support them. The alternative model in Section III of the *DSM-5* appears to be the most effective approach, as it uses both categorical and dimensional methods – allowing for subtypes to be diagnosed, as well as an individualised PD diagnosis, for those who do not meet the criteria for a subtype.

Structured clinical interviews

Despite the difference in the *ICD-10* and *DSM-5* criteria for diagnosis, there are several standardised interviews to aid the process. On the ward where I work, the consultant psychiatrist predominantly uses *SCID 11 – Structured Clinical Interview for DSM-IV Personality Disorders* (First et al., 1997), which he described as "a good instrument that leads to a useful discussion with the patient that can bring them alive as individuals with their own specific issues, while still testing for the presence of diagnostic criteria for a number of diagnostic groups". The service user's history is considered and he or she is continually assessed by the multidisciplinary team (MDT) through interactions with staff and peers on the ward and within therapy groups (including dramatherapy) and one-to-one therapy. It is important to note that diagnosis is not immovable and, at times, individuals referred to us with a BPD or Emerging EUPD diagnosis will later be re-diagnosed with an alternative, more appropriate condition.

As well as *SCID 11*, NICE lists five other interviews to aid diagnosis (2009b, p. 19): *DIPD-IV, Diagnostic Interview for DSM-IV Personality Disorders* (Zanarini, 1983); *SIDP-IV, Structured Interview for DSM-IV Personality* (Pfohl et al., 1997); *IPDE, International Personality Disorder Examination* (Loranger et al., 1996); *PAS, Personality Assessment Schedule* (Tyrer et al., 1979); and *SAP, Standardised Assessment of Personality* (Mann et al., 1999). Whilst each is said to have advantages and disadvantages, NICE indicates that "all of the schedules allow for a reliable diagnosis of borderline personality disorder to be made" (2009b, p. 18). Most importantly, the individual assessed must be treated with sensitivity and respect. As Bolton et al. advise, "How a person is given a diagnosis, and what happens afterwards, can make all the difference between someone feeling recognised and helped, or labelled and stigmatised" (2014, p. 29).

Aetiology

The Biopsychosocial Model relates to or involves "the interaction of biological, psychological, and social factors, especially in medicine" (Oxford University Press, 2017). The DH (Department of Health, UK) suggests it is the most helpful approach to understanding the development of personality disorders. It includes: biological sensitivity (the characteristics with which we are born) and early childhood experiences (with significant others) plus social and environmental factors (e.g. schools, neighbourhoods and cultures) (Bolton et al., 2014, p. 31). This will be explored in depth, with examples in the following section.

NICE explains that BPD may develop in individuals who were prevented from developing healthy cognitive functioning as children, caused by problems such as early neglect. They also indicate that natural vulnerability may have been present, and with or without further trauma (e.g. severe neglect and abuse) changes can occur "in the neural mechanisms of arousal and lead to structural and functional changes in the developing brain" (2009b, p. 25). The following are listed as potential factors that may contribute to the development of BPD: "Genetics and constitutional vulnerabilities; neurophysiological and neurobiological dysfunctions of emotional regulation and stress; psychosocial histories of childhood maltreatment and abuse; and disorganisation of aspects of the affiliative behavioural system, most particularly the attachment system" (Nice, 2009b, p. 21).

Mosquera et al. emphasise the significance of attachment issues in the development of BPD, though stress they are not the sole cause of the disorder and will affect each person differently (2014, p. 6). Gunn and Potter describe the condition as 'untreated trauma' (2015, p. 47) and in a study of over 300 people with BPD, 84% revealed they had experienced some type of bi-parental abuse or neglect before the age of 18, from parents who did not validate their thoughts and feelings, failed to protect them adequately, neglected their physical care, emotionally withdrew from them or treated them inconsistently (Zanarini et al., 2000, p. 264).

Fonagy and Batemen also reveal consistent evidence that people with BPD have experienced problematic parenting (2007, p. 87). They explain how challenging aspects within a family environment could affect children's capacity to make sense of themselves and others (described as effective mentalisation), potentially leading to the development of BPD. These include a chaotic family, disrupted attachments, multiple caregivers, parental neglect, alcoholism and emotional instability among family members (2007, p. 88). Mosquera and colleagues predict that people with BPD will have experienced either insecure or disorganised attachments as children (2014, p. 3). Bowlby explains that a secure attachment relies on the ability of parents to create a secure base for their children, which they can journey from into the outside world and return to, knowing they will be welcomed, "nourished physically and emotionally, comforted if distressed, reassured if frightened" (2005, p. 12). When deprived of this, a child may develop anxious, resistant or avoidant attachment behaviours, which can persist into adolescence and adulthood (Bowlby, 2005, pp. 139–140).

Investigating childhood maltreatment within a large number of adults with multiple and specific personality disorders, Battle and colleagues found that whilst the rate of abuse and neglect was high across every group, BPD was the most consistently connected to multiple forms of mistreatment during childhood (2004, p. 208). Reflecting on past studies, they confirm that although sexual abuse is common to people with BPD, it often coincides with other forms of abuse and neglect from both parents (p. 194). Bradley and Weston also reveal that people with BPD are more likely to have experienced lengthy separations (or the permanent loss) of either one or both parents than people with schizophrenia, depression and other personality disorders (2005, p. 943). Trauma can lead to dissociation, which has been estimated to affect up to two thirds of the BPD population (Vermetten and Spiegel, 2014, p. 434).

Fruzzetti et al. suggest that the interaction between biological sensitivity (the characteristics with which we are born) and an invalidating family environment is a significant precursor to developing BPD (2005, p. 1026). They explain that a child who is particularly sensitive or volatile may be more challenging for parents, especially if those parents are struggling with their own problems (e.g. depression, substance abuse or money difficulties). Such parents may then engage in invalidating behaviours that intensify their child's sensitivity, thus exacerbating their own distress. If this cycle continues, the child will become increasingly vulnerable and the family environment more invalidating. Serious and chronic problems may then arise, such as the development of BPD (Fruzzetti et al., 2005, p. 1026). A secure attachment is therefore vital, as without it, a child is at risk of developing "significant emotional and mental health difficulties in later life" (Balbernie, 2013, p. 210).

Recent studies have also revealed a neurophysiological component of BPD, as summarised by Zeichner: regions of the central nervous system believed to monitor, evaluate and regulate emotion have shown abnormalities in people with BPD, as have the two limbic regions responsible for emotional regulation and memory. As these parts develop during childhood, their abnormalities can be connected to childhood trauma, which relates to the idea that such trauma is a precursor to BPD (2013, p. 4). Studies have also revealed that certain genetic traits may contribute to the development of BPD (Fruzzetti et al., 2005, p. 1009) and that people with BPD show consistent differences in their serotonergic functioning (p. 1010).

Diagnosis in adolescence

Diagnosing BPD (and other personality disorders) in children and adolescents is another area of contention, although the *DSM-5* (unlike the *DSM-IV*) advises that personality disorders may begin in adolescence or early adulthood (2013a, p. 644). Laurenssen et al. analysed the results of an online survey sent to 566 psychologists. Whilst 57.8% agreed that it was possible to diagnose PD in adolescents, only 8.7% of the 367 working with adolescents stated that they had made a PD diagnosis. Their most common reasons for not doing so were the fluctuating, transient nature of personality during adolescence; the criteria in the *DSM-IV* (which did not allow for it); and the stigmatisation of a PD diagnoses (2013, p. 2). Laurenssen et al. reflect, however, that by avoiding the diagnosis, clinicians may impede the development and application of necessary interventions for adolescents with PD (2013, p. 3).

Whilst research on personality disorders in young people remains minimal, NICE currently recommends that young people meeting the criteria for BPD should have access to the recommended treatments, via the Child and Adolescent Mental Health Service (CAMHS) (Meier et al., 2011, p. 15). As both adults and adolescents with BPD are known to use both inpatient and outpatient services more frequently than people with other personality disorders, Beck and colleagues suggest that "the development of early and effective treatment programs which include adolescents with BPD at the threshold level is important and may have long-term benefits for patients, their families and society" (2016, p. 2). The diagnosis of 'Emerging EUPD' is used within the services where I work, for young adults often transferring from CAMHS to adult services. This is useful, as it allows time for ongoing assessment and treatment before deciding whether an EUPD (or BPD) diagnosis is appropriate.

Co-morbidity

Bender et al. report that 98% of the people diagnosed with BPD will have at least one co-morbid mental illness within their lifetime (2001, p. 296). It is therefore imperative to have a thorough understanding of a wide range of mental health difficulties whilst working with the client group. NICE describes the symptoms of BPD as highly variable, overlapping with depressive, schizophrenic, impulsive, dissociative and identity disorders (2009b, p. 17) and co-morbid with post-traumatic stress disorder (PTSD), depression, anxiety, eating disorders, substance misuse disorders and bipolar disorder, with which it is sometimes confused (p. 15).

A large study of the co-morbidity between BPD and PTSD and the significance of childhood sexual abuse and other trauma (Scheiderer et al., 2015, p. 5) revealed that 53.11% of those who met the criteria for BPD also met the criteria for lifetime PTSD. Of this co-morbid group, 43.42% of the women and 19.14% of the men had experienced childhood sexual abuse (Scheiderer et al., 2015, p. 5). Examining the research between 1998 and 2009, Sansone and Sansone reveal that whilst men with BPD are more likely to be diagnosed with co-morbid substance use disorders and antisocial personality disorder, women are more likely to present with eating, mood, anxiety and post-traumatic stress disorders (2011, p. 1).

Conclusion

Borderline personality disorder is a complex yet treatable condition, with causes and symptoms varying greatly between individuals. Hundreds of variations may be diagnosed through the current *DSM*'s categorical approach (Fruzzetti et al., 2005, p. 1008). Whilst this acknowledges the individuality of people, it may also stimulate further inconsistencies over diagnosis and increases the challenge of finding effective treatment for each person. Historically, BPD was a diagnosis that people wanted to avoid giving, receiving and even treating. After twenty years of positive research and advocacy, however, views are shifting and prognosis has improved. In the following chapter, I will explore the treatment options recommended for people with BPD.

References

APA (1980) *DSM-III – Diagnostic and Statistical Manual of Mental Disorders.* Third edition. Washington, DC: American Psychiatric Association.

APA (2000) *DSM 1V – Diagnostic and Statistical Manual of Mental Disorders.* Fourth edition. Washington, DC: American Psychiatric Association.

APA (2013a) Borderline Personality Disorder, Diagnostic Criteria. *Diagnostic and Statistical Manual of Mental Disorders, Fifth Edition (DSM-5)*, 301(83), pp. 663–666. Arlington, VA: American Psychiatric Association.

APA (2013b) Alternative DSM-5 Model for Personality Disorders. *Diagnostic and Statistical Manual of Mental Disorders, Fifth Edition (DSM-5)*, pp. 761–783. Arlington, VA: American Psychiatric Association.

APA (2013c) Personality Disorder [Online]. *American Psychiatric Association.* PDF available from: www.psychiatry.org/psychiatrists/practice/dsm/educational-resources/dsm-5-fact-sheets [Accessed: 04.09.17].

APA (2016) Post–World War II [Online]. *American Psychiatric Association.* Available from: https://psychiatry.org/psychiatrists/practice/dsm/history-of-the-dsm?_ga=1.26165377 4.2023233716.1478107218 [Accessed: 02.11.16].

Balbernie, R. (2013) The Importance of Attachment for Infant Mental Health. *Journal of Health Visiting*, 1(4), pp. 210–217.

Bateman, A. and Fonagy, P. (2013) Mentalization-Based Treatment. *Psychoanalytic Inquiry*, 33(6), pp. 595–613. Taylor & Francis Online.

Bateman, A. and Krawitz, R. (2013) *Borderline Personality Disorder: An Evidence-Based Guide for Generalist Mental Health Professionals.* Kindle edition. Oxford: Oxford University Press.

Battle, C. L., Shea, M. T., Johnson, D. M., Yen, S., Zlotnick, C., Zanarini, M. C., Sanislow, C. A., Skodol, A. E., Gunderson, J. G., Grilo, C. M., McGlashan, T. H. and Morey, L. C. (2004) Childhood Maltreatment Associated with Adult Personality Disorders: Findings from the Collaborative Longitudinal Personality Disorders Study. *Journal of Personality Disorders*, 18(2), pp. 193–211.

Beck, E., Bo, S. and Poulsen, S. (2016) Mentalization-Based Treatment in Groups for Adolescents with Borderline Personality Disorder (BPD) or Subthreshold BPD versus Treatment as Usual (M-GAB): Study Protocol for a Randomized Controlled Trial [Online]. *Trials.* Available from: www.researchgate.net/publication/305271914

Bender, D. S., Dolan, R. T., Skodol, A. E., et al. (2001) Treatment Utilization by Patients with Personality Disorders. *American Journal of Psychiatry*, 158, pp. 295–302.

Bolton, W., Lovell, K., Morgan, L. and Wood, H. (2014) *Meeting the Challenge, Making a Difference: Working Effectively to Support People with Personality Disorder in the Community* [Online]. Commissioned by the UK's Department of Health (DH). PDF available from: http://repository.tavistockandportman.ac.uk/864/1/Heather_Wood_-_MeetingThe Challenge.pdf [Accessed: 01.10.17].

Bowlby, J. (2005) *A Secure Base: Clinical Applications of Attachment Theory.* Second edition. Routledge Classics. Kindle edition. London: Taylor & Francis Online.

Bradley, R. and Westen, D. (2005) The Psychodynamics of Borderline Personality Disorder: A View from Developmental Psychopathology. *Development and Psychopathology*, 17, pp. 927–957.

Crocq, Marc-Antoine (2013, June) Milestones in the History of Personality Disorders. *Dialogues in Clinical Neuroscience*, 15(2), pp. 147–153.

Farmer, P. and Dyer, J. (2016) Foreword [Online]. In *The Five-Year Forward View for Mental Health for the NHS in England.* Commissioned by Simon Stevens for the NHS, England: Independent Mental Health Task Force. Available from: www.england.nhs.uk/mentalhealth/taskforce/ [Accessed: 01.09.17].

First, M. B., Gibbon, M., Spitzer, R. L., et al. (1997) *The Structured Clinical Interview for DSM-IV Axis II Personality Disorders (SCID-II).* Washington, DC: American Psychiatric Press. Cited within NICE (2009b) *Borderline Personality Disorder: Treatment and Management – Clinical Guideline 78*, p. 19.

Fonagy, P. and Bateman, A. (2007) Mentalizing and Borderline Personality Disorder. *Journal of Mental Health*, 16(1), pp. 83–101.

Friedel, R. O. (2004) *Borderline Personality Demystified: The Essential Guide to Understanding and Living with BPD.* New York: Marlowe.

Fruzzetti, A., Shenk, C. and Hoffman, D. (2005) Family Interaction and the Development of Borderline Personality Disorder: A Transactional Model. *Development and Psychopathology*, 17, pp. 1007–1030.

Grant, B. F., Chou, P. S., Goldstein, R. B., Huang, B., Stinson, F. S., Saha, T. D., Smith, S. M., Dawson, D. A., Pulay, A. J., Pickering, R. P. and Ruan, J. W. (2008) Prevalence, Correlates, Disability, and Comorbidity of DSM-IV Borderline Personality Disorder: Results from the Wave 2 National Epidemiologic Survey on Alcohol and Related Conditions. *Journal of Clinical Psychiatry*, 69(4), pp. 533–545.

Grinker, R., Werble, B. and Drye, R. (1968) *The Borderline Syndrome: A Behavioral Study of Ego Functions.* New York: Basic Books.

Gunderson, J. G. (2009) Borderline Personality Disorder: Ontogeny of a Diagnosis. *American Journal of Psychiatry*, 166(5), pp. 530–539.

Gunderson, J. G. (2011) *A BPD Brief for the NEA. BPD (National Education Alliance. Borderline Personality Disorder): Revised Version.* Available from: www.borderlinepersonalitydisorder. com [Accessed: 01.06.17].

Gunderson, J. G. and Singer, M. T. (1975) Defining Borderline Patients: An Overview [Online]. *Am J Psychiatry*, 132(1), pp. 1–10. Available from: http://dx.doi.org/10.1176/ajp.132.1.1

Gunderson, J. G., Stout, R. L., McGlashan, T. H., Shea, M. T., Morey, L. C., Grilo, C. M., Zanarini, M. C., Yen, S., Markowitz, J. C., Sanislow, C. A., Ansell, E. B., Pinto, A. and

Skodol, A. E. (2011b) Ten-Year Course of Borderline Personality Disorder: Psychopathology and Function from the Collaborative Longitudinal Personality Study [Online]. *Archives of General Psychiatry*, 68, pp. 827–837. Available from: http://wesscholar.wesleyan. edu/div3facpubs/149/ [Accessed: 20.11.16].

Gunn, J. and Potter, B. (2015) *Borderline Personality Disorder: New Perspectives on a Stigmatizing and Overused Diagnosis*. Santa Barbara, CA: Praeger.

Hamilton, L., Thompson, K. and Slade, S. (2015) Psychopathology: Theories and Causes. In Banyard, P., Dillon, G., Norman, C. and Winder, B. (eds.) *Essential Psychology*. Second edition. Kindle edition. London: SAGE.

Hinshaw, S. P. (2006) *The Mark of Shame: Stigma of Mental Illness and an Agenda for Change*. Oxford: Oxford University Press.

HMG/DH (2011) No Health without Mental Health: A Cross-Government Mental Health Outcomes Strategy for People of All Ages [Online]. Available from: www.gov. uk/government/publications/no-health-without-mental-health-a-cross-government-outcomes-strategy [Accessed: 20.10.17].

HMG/DH (2017) Preventing Suicide in England: Third Progress Report on the Cross-Government Outcomes Strategy to Save Lives [Online]. Available from: www.gov.uk/ government/publications/suicide-prevention-strategy-for-england [Accessed: 03.07.17].

Independent Mental Health Taskforce (2016) *The Five-Year Forward View for Mental Health for the NHS in England*. Commissioned by Stevens, S. for NHS, England. Available from: www.england.nhs.uk/mentalhealth/taskforce/ [Accessed: 01.09.17].

Laurenssen, E., Hutsebaut, J., Feenstra, D., Van Busschbach, J. and Luyten, P. (2013) Diagnosis of Personality Disorders in Adolescents: A Study among Psychologists [Online]. *Child and Adolescent Psychiatry and Mental Health*, 7, p. 3. PDF available from: www.capmh.com/ content/7/1/3

Linehan, M. M., Armstrong, H. E., Suarez, A., Allmon, D. and Heard, H. L. (1991) Cognitive-Behavioral Treatment of Chronically Parasuicidal Borderline Patients. *Archives of General Psychiatry*, 48, pp. 1060–1064.

Loranger, A. W., Sartorius, N. and Janca, A. (1996) *Assessment and Diagnosis of Personality Disorders: The International Personality Disorder Examination (IPDE)*. New York: Cambridge University Press. Cited within NICE (2009b) *Borderline Personality Disorder: Treatment and Management – Clinical Guideline 78*, p. 19.

Mann, A. H., Raven, P., Pilgrim, J., et al. (1999) An Assessment of the Standardized Assessment of Personality as a Screening Instrument for the International Personality Disorder Examination: A Comparison of Informant and Patient Assessment for Personality Disorder. *Psychological Medicine*, 29, pp. 985–989. Cited within NICE (2009b) *Borderline Personality Disorder: Treatment and Management – Clinical Guideline*, 78, p. 19.

Meier, R., Dr Murphy, M., Prof Singh, S. and Dr Lamb, C. (2011) Developing Services to Improve the Quality of Life of Young People with Neurodevelopmental Disorders, Emotional/Neurotic Disorders and Emerging Personality Disorder. Occasional Paper 77. *Royal College of Psychiatrists London*. PDF available from: www.rcpsych.ac.uk/files/ pdfversion/OP77.pdf

Mental Health Foundation (2015) Fundamental Facts about Mental Health [Online]. *Mental Health Foundation*. Available from: www.mentalhealth.org.uk [Accessed: 10.11.16].

MIND (2015) Public Mental Health in England [Online]. *Mind: For Better Mental Health*. Available from: www.mind.org.uk/media/3007803/public-mental-health-fois-2015-one-pager.pdf [Accessed: 16.11.16].

Mosquera, D., Gonzalez, A. and Leeds, A. (2014) Early Experience, Structural Dissociation, and Emotional Dysregulation in Borderline Personality Disorder: The Role of Insecure and Disorganized Attachment. *Borderline Personal Disorder and Emotional Dysregulation*, 1(15).

NHS England (2016a) Implementing the Mental Health Forward View [Online]. *NHS England.* Available from: www.england.nhs.uk/mental-health/taskforce/imp/ [Accessed: 16.11.16].

NHS England (2016b) Implementation Plan. PDF available from: www.england.nhs.uk/mental-health/taskforce/imp/ [Accessed: 16.11.16].

NHS England and NOMS (National Offender Management Service) (2015) *Working with Offenders with Personality Disorder: A Practitioners' Guide.* Second edition. NHS England Publications Gateway, Ref. 04004. © Crown copyright. Available from: www.gov.uk and www.england.nhs.uk

NICE (2009a) *Borderline Personality Disorder: Recognition and Management: Clinical Guideline 78* [Online]. National Institute for Health and Care Excellence. Developed by the National Collaborating Centre for Mental Health. Available from: www.nice.org.uk/guidance/cg78/chapter/1-Guidance

NICE (2009b) *Borderline Personality Disorder: Treatment and Management: National Clinical Practice Guideline 78* [Online]. National Institute for Health and Care Excellence. Developed by the National Collaborating Centre for Mental Health. UK: The British Psychological Society and The Royal College of Psychiatrists. [Reproduced with Permission of the Licensor through PLSclear]. PDF available from: www.nice.org.uk/guidance/cg78/evidence [Accessed: 10.10.17].

NIMH(E) (2003) *Personality Disorder: No Longer a Diagnosis of Exclusion – Policy Implementation Guidance for the Development of Services for People with Personality Disorder.* London: National Institute for Mental Health in England. Gateway Reference 1055. Available from: http://personalitydisorder.org.uk/resources-and-documents [Accessed: 10.11.16].

Oldham, J. M. (2006) Treatment in Psychiatry: Borderline Personality Disorder and Suicidality [Online]. *Am J Psychiatry,* 163(1), pp. 20–26. Available from: http://dx.doi.org/10.1176/appi.ajp.163.1.20 [Accessed: 10.11.16].

Oxford University Press (2017) Biopsychosocial [Online]. *English Oxford Living Dictionary.* Available from: https://en.oxforddictionaries.com/definition/biopsychosocial [Accessed: 20.10.17].

Pfohl, B., Blum, N. and Immerman, M. (1997) *Structured Interview for DSM-IV Personality (SIDP-IV).* Washington, DC: American Psychiatric Press. Cited within NICE (2009b) *Borderline Personality Disorder: Treatment and Management – Clinical Guideline 78,* p. 19.

Ritschel, L. A. and Kilpela, L. S. (2014) Borderline Personality Disorder [Online]. *The Encyclopedia of Clinical Psychology,* pp. 1–6. John Wiley & Sons. Available from: http://onlinelibrary.wiley.com/doi/10.1002/9781118625392.wbecp478/full [Accessed: 01.11.16].

Sansone, R. A. and Sansone, L. A. (2011, May) Gender Patterns in Borderline Personality Disorder. *Journal Innovations in Clinical Neuroscience,* 8(5), pp. 16–20.

Scheiderer, E. M., Wood, P. and Trull, T. (2015) The Comorbidity of Borderline Personality Disorder and Posttraumatic Stress Disorder: Revisiting the Prevalence and Associations in a General Population Sample [Online]. *Borderline Personality Disorder and Emotion Dysregulation,* 2(11). Available from: http://bpded.biomedcentral.com/articles/10.1186/s40479-015-0032-y [Accessed: 20.11.16].

Seebohm, H. (2011) On Bondage and Liberty: The Art of the Possible in Medium-Secure Settings. In Dokter, D., Holloway, P. and Seebohm, H. (eds.) *Dramatherapy and Destructiveness: Creating the Evidence Base, Playing with Thanatos.* Kindle edition. Hove, UK: Routledge.

Senol, S. (2016) Borderline Personality Disorder [Online]. *Encyclopaedia Britannica, Inc.* Available from: www.britannica.com/contributor/Selahattin-Senol/9421928 [Accessed: 29.10.16].

Sperry, L. (2016) *Handbook of Diagnosis and Treatment of DSM-5 Personality Disorders: Assessment, Case Conceptualization, and Treatment.* Third edition. Kindle edition. New York: Routledge.

Taylor, S. (2010) *The Fall: The Insanity of the Ego in Human History and the Dawning of a New Era*. Kindle edition. Ropley, UK: John Hunt.

Tyrer, P., Alexander, M. S., Cicchetti, D., Cohen, M. S. and Remington, M. (1979) Reliability of a Schedule for Rating Personality Disorders. *British Journal of Psychiatry*, 135, pp. 168–174. Cited within NICE (2009b) *Borderline Personality Disorder: Treatment and Management – Clinical Guideline 78*, p. 19.

Tyrer, P., Reed, G. and Crawford, M. J. (2015) Classification, Assessment, Prevalence, and Effect of Personality Disorder [Online]. *The Lancet*, 385(9969), pp. 717–726. Available from: www.thelancet.com/journals/lancet/article/PIIS0140-6736(14)61995-4/fulltext [Accessed: 19.11.16].

Vermetten, E. and Spiegel, D. (2014) Trauma and Dissociation: Implications for Borderline Personality Disorder. *Current Psychiatry Reports*, 16(2), p. 434.

WHO (1948) ICD Revision 6 [Online]. Available from: www.wolfbane.com/icd/icd6h.htm [Accessed: 01.11.16].

WHO (1955) ICD Revision 7 [Online]. Available from: www.wolfbane.com/icd/icd7h.htm [Accessed: 01.11.16].

WHO (1965) ICD Revision 8 [Online]. Available from: www.wolfbane.com/icd/icd8h.htm [Accessed: 01.11.16].

WHO (1975) ICD Revision 9 [Online]. Available from: www.wolfbane.com/icd/icd9h.htm [Accessed: 01.11.16].

WHO (2016a) Classifications [Online]. *World Health Organization*. Available from: http://who.int/classifications/icd/revision/en/ [Accessed: 19.11.16].

WHO (2016b) F60-F69 – Disorders of Adult Personality and Behaviour [Online]. *ICD-10 Version: 2016*. Available from: http://apps.who.int/classifications/icd10/browse/2016/en#/F60-F69 [Accessed: 08.10.16].

WHO (2016c) F60 – Specific Personality Disorders [Online]. *ICD-10 Version: 2016*. Available from: http://apps.who.int/classifications/icd10/browse/2016/en#/F60 [Accessed: 08.10.16].

WHO (2016d) F60.3 Emotionally Unstable Personality Disorder [Online]. *ICD-10 Version: 2016*. Available from: http://apps.who.int/classifications/icd10/browse/2016/en#/F60.3 [Accessed: 08.10.16].

Zanarini, M. (1983) *Diagnostic Interview for Personality Disorders (DIPD)*. Belmont, MA: McLean Hospital. Cited within NICE (2009b) *Borderline Personality Disorder: Treatment and Management – Clinical Guideline 78*, p. 19.

Zanarini, M. (2006) *10-Year Course of Borderline Personality Disorder* [Online]. McLean Hospital Harvard Medical. Available from: www.borderlinepersonalitydisorder.com/wp-content/uploads/2012/07/Zanarini10-yearCourseofBPD-10-23-12.pdf [Accessed: 21.11.16].

Zanarini, M., Frankenburg, F., Reich, D., Marino, M., Lewis, R., Williams, A. and Khera, G. (2000) Biparental Failure in the Childhood Experiences of Borderline Patients. *Journal of Personality Disorders*, 14(3), pp. 264–273.

Zeichner, S. (2013) Borderline Personality Disorder: Implications in Family and Pediatric Practice. *Psychology and Psychotherapy*, 3(122). Available from: www.omicsonline.org [Accessed: 01.11.16].

3

PSYCHOLOGICAL
TREATMENTS FOR BPD

I want to be healed,
But I don't know how.
I want to be healed,
I want to be wowed.
I feel so broken,
But I don't know why,
I want to be healed NOW
                    —*Millie, 2016*

A desire for positive change may be the first step towards achieving it. The author of the foregoing poem made a conscious effort to express and unravel her inner turmoil through the dramatherapy (and concurrent art and writing–focused dramatherapy) group process on a secure ward for women with BPD. She also discovered new coping strategies within dialectical behavioural therapy (DBT), regained her confidence in life skills through occupational therapy (OT) groups and tackled personal issues in family therapy, facilitated by the ward's consultant psychiatrist. She wanted her life to change and discovered that genuine change takes courage, patience and time.

Introduction

There is no specific medication for BPD and for decades it was considered untreatable. The role of psychological treatment and the development of new approaches have therefore been vital. NHS Choices describes four examples of recommended treatment for BPD, which includes the arts therapies (dramatherapy, music, art and dance movement therapy), together with DBT, mentalisation-based therapy (MBT) and therapeutic communities (2017). The arts therapies are often incorporated in therapeutic communities and therapeutic programmes with an MBT or DBT focus. NICE recommends long-term, flexible, psychological approaches, as symptoms and needs vary greatly between individuals.

Furthermore, evidence reveals that despite significant improvement over the past decade, stigma attached to people with PD continues, even within mental health services. Individuals do not always have access to the most appropriate treatment and are at times excluded from services due to their diagnosis or behaviour (NICE, 2015, pp. 7–8). The UK's Department of Health (DH) advises that primary care trusts (PCTs) should have a range of Tiers 1 to 3 services for people with moderate to severe personality disorder (PD), offering a selection of interventions (DH/Care Pathways Branch/Mental Health Division, 2009, p. 30).

For women with complex and severe PD, the DH recommends specialist residential Tier 4 services (DH/Care Pathways Branch/Mental Health Division, 2009, p. 57). These are commissioned by NHS England and offer more intensive treatment (NHS England, 2017, p. 314). Female service users on the private, Tier 4 ward where I work are funded by the NHS. They are encouraged to attend all the groups on offer and formally agree to engage in the treatment programme before admission. This includes DBT, OT and dramatherapy (with an allied art and writing–focused dramatherapy group). Most service users are on a mental health section, however, and despite the promotion of less restrictive practice, firm boundaries are vital, and choices limited. Within the dramatherapy group, the theme of freedom is frequently visited. Choosing to attend and staying until the end are recognised as positive acts that take courage and effort. Choice is also promoted throughout, and clients are invited, rather than instructed, to participate in each activity.

Current research indicates a more hopeful prognosis for people with BPD. With unique personalities, histories, symptoms and needs, however, they will respond differently to the various treatments on offer and to the clinicians who administer them. Evidence-based approaches are thought to be most effective, when facilitated by professionals with an expertise in the field (NEA.BPD, 2016). A multidisciplinary approach allows the flexibility recommended by NICE and supportive, positive teamwork is crucial. As Bateman and Krawitz suggest, "All clinicians should have chosen to work with people with BPD, be enthusiastic about the work, optimistic about outcomes, compassionate, and willing to organize around a shared understanding of the disorder" (2013, p. 115).

Treatment pathway

Treatment for BPD in the UK usually includes either individual or group psychotherapy, facilitated by professionals within a community mental health team (CMHT). Should someone deteriorate, they may enter the Care Programme Approach (CPA) for extra support (NHS Choices, 2017). NICE advises that young people with severe BPD (under the age of 18) should also have access to specialist services within both inpatient and outpatient services (NICE, 2009a, p. 24). Treatment for BPD is predicted to last for a year or longer and the type of psychotherapy offered will depend on what is available locally, as well as personal choice (NHS Choices, 2017).

Whilst in the community, individuals should have telephone numbers for their community mental health nurse, an out-of-hours social worker and their local CRT (crisis resolution team) to help to avoid or manage a crisis (NHS Choices, 2017). Should symptoms become severe, individuals may need hospitalisation. Before admitting them, however, NICE advises they should first be referred to their local CRT. Admission may be necessary, however, following a crisis, for people at significant risk to themselves or others, and for those detained under the Mental Health Act (2009a, p. 24).

Research suggests that over 50% of psychiatric service users in the UK have a personality disorder, of which BPD is the most prevalent in non-forensic settings (NICE, 2009b, p. 20). Similarly, Gunderson has estimated that in the US, 20% of all psychiatric inpatients have BPD (2011, p. 3). Registered mental health nurses (RMNs) and health care assistants (HCAs) play a major part in the treatment process within inpatient settings, spending more time with service users than any other member of the MDT (multidisciplinary team). Consistent communication between all members of the MDT is essential (including the ward doctor, manager, consultant psychiatrist, occupational therapist, psychologist, social worker and sessional therapists). Family therapy may also be crucial to the inpatient process.

Treating co-morbidity

Managing co-morbidity is another challenge with the BPD population, as 98% are predicted to have at least one co-morbid mental illness within their lifetime (Bender et al., 2001, p. 296). Australia's NHMRC (National Health and Medical Research Council) advises that co-morbid disorders should be treated simultaneously and within the same service if possible. If not, the additional health service or therapist must communicate closely with the client's main clinician (2013, p. 12). NICE also recommends that co-morbid depression, anxiety or PTSD (post-traumatic stress disorder) be treated within a structured treatment programme for BPD (2009a, p. 20).

Should substance misuse become severe or life-threatening, the NHMRC advises that it should be stabilised before treatment for BPD begins (2013, pp. 12–13), whilst in the UK, NICE recommends referral to appropriate services for someone who has major psychosis, a severe eating disorder or Class A drug or alcohol dependence, in addition to BPD (NICE, 2009a, p. 20). Medication is another area that requires careful attention, due to inconsistent effects, potential suicide risk and co-morbid addictions (NHMRC, 2013, p. 10). NICE advises that short-term psychiatric medicines may be used in the temporary management of a crisis, or in conjunction with psychological treatment. This may relieve some of the symptoms associated with co-morbid disorders, such as depression, anxiety and transient psychosis (NICE, 2015, p. 26).

Therapeutic interventions

In 2014, the UK's Department of Health (DH) commissioned a handbook on how to support people with BPD. Ten treatments are advocated, which vary significantly in structure and ideology: arts therapies (dramatherapy, art, music and dance movement therapy), DBT, MBT, intensive therapeutic programmes (with a DBT or MBT focus), CAT (cognitive analytical therapy), TFP (transference-focused therapy), IGP for BPD (interpersonal group psychotherapy adapted for BPD), CBT for PD (cognitive behavioural therapy adapted for borderline and antisocial PDs), schema therapy (ST) and therapeutic communities (TCs) (Bolton et al., 2014, pp. 76–78).

Whilst this book focuses on how dramatherapy can help people with BPD, it is useful to gain a thorough understanding of other approaches, particularly as dramatherapists often work within multidisciplinary teams (MDTs) offering a range of interventions. Through exploring them, we broaden our understanding of the client group: "The history of specific psychological interventions designed to help people with borderline personality disorder is intertwined with changing conceptions of the nature of the disorder itself" (NICE, 2009b, p. 27). Understanding the rationale and methods employed by our colleagues also enables us to put our work into context when considering the role of dramatherapy within each client's journey. The ten treatments recommended in the handbook (Bolton et al., 2014) will therefore be summarised in this chapter. More detail will be offered about the methods most relevant to dramatherapy, including occupational therapy (OT) for BPD, which is consistently used in both community and ward settings. The others are: schema therapy, from a concept perspective; and both DBT and MBT, as they form the basis of several therapeutic programmes, which often include dramatherapy. I will begin with DBT, the model employed on a Tier 4 secure female ward for BPD where I have worked for many years.

DBT – dialectical behaviour therapy

In the late 1970s, Linehan and her colleagues explored the impact of cognitive behaviour therapy (CBT) on women with a history of chronic suicide attempts, suicidal ideation and non-suicidal injury. These women met the criteria for BPD. Many of them responded negatively and withdrew from treatment (The Linehan Institute, 1996–2016c). As a result, Linehan and her research team made significant changes to the traditional CBT model to address the extent and severity of their clients' problems: acceptance and validation strategies were added, together with a dialectical approach that offered the therapist a way to balance acceptance and encourage change in each session, helping to prevent both therapist and client from becoming stuck. Regular supervision and weekly consultation team meetings became integral to the model, helping to enhance a therapist's capabilities and to prevent burnout.

Linehan published her first book on DBT, together with a skills training manual, in 1993. Dimeff and Linehan describe the approach as a combination of behaviour therapy and eastern mindfulness (2001, p. 1). The aim is to enable clients to replace rigid, split thought patterns with flexible dialectical thinking. Feigenbaum defines dialectics as a concept grounded in philosophy and science, with three core facets: "the interconnectedness of the world; that truth can be found as a synthesis of differing views; and change is inevitable and constant" (2007, p. 53). The term 'dialectical' is also used to capture the numerous tensions that may concurrently arise in therapy with suicidal clients. As Dimeff and Linehan explain, "The fundamental dialectic in DBT is between validation and acceptance of the client as they are, within the context of simultaneously helping them to change" (2001, p. 1).

DBT is a complex biosocial model of therapy, designed to be delivered over one year. It consists of weekly one-to-one sessions, skills group training and access to an individual therapist if in crisis. The main goals are to reduce parasuicidal and life-threatening behaviours, therapy-interfering behaviours (from both client and therapist) and any behaviours that may seriously hinder a person's quality of life (O'Connell and Dowling, 2014, p. 519). DBT regards emotional dysregulation as the core problem for people with BPD, resulting from the variety of factors discussed in the previous chapter. Whilst it was initially developed as an outpatient treatment, it has also been shown to reduce the symptoms of people treated as inpatients (O'Connell and Dowling, 2014, p. 519). NICE advises that DBT should be considered for people when the priority is to reduce self-harm (2009b, p. 205).

There are four stages of DBT, which follow a pre-treatment stage: initially, client and therapist decide if they are compatible and if agreed, formulate a plan. The goal of the first stage is for the client to achieve behavioural control. The second aims to transform the client's state of quiet desperation into one of full emotional experiencing. The third stage challenges the client to define life goals, build self-respect and find peace and happiness. The final stage is for those wanting to find a deeper, spiritual meaning in life and to move from feeling incomplete "towards a life that involves an ongoing capacity for experiences of joy and freedom" (The Linehan Institute, 1996–2016b). During treatment, three core strategies are employed: behavioural change, validation and dialectic (Koerner, 2012, pp. 13–17). There are also four sets of behavioural skills: mindfulness, distress tolerance and acceptance, interpersonal effectiveness and emotion regulation (Koerner, 2012, p. 21; The Linehan Institute, 1996–2016a).

DBT and dramatherapy are clearly very different approaches: one is highly structured and behaviour-focused, employing specific modules and homework; the other is flexible and creative, adapting to individual needs, through a multitude of potential strategies. It is helpful to consider the elements that underpin both methods, however, especially if a dramatherapist is working in a setting that employs the DBT model:

- The four stages of DBT encompass therapeutic aims that a dramatherapist would also work towards, via the creative process.

- One of the five core functions of DBT stresses the importance of therapists receiving regular supervision and continuing to develop their skills. Dramatherapists follow very similar guidelines, as stipulated by the HCPC (2013, p. 11, 2016, p. 7).
- Another of the five core functions highlights the importance of structuring a client's environment. This is also vital within dramatherapy, where a safe space is defined and protected (Jones, 2007, l.524–525) and the process structured through familiar creative rituals.
- Dramatherapists are encouraged to be transparent and informative about their work, offering feedback to their colleagues and seeking information between sessions to develop their understanding of their clients and to refine the dramatherapy process (Benbow and Jackson, 2017, p. 131). Similarly, the last of the five core functions of DBT stresses the importance of communicating with everyone involved in a service user's care.
- Of the three core strategies of DBT, the validation methods are particularly relevant to dramatherapy. Validation and acceptance are essential features of DBT. Together, they mirror the notion of 'unconditional positive regard', which defines acceptance within the humanistic, person-centred approach (Rogers, 2004, p. 62) and is applied by dramatherapists. Certain dialectical strategies likewise relate to dramatherapy, such as entering the paradox, using metaphor and allowing natural change.
- Of the four sets of behavioural skills used in DBT, mindfulness is most relevant to dramatherapy: "A mental state achieved by focusing one's awareness on the present moment, while calmly acknowledging and accepting one's feelings, thoughts, and bodily sensations, used as a therapeutic technique" (Oxford University Press, 2016, number 2). In dramatherapy, working in the 'here and now' is a very similar process (Cassidy et al., 2014, p. 12). As Gluck explains, "The client in drama therapy is fully engaged in the therapy process in the same ways an actor is fully engaged in a performance, mentally, physically, vocally, and emotionally" (2014, p. 86).
- Another of the four sets of behavioural skills relating to dramatherapy is 'distress tolerance and acceptance', which includes techniques such as self-soothing with the five senses, positive distraction and improving the moment through imagery, meaning and relaxation.
- DBT therapists adhere to a set of assumptions about their clients, most of which are relevant to dramatherapists. These include the belief that clients will do their best and cannot fail in therapy, but will need to resolve their own conflicts and find the motivation to change their lives.
- They also agree to set of assumptions about therapy and therapists, most of which are applicable to dramatherapists. These include the belief that client and therapist are equals within a genuine relationship; that therapists will understand the therapy may fail to help their clients to achieve their goals, even when facilitated effectively; and that ongoing supervision and peer support are a necessity.

DBT and dramatherapy clearly share significant aims and beliefs, despite fundamental differences regarding structure and delivery. They should therefore enhance one another. Congruency between professionals is another factor to consider, however, and will be explored towards the end of this chapter.

MBT – mentalisation-based therapy

Fonagy and Bateman began to develop MBT for people with BPD in the early 1990s. Rather than claim originality, they describe it as an approach that identifies developmental processes that exist within each of our histories. The focus is on developing an intense therapeutic relationship that models positive attachment – a concept closely relating to dramatherapy. The aim is that through the experience, patients will learn to understand their mental states. Their feelings and thoughts will be clearly reflected, enabling them "to identify themselves as thinking and feeling in the context of powerful bonds and high levels of emotional arousals" (Fonagy and Bateman, 2010, pp. 14–15).

Fonagy and Bateman describe mentalisation as the process we use to make sense of ourselves and others (2010, p. 11). They suggest that whilst difficulties in this area may relate to most mental health disorders, it is central to people with BPD, due to their "fragile mentalizing capacity vulnerable to social and interpersonal interaction" (2010, p. 12). They believe that mentalisation is therefore essential to any treatment offered to the client group, helping to regulate their thoughts and feelings and enabling them to develop genuine relationships (Fonagy and Bateman, 2010, p. 14). Mentalisation techniques are often used by dramatherapists working with the BPD client group. ICAPT (International Centre for Arts Psychotherapies Training) describes an MBT model for arts therapists that "focuses on the re-representations (image, sound, movement, narrative) of self and other and alternative perspectives that underpin affect regulation and interpersonal dynamics" (CNWL, 2013, p. 4).

In the NICE guideline for the treatment and management of BPD, MBT with partial hospitalisation is reported to reduce anxiety and the general symptoms of BPD, whilst improving general functioning and employment outcomes. Both MBT and DBT with partial hospitalisation are also indicated as effective treatments in reducing suicide attempts, self-harm, anger, aggression and depression (2009b, p. 205). MBT is described by NICE in the context of an RCT conducted by Fonagy and Bateman in 1999. Their clients attended a day hospital for a maximum of eighteen months, where they had weekly individual therapy, expressive therapy with psychodrama, a community meeting and group analytic therapy three times a week (2009b, p. 153).

The concept of mentalising is grounded within Bowlby's attachment theory and the related work of developmental psychologists. The essence is that "infants have an inborn need to seek closeness with their caregiver" (Sperry, 2016, l.899). Sperry explains that if a child's main caregiver (or caregivers) does not respond adequately to this, an insecure attachment will form, and the child may struggle to develop self-soothing and self-regulating abilities. He describes mentalisation as "the ability to reflect upon, and to understand, one's own state of mind" (2016, l.906–907), a skill learnt when a caregiver responds appropriately to a child's distress, forming a secure attachment.

Fonagy and Bateman recommend a therapeutic attitude of 'not knowing', reminding us that "the therapist can have no more idea of what is in the patient's mind than the patient himself" (2007, p. 12). Essentially, their approach may be adapted across various schools of therapy. Rather than learning a new treatment model, practitioners are encouraged to adjust their practice by focusing on mentalising, as opposed to behaviour, cognition or insight (2010, p. 13). Aims and outcomes are therefore more significant than the type of intervention used, and whatever the specific approach, the primary aim is to restore a client's capacity for mentalising. Therapists are encouraged to imagine sitting side-by-side with their patient. Empathy, support and clarity are key to the approach, with an emphasis on the patient-therapist relationship (Fonagy and Bateman, 2010, p. 13). MBT also employs a system of continuous feedback, applied every session via specific measures. This allows client and therapist to discuss relevant themes, such as "quality of life, symptoms, social and interpersonal function, therapy process, and goal-based outcomes" (Bateman and Krawitz, 2013, p. 202).

Fonagy and Bateman advocate the following steps within MBT (2010, p. 13):

- The first step is to establish the patient's perspective by validating the feelings he or she experiences through the transference within the therapeutic relationship.
- The second step is to explore the events that caused those feelings, followed by the behaviours which connect to them.
- The third step is for the therapist to acknowledge his or her part in the transference. This is vital in helping the patient to understand and accept that unintentional comments or gestures from the therapist (which they are willing to admit) do not discount the validity of the therapy or therapist. Distortions can then be genuinely explored.
- The fourth step is a collaboration between patient and therapist through which they interpret the transference from an inquisitive perspective.
- During the fifth step, the therapist offers an alternative view, and finally, the therapist carefully observes the patient's reaction as well as his or her own.

Therapeutic communities

Therapeutic communities (TCs) developed in the UK towards the end of World War II, the first established within Northfield Military Hospital, for soldiers psychologically traumatised by their experiences. Here, Foulkes introduced psychodrama and a hospital-based theatre (Harrison, 2000, p. 247). Several psychological treatment programmes then arose, including those at the Tavistock Clinic and Cassel Hospital. NICE also acknowledges the positive impact of the Northfield experiments on the use of psychological treatments in mental health hospitals worldwide (2009b, p. 29). Drama, art, music and creative writing were utilised within the first

TC and the arts therapies have endured within modern TCs, such as the inpatient service for PD at the Cassel Hospital (WLMHT, 2017). Several TCs now offer specific treatment for people with personality disorders and positive reports from past and current service users are included in the detailed version of the NICE guideline on BPD (2009b, p. 81).

TCs may be residential or will offer weekly programmes, including community meetings and a variety of activities and therapy groups. These often include arts therapy groups, psychodrama, analytical groups, cognitive therapy, problem-solving groups, psychoeducation and Gestalt therapy (NICE, 2009b, p. 30). Staff and service users are recognised as valuable members within a TC, working together in many ways, such as managing crises and deciding when people are ready to leave: "The aim is that individuals will be helped with their own problems, but will also be empowered by discovering their capacity to take responsibility and to help others" (Bolton et al., 2014, p. 81). The interactive community is the core therapeutic structure, enhanced by everything else that takes place. Dramatherapy group work would be an asset to any TC, focusing on communication skills, self-awareness and understanding others.

The arts therapies

NICE acknowledges the prevalence of the arts therapies within BPD treatment programmes and therapeutic communities (TCs). In the absence of quantitative research, however (e.g. RCTs), they are yet to be formerly recommended (2009b, pp. 115–117). Despite this, they were included as one of the ten relevant treatments for people with BPD, in the handbook commissioned by the DH (Bolton et al., 2014, p. 80). They are also one of four examples of recommended treatments for BPD, described by NHS Choices (2017). As Malchiodi reflects, "the expressive therapies help individuals to quickly communicate relevant issues in ways that talk therapy cannot do" (2005, p. 2). Dramatherapy, art, music and dance movement therapy share the philosophy that "creative processes encourage self-expression, promote self-awareness and increase insight, in the context of a reparative therapeutic relationship, thereby enhancing a person's psychological wellbeing" (NICE, 2009b, p. 115).

Arts therapists use creative tools to work both non-verbally and with words, at whatever level suits the individual or group with whom they are working. Malchiodi acknowledges the significance of verbal communication within the arts therapies, whilst also emphasising the power of the non-verbal: for children with restricted language, older adults who have lost the capacity to speak and individuals who have experienced trauma. He explains that "art, music, movement, or play can be ways to convey oneself without words and may be the primary form of communication in therapy" (Malchiodi, 2005, p. 4).

Historically, the arts have been linked to healing. Whilst their role decreased in many cultures with the rise of Western medicine, it was revived in the twentieth century in the form of the arts therapies (Jones, 2007, p. 66). Jones reports that they began to appear as distinct professions in the 1940s and are now recognised in many countries as an integral part of health and care systems (2007, p. 3). In 1991, the European Consortium of Arts Therapies Training and Education (ECArTE) was established, helping to develop courses throughout Europe. It currently has thirty-two member institutions from fourteen countries (ECArTE, 2017). Arts therapists train at the master's level to become state registered professionals in the UK. Dramatherapists, art and music therapists are regulated by the HCPC (Health and Care Professions Council), which describes four significant psychological approaches used by arts therapists: psychosocial interventions, mentalisation-based treatment, mindfulness and compassion-based treatment (2017, p. 1).

Dramatherapy

A history of dramatherapy and a detailed description of effective approaches for clients with BPD will feature in the next chapter. A brief introduction is included here, and throughout this chapter, dramatherapy is considered in relation to the most relevant interventions.

> Dramatherapy is a form of psychological therapy in which all of the performance arts are utilised within the therapeutic relationship. Dramatherapists are both artists and clinicians and draw on their trainings in theatre/drama and therapy to create methods to engage clients in effecting psychological, emotional and social changes.
>
> *(BADth, 2011, Dramatherapy)*

Although dramatherapy began to emerge as a specific profession in the 1960s, history reveals an ancient connection between theatre, dramatic ritual and healing (Schrader, 2012, pp. 32–33). During the twentieth century, the role of drama within education, health and social care began to expand, and from the 1930s, the therapeutic application of drama advanced (Jones, 2007, l.1328–1356). This was a multifaceted transition, influenced by several pioneering individuals, experimental theatre practitioners and developments in related areas, such as hospital theatre, therapeutic theatre, drama-in-education and psychodrama (Jones, 2007, l.797–1327). As Jones explains, "Dramatherapy evolved gradually with a number of starting points which, to an extent, began to converge, rather than being started in one place at one time by one person or group" (2007, l.1588).

In both the UK and North America, formal training for dramatherapy began in the 1970s, and in 1977, the British Association of Dramatherapy (BADth) was established, followed by the North American Drama Therapy Association (NADTA) in 1979 (Cassidy et al., 2014, p. 353). The arts therapies gained prominence in the Netherlands from the 1960s, and in 1981, a branch of The Netherlands Society for Creative Expressive Therapy was dedicated to dramatherapy (Jones, 2007, l.1604–1607). By the end of the twentieth century, dramatherapy was recognised across many parts of the world as a distinct form of psychological treatment for adults and children within health, social care and education.

Drama therapy focuses on the expression and control of emotions, the development of reflectivity, the expansion of role repertoire, and the expansion of interpersonal and communicative skills. In drama therapy methodical work is done with a fictional reality through drama and theater work forms, drama-therapeutic play, scene work (fictional play), role play and psychodrama techniques as role changes and rescripts.

(Dutch Association of Dramatherapy, 2018)

BADth explains that the healing aspects of drama and theatre are core to the process and that creative techniques which give attention to both body and mind allow people to work through intense feelings and difficult memories in an indirect manner (2011). This is a particularly useful approach for the BPD client group, who are often overwhelmed by their emotions and experiences. As Jones explains, "The drama does not serve the therapy. The drama process contains the therapy" (2007, l.486–487). Such containment is paramount, especially when offering clients an alternative way in which to express their inner rage and other intense emotions. Dramatherapy interventions for BPD will be described in detail in Chapter 4.

Art therapy

"Art has been used since the beginning of human history as a medium for communicating thoughts and ideas" (Art Therapy Journal, 2017). In the late 1940s, it began to emerge as a specific form of psychotherapy. In the UK, the artist Hill coined the term 'art therapy' when discovering that immersing oneself in the act of image making whilst hospitalised occupied the mind and released energy (Edwards, 2014, p. 1). Simultaneously, in the US, Naumberg began to describe the work she was developing as art therapy. Her approach was psychoanalytic, with attention given to transference within the therapeutic relationship and image making as a tool to release unconscious thoughts and feelings (Edwards, 2014, p. 1). Art therapy continued to develop and thrive across the world. The British Association of Art Therapists (BAAT) was established in 1964 (Case and Dalley, 2014, p. 23), followed by the American Art Therapy Association (AATA) in 1969 (Junge, 2010, p. 9).

The first art therapy post was created in the UK's National Health Service (NHS) in 1946 (Case and Dalley, 2014, p. 6). It was not until 1997, however, that it became a state registered profession under the CPSM (Council for Professions Supplementary to Medicine [CPSM]) (UK Government, 1997). There remain two approaches in the UK: art as therapy and art psychotherapy. BAAT defines it as "a form of psychotherapy that uses art media as its primary mode of expression and communication" (2017). The American Association currently describes it as

an integrative mental health profession that combines knowledge and understanding of human development and psychological theories and techniques with visual arts and the creative process to provide a unique approach for helping clients improve psychological health, cognitive abilities, and sensory-motor functions.

(AATA, 2017)

Art therapists can work with individuals and groups across a wide range of settings. Their approach will depend on the client group, and whilst influenced by psychoanalysis, they may utilise various theories, including attachment-based psychotherapy, psycho-educational, mindfulness and mentalisation-based treatments, and compassion-focused and cognitive analytic therapies (BAAT, 2017).

The AATA explains that "Art therapy provides an alternative means of communicating for those who cannot find the words to express anxiety, pain or emotions as a result of trauma, combat, physical abuse, loss of brain function, depression, and other debilitating health conditions" (2017). With a specific focus on BPD, Springham and Whitaker published the results of an international survey that explored the approach of art therapists working with the BPD client group. The results revealed that most of them prepared their clients carefully for treatment, giving "particular attention to the attachment issues involved" (2015, p. 31).

Music therapy

"Music has been used extensively throughout history as a healing force to alleviate illness and distress" (Bunt, 2014, p. 5). In the US, training for music therapists began in the mid-1940s. The National Association for Music Therapy (NAMT) was established in New York in 1950, and in 1971, the American Association for Music Therapy (AAMT) was established. The two then merged to become the American Music Therapy Association (AMTA) in 1988 (AMTA, 2017a). In the UK, the British Society for Music Therapy (BMST) was founded in 1958, followed by the Association of Professional Music Therapists (APMT) in 1976. They subsequently merged to become the British Association for Music Therapy (BAMT) in 2011 (BAMT, 2017a).

The definition and essence of music therapy differ across the world and have changed over time. In the UK, BAMT now describes it as a clinical approach for either individuals or groups through which a musical language develops, enabling clients to connect their inner selves and those around them (1998–2017). They explain it is "an effective psychological therapy in supporting and enabling people with mental health problems to manage their condition" (2017b, p. 1). The AMTA currently defines it as "an established health profession in which music is used within a therapeutic relationship to address physical, emotional, cognitive, and social needs of individuals" (2017b).

Describing the potential benefits of music therapy for people with BPD, Odell-Miller stresses the importance of forming close working relationships with all members of the MDT involved in a person's care (2011, p. 34). She suggests that "music therapy that can shift between structured and unstructured forms, and that allows for discussion and interpretation, can help patients to break rigid patterns of thought" (2011, p. 35), encouraging them to gain some control over their destructive behaviours.

Dance movement therapy

The American Dance Therapy Association (ADTA) was founded in 1966. It defines dance movement therapy as "the psychotherapeutic use of movement to promote emotional, social, cognitive and physical integration of the individual" (2016). In the UK, the Association for Dance Movement Psychotherapy (ADMP UK) was established in 1982. Its definition states that "Dance Movement Psychotherapy (DMP) recognises body movement as an implicit and expressive instrument of communication and expression" (2013). ADMP UK describes it as "a relational process in which client/s and therapist engage in an empathic creative process using body movement and dance to assist integration of emotional, cognitive, physical, social and spiritual aspects of self" (2013). DMP is offered as either individual or group therapy in a variety of public and private settings in the UK.

ADTA explains how DMT can help with various functional and organic disorders. With regards to working with trauma, it explains that both the mind and body are affected, and research has revealed that optimum treatment will address both aspects (2016, p. 1). DMT then fulfils these criteria, as movement is central to the approach and "the body is not merely addressed in therapy but actually given a voice" (ADTA, 2016, p. 1). As shared in Chapter 2, Scheiderer and colleagues conducted a large study of the co-morbidity between BPD and PTSD, exploring the significance of childhood sexual abuse and other trauma. It revealed that 53.11% of those who met the criteria for BPD also met the criteria for lifetime PTSD (2015, p. 5). Trauma work is therefore relevant to the BPD client group and has been explored in depth, with a focus on DMP, by Levine and Land:

> The body is deeply connected to the mind, and as the body engages in the movement process, the mind awakens and becomes more aware. Once clients gain awareness, they can begin to attach meaning to what they are feeling, what they experienced, and how they will accept their past as a part of their narrative and integrate the meaning of their experience into their lives in a healthy manner. This process is how resolution of trauma is ultimately achieved.
>
> *(2015, p. 337)*

CBT – cognitive behaviour therapy

CBT integrates two approaches that developed in the early 1960s – primarily Beck's cognitive therapy and partly Ellis's rational emotive behaviour therapy. Based on the concept that behaviour and feelings result from our understanding and thoughts about them, the goal of CBT is to help people develop rational thinking (Slade et al., 2015, pp. 452–453). Supported by extensive research, hundreds of studies have revealed its effectiveness with mental health issues, such as depression, anxiety and

PTSD. When psychological input is required, therefore, it is often the first treatment option. Slade, Hamilton and Thompson reflect that its methods are easier to test, unlike those of psychodynamic models (2015, pp. 457–458).

CBT starts by examining the thoughts and emotions behind a problem behaviour, focusing on the present, rather than the past or the unconscious (Slade et al., 2015, 453). Originally developed for depression, it has since been adapted for people with personality disorders, for whom past experiences are considered within the process, in relation to their core beliefs, also known as schemas (NICE, 2009b, p. 126). The cognitive model describes three levels of belief: (1) automatic thoughts: daily, spontaneous thoughts that directly influence our mood and behaviour; (2) conditional beliefs: which we are usually aware of and are often based on assumptions; (3) core beliefs: our deepest beliefs, developing in childhood and reinforced throughout our lives; they influence our interpretation of the world and are the most resistant to change (Slade et al., 2015, pp. 453–454).

Sperry reports that although CBT, behaviour therapy and cognitive therapy were the choice psychosocial treatments for personality disorders in the mid-1980s, more focused treatments have since developed, with a stronger research base (2016, l.612–614). These include DBT, CBASP (cognitive behaviour analysis system of psychotherapy) and MBCT (mindfulness-based cognitive therapy). Sperry explains, however, that DBT (described earlier in this chapter) maintains many similarities with cognitive therapy. Both encourage a collaborative therapeutic relationship and empathy from the therapist. They also share a teaching element, analyse personal triggers, explore plans and emotions, and employ homework and imagery (2016, l.631–634).

NICE describes CBT for people with BPD as a "structured psychological treatment that focuses on helping a person make connections between their thoughts, feelings and behaviour" (2009b, p. 126). It consists of weekly one-to-one sessions and is facilitated from nine months up to three years (significantly longer than when it is used to treat other conditions); clients are given homework in between sessions and some services offer telephone support (NICE, 2009b, p. 126). Group dramatherapy would complement one-to-one CBT sessions for people with BPD, as it would give them a safe space in which to practise the skills they are learning. As in Grotowski's rehearsal process, each client is offered "a terrain of discoveries, about himself, his possibilities, his chances to transcend his limits" (1995, p. 118).

CAT – cognitive analytic therapy

Ryle developed the CAT model in the early 1980s, in response to the challenging mental health needs in a busy inner London area in the UK. His aim was to create a short-term, focused treatment, integrating different approaches, which could be fairly accessed within the NHS (ACAT, 2016a, p. 1). NICE describes CAT as an approach that uses aspects of CBT, whilst focusing on the therapeutic relationship as a vehicle for change (2009b, p. 127). Initially, the client learns that the negative reciprocal roles learnt in childhood are re-enacted within his or her relationships with both self and others. This is key to the approach. CAT integrates ideas from cognitive psychotherapy and psychoanalysis (ACAT, 2016a, p. 1). Initially developed as a form of one-to-one therapy, its concepts are now applied on a wider scale, enhancing our understanding of how individuals relate to one another within couples, families, teams, systems and society (ACAT, 2016b, p. 1). For people with BPD, CAT aims to create "a reparative relational experience" that allows them to learn new ways to relate to themselves and others (NICE, 2009b, p. 127).

ST – schema therapy

Schema therapy (originally named schema-focused cognitive therapy) was developed by Young as a treatment for people with complex and enduring mental health problems, particularly those diagnosed with personality disorders. The model was inspired by his work with Beck, treating people with cognitive therapy (CT). It became apparent that those who failed to respond had "more rigid cognitive structures; more chronic, often lifelong psychological problems; and more deeply entrenched, dysfunctional belief systems" (Kellogg and Young, 2006, p. 446). It was for individuals like them that Young adapted the CT approach, focusing on the schemas (also known as core beliefs) that were preventing them from progressing. He extended the treatment, allowing more time to explore childhood experiences and placing more significance on the therapeutic relationship (Kellogg and Young, 2006, p. 446). This culminated in a model of eighteen schemas, with guidelines to treat maladaptive coping styles. The techniques used are cognitive, behavioural and emotion-focused.

Kellogg and Young explain that the original model of ST needed further adaptation to help people with BPD, however, due to their rapidly fluctuating moods (2006, p. 446). They suggest an approach allowing for psychological and emotional immaturity "in which patients can grow from functioning as children to functioning as healthy adults" (Kellogg and Young, 2006, p. 450). As NICE explains, schema therapy "aims to facilitate affective engagement and re-learning, which may sometimes involve elements of reparenting" (2009b, p. 127). Working with different aspects of an individual's personality, referred to as modes, has become a key part of ST for people with severe personality disorders. The concept is that three groups of modes exist within each of us: child, parent and coping modes (Kellogg and Young, 2006, p. 447).

For people with BPD, five central modes are identified:

1. The abandoned and abused child: their central state of being.
2. The angry and impulsive child: the part that knows it has suffered injustice.
3. The detached protector: a regular coping mechanism; emotionally withdrawn, isolative and disconnected.
4. The punitive parent: an internalised experience of parenting.

5. The healthy adult: very limited in a person with BPD (Kellogg and Young, 2006, pp. 447–449).

Kellogg and Young suggest that the detrimental interaction between these five modes offers insight into the emotional, often chaotic mental state of individuals with BPD (2006, p. 447). One of the core goals is to help clients to develop their healthy adult mode. The therapist initially embodies this, and further into the process, the client begins to internalise it (2006, p. 449). Schema therapists work with each of the modes using various techniques, within four key strategies:

1. Limited reparenting: This is the central approach, as it addresses the client's core mode of the abandoned and abused child. The therapist employs strategies to reparent the client (within professional boundaries). This may include relevant disclosures, telephone or email contact in between sessions and flash cards given as transitionary objects (Kellogg and Young, 2006, p. 450).
2. Emotion-focused work: This involves experiential techniques, mainly imagery work, dialogues and letter writing. Whilst trauma is carefully explored, the therapist acts as a protective adult and the client then mirrors this for him- or herself. The therapist and client also have frequent dialogues to fight the internalised punitive parent together, thus reassuring and nurturing the abandoned/abused inner child. These internal aspects can be expressed through techniques such as imagery and Gestalt chair work (Kellogg and Young, 2006, p. 450).
3. Cognitive restructuring and education: The underlying philosophy of ST is that all children deserve to have their core needs met, and when this does not happen, developmental problems are likely to emerge (Kellogg and Young, 2006, p. 451). Clients' needs and emotions are validated within therapy and they are taught that in adult relationships, they will need to "negotiate their desires on the basis of respect for, and reciprocity with, others" (Kellogg and Young, 2006, p. 451). Cognitive restructuring also teaches them that it was not their fault that their needs were not met and their feelings not validated, as this was caused by their parents' own difficulties. The client's positive qualities are also emphasised "to help to combat the toxic messages of the punitive parent" (Kellogg and Young, 2006, p. 451).
   Validating their anger and helping them to manage it in a non-destructive manner are also important and positive reinforcement and shaping are two of the strategies used to replace punishment.
4. Behavioural pattern breaking: This is usually the last and longest phase of the ST process, through which clients learn to apply what they have learnt within previous sessions to their current life and relationships. Flash cards, imagery and dialogues are some of the techniques used, together with more traditional behavioural methods, including: relaxation training, assertiveness training, anger management, self-control strategies (e.g. self-monitoring, goal-setting and self-reinforcement) and gradual exposure to feared situations (Kellogg and Young, 2006, p. 452).

Schema therapy takes time and patience, requiring a minimum of two years. There are three treatment phases for BPD: (1) bonding and emotional regulation; (2) schema mode change; and (3) development of autonomy. To begin with, attention is given to the validation of emotions and reparenting. This gradually shifts towards problem solving and, finally, empowering clients to parent themselves. In the third stage, clients are encouraged to become more independent, with an emphasis on interpersonal relationships and self-identity (Kellogg and Young, 2006, p. 449–452).

As a form of individual therapy, the schema approach could work in harmony with group dramatherapy, particularly in relation to techniques employing Jung's archetypes (1978) and Rowan's theory of subpersonalities (1989). The concepts of ST could also enhance the individual dramatherapy process. Whilst researching the method, I recognised many similarities in the trauma-focused dramatherapy approach I employed with a client (pseudonym Jean) whose case is presented in detail in Chapter 5. Poignantly, Kellogg and Young describe the internal world of a person with BPD and his or her conflicting inner modes in theatrical terms: "In this interaction, the patient is living in a kind of inner theater in which the forces of cruelty, rage, submission, and self-numbing each take their turn on the stage" (2006, p. 447).

The Schema Therapy Institute in the UK offers ISST-approved (International Society of Schema Therapy) standard, advanced and group schema therapy training to experienced mental health professionals – or professionals with doctoral or master's-level qualifications in mental health fields – with intermediate or advanced levels of general psychotherapy experience (2017). Training such as this could be invaluable to dramatherapists working with people with BPD, who could then apply a schema-focused model of dramatherapy.

TFP – transference-focused psychotherapy

TFP is a complex, evidence-based form of one-to-one psychodynamic therapy, which can help people with BPD. It focuses on the split between their desire for perfect care and their real experience of care, which has often been disappointing, neglectful or abusive (Bolton et al., 2014, p. 77). The studies that led to the emergence of TFP began in 1972, with the Menninger Foundation's psychotherapy research project, led by Kernberg and colleagues (1972). Their findings directed them towards an approach based on contemporary psychoanalytic object relations theory (Kernberg et al., 2008, p. 602), which continues to develop under the leadership of Kernberg and Clarkin at the Personality Disorders Institute in the US. With their colleagues, they have promoted the use of TFP, helping to establish clinics worldwide (PDI, 2016). The original research team wanted to develop a treatment for people with severe personalities and borderline personality organisation, to reduce suicidal behaviour, anxiety and depression whilst helping them to manage their personal and work-related relationships (PDI, 2016). They discovered that treatment had to focus on how people thought about themselves and others, as well as on their behaviours.

TFP works on the assumption that people with severe personality disorders and borderline personality organisation struggle with identity diffusion, an enduring lack of integration of the self and significant others (Kernberg et al., 2008, p. 602). Defensive coping mechanisms will then emerge, distorting an unwanted reality, such as dissociation and splitting (Sperry, 2016, l.2670–2671). In response to this, the goal within TFP is to help people to integrate their "polarized affect states and representations of self and other into a more coherent whole" (Levy et al., 2006, p. 486). Similarly, dramatherapists may work towards reviving and then integrating their client's alienated aspects of self, using creative techniques, such as subpersonality dialogues (Rowan, 1989, p. 86). To achieve this, therapists use the basic skills of psychoanalysis – interpretation, transference analysis and technical neutrality – together with a significant added technique: the analysis of countertransference (Kernberg et al., 2008, p. 608). TFP also recognises and addresses "the aggression and rage which may be felt very acutely by people with BPD, and the ways in which this may be a response to disappointment in relationships" (Bolton et al., 2014, p. 77).

IGP – interpersonal group psychotherapy

In this model, key themes that cause people difficulty are revealed through their interactions with both the therapist and other members of the group. Attention is also given to the conflict between an individual's desire to be cared for and his or her negative expectations of others (fear of rejection or abuse) (Bolton et al., 2014, p. 77). Within the group process, these conflicting desires and expectations are also explored in relation to each person's childhood.

OT – occupational therapy

Occupational therapists (OTs) work across a wide variety of physical and mental health settings. Their role adapts to their client group, and for individuals with BPD, they assess occupational functioning and formulate occupational, rehabilitation care plans. NICE advises this work should be done (2009b, p. 382), although it does not describe their interventions (2009b, p. 13). I have worked closely with OTs for many years and several have assisted me in weekly dramatherapy and art and writing–focused dramatherapy groups. I have also witnessed the significance of their role with our clients. Georgia Ntzimani supported me in this manner for two years and has summarised the specific role of OT for the BPD client group.

OT for BPD, by Georgia Ntzimani

WFOT (World Federation of Occupational Therapy) describes OT as a client-centred health profession, concerned with promoting health and well-being through occupation (2016). It emerged as a profession early in the twentieth century in the US, as a response to increased health needs following World War I. The connection between well-being and occupation is strong and has been recognised historically. Modern science now confirms what the Greek physician Galen wrote in AD 172:

"Employment is nature's physician, and is essential to human happiness" (Christian et al., 2016, p. 1).

In my role as OT on a secure ward for women with BPD, I worked closely with the dramatherapist (and author of this book), supporting her in group sessions. I learnt that our two approaches worked harmoniously, both encouraging clients to explore interests, form relationships and identify their strengths and limitations, through their participation in creative activities. This helps them to build or rebuild life roles. Whilst dramatherapy invites them to explore their emotions in a safe way and to perform life roles in a creative, imaginary world, OT creates opportunities where the patients practise their life roles in their daily environments.

I start my OT assessment with a question: Can you tell me what you do during the day? This can prompt someone to describe his or her life story. Every daily routine is significant and unique. You can learn how people spend their day, what is most and least important to them, who they spend time with and the life roles with which they identify. A simple question can help an OT meet a person, imagine the person's life and understand the difficulties that form barriers to his or her ambitions. Individual strengths and qualities may be hidden, which an OT can help to uncover. As written in one of my favourite books, *The Little Prince*, "Anything essential is invisible to the eyes" (Saint-Exupéry, 1943, p. 50).

OT interventions focus on enabling individuals to change aspects of themselves, their occupation, the environment or some combination of these to enhance occupational participation. The outcomes are patient-driven and diverse, measured in terms of participation and satisfaction, as well as improvement in occupational performance (WFOT, 2013, p. 4). Occupation refers to activities of daily life that have value and meaning for individuals and their environments (Law et al., 1998). As Glass et al. explain, activity, from a social, productive and fitness perspective, is vital to one's physical and mental health, with the potential to extend our lives and protect us against certain causes of mortality (1999, p. 480).

The value of occupation remains widely underestimated in mental health services and the role of OT is often undermined (Jones, 2010, p. 206). A common misconception is that OTs should set daily activities and keep patients occupied, or teach classes such as baking or needlework. Many staff members expect them to work outside of their roles and do not recognise the complexity of the OT intervention (Creek, 2010, pp. 11–12). Occupation is used as a therapeutic medium to enable clients to address problems with skills, habits and beliefs, whilst supporting them to overcome restricting environmental barriers (Jones, 2010, p. 201).

The occupational needs of people with BPD are often overlooked, despite their significance. Clients may have impairment in social and occupational areas, including leisure, work and self-care (Skodol et al., 2002, p. 276, 2005, p. 1919). Zanarini et al. suggest the presence of greater functional impairment in BPD clients, compared to those with other mental illnesses (2005, p. 19). Falklof and Haglund reveal they may struggle to set realistic goals or tend to rely on others to solve their problems (2010, p. 365). Emotional dysregulation in areas such as volition, habituation and personal causation can lead to maladaptive behaviours that have a negative impact on their daily occupational participation. Previous life experiences and an invalidating environment can also affect their ability to adapt their occupations (Lee and Harris, 2010, p. 560). Jones states that if they lack a clear sense of occupational identity and have difficulty differentiating self from others, clients with BPD may find it difficult to form a future image of themselves, struggling to identify meaning in their lives and set goals for the future (2010, p. 203).

People with BPD might appear competent in one occupational area, such as work, giving the impression of a general competence in life. Jones describes this as "An illusion of competence" (2010, p. 203). She suggests that despite occupational competence in one area, investigation can reveal deficits in others, such as leisure and self-care. The individual may then struggle to maintain a balanced occupational routine. Moreover, she notes that potential trust issues and feelings of shame contribute greatly to their tendency of hiding difficulties and occupational dysfunctions (Jones, 2010, p. 204). Clients with BPD may then avoid OT engagement, as they tend to focus on areas in which they are successful. Furthermore, they often resist building independent living skills, due to their fear of receiving less support and becoming abandoned (Jones, 2010, p. 213). OTs can provide interventions that enable clients with BPD to explore interests, build routines and, through occupational participation, achieve a sense of identity and hope of a meaningful life. One client said, "Occupational therapy is not just about learning new skills; it is about relearning things about your identity and who you are".

Multidisciplinary communication

Words are a complex and significant part of communication: the words we choose, the way we say them and how we hear and interpret the words of others. Every clinical model has its own vocabulary. Within an MDT, however, clinicians from various disciplines need to communicate via a shared language and understanding to avoid misinterpretation. This should include a willingness to understand one another's approaches and may involve adapting individual styles of communication and choice of words. As Colkett reflects, dramatherapy was both valued *and* misunderstood in a psychiatric institution where she was working: "for the dramatherapy to be understood it is often diluted or compromised: perhaps in order to coexist with the other therapies on offer" (2012, p. 258). The challenge for dramatherapists working in these settings may then be to adapt the way they communicate with other professionals, without losing their integrity.

At one stage, the question of compatibility between dramatherapy and DBT arose in my workplace: a clinical psychologist specialising in DBT expressed concern that the nurturing approach employed within the dramatherapy group sabotaged the service users' potential to engage with their individual DBT therapist. In relation to my work, I referred to 'unconditional positive regard' (Rogers, 2004, p. 62). She thought the concept naïve and, considering our methods incompatible, stressed that NICE recommended DBT for BPD and not dramatherapy. Having facilitated sessions on DBT-focused wards for over a decade, however, experience had taught me that despite key differences in structure and delivery, they complemented one another and share significant aims and beliefs.

It became clear that the issue on this occasion was due to professional dynamics, rather than a clash of methods. Offering a variety of interventions requires positive communication between professionals, together with an understanding and respect of one another's work. As Holloway and Seebohm reflect, "There is a concomitant risk that innovative and creative practice may be experienced as a threat towards the established tradition" (2011, p. 5). Healthy working relationships will enhance service users' experience and serve as a positive example. It should also be noted that challenging dynamics within teams may reflect the complex dynamics their clients present. Regular clinical supervision and staff support are then integral to clinical practice in these settings.

Final reflection

In 2009, NICE explored the evidence base for psychological treatments for BPD, in relation to an improvement in mental state and quality of life; reduction in self-harm and risk-related behaviour; and improved social and personal functioning and engagement in treatment (2009b, p. 103). Considering randomised control trials (RCTs) its most reliable source, it focused on several RCTs on DBT and one on MBT. All revealed some benefit in reducing symptoms such as anxiety, depression and self-harm (2009b, p. 170). NICE acknowledges, however, that older adults, males, black people and ethnic minorities with BPD were underrepresented within these RCTs (2009b, p. 110). Other studies have shown that outpatient psychosocial treatments for BPD have the potential to help individuals with less severe symptoms and fewer co-morbidities. They include: CBT, CAT, ST and TFP (NICE, 2009b, p. 209). For these interventions and other relevant therapies, including dramatherapy, NICE encourages further evidence-based research and the development of shared outcome measures between professions to improve and broaden their recommendations (2009b, p. 209).

Dramatherapy works harmoniously with art, music and dance movement therapy. As a form of group therapy, it also complements both DBT- and MBT-focused therapeutic programmes. Similarly, it would work well within therapeutic communities and in combination with psychosocial treatments, such as CBT, CAT, ST and TFT. Moreover, the philosophy and techniques of ST closely relate to a trauma-focused model of one-to-one dramatherapy (explained further in Chapter 5) and clear links have been established by ICAPT with the MBT approach. Finally, there are qualities within TFP and CAT that resonate with the underlying principles of dramatherapy. Building an evidence base to support the use of dramatherapy and demonstrating its genuine value, however, remain an enormous challenge to a profession that is relatively small, particularly in comparison to the field of psychology. This is also true for the other arts therapies. There are many efforts to increase the research and evidence base by professional bodies in the UK and abroad, as well as institutions, such as the Centre for Arts Therapies Research (CATR) at Roehampton University in the UK and the Creative Arts Therapies Research Unit (CATRU) at the Victorian College of the Arts (VCA), University of Melbourne, Australia.

Finding the best treatment for an individual with BPD may take time and will potentially involve a combination of approaches. Antonsen and colleagues conclude that "patients who received combined treatment fared better in the long run, on crucial parameters, than patients allocated to individual therapy alone" (2017, p. 63). Furthermore, O'Connell and Dowling surmise that DBT has become the leading treatment for BPD partly due to the lack of evidence supporting other therapies, rather than evidence for its effectiveness over them (2014, p. 522). Dokter also reflects that the focus on evidence-based practice has created "a situation where the methodology of the randomised control trial (RCT) is privileged as evidence above all others" (2011, p. 36).

To conclude, a combination of long-term individual and group therapy is preferable, within specialist yet flexible BPD services, offering choice wherever possible, empathy and appropriate medication if required. Collaborative teamwork is also essential, with effective communication between colleagues, services and individuals involved in each person's care. Finally, regular clinical supervision and staff support are vital for all mental health professionals working with the client group (NICE, 2009a, p. 14).

References

AATA (2017) What Is Art Therapy? [Online]. *American Art Therapy Association.* Available from: http://arttherapy.org/aata-aboutus/ [Accessed: 20.01.17].

ACAT (2016a) What Is CAT? [Online]. *Association of Cognitive Analytic Therapy.* Available from: www.acat.me.uk/factsheets/What-is-CAT.pdf [Accessed: 29.12.16].

ACAT (2016b) What Is CAT Understanding? [Online]. *Association of Cognitive Analytic Therapy.* Available from: www.acat.me.uk/factsheets/What-is-CAT-Understanding.pdf [Accessed: 29.12.16].

ADMP UK (2013) Home [Online]. *Association for Dance Movement Psychotherapy UK.* Available from: http://admp.org.uk/ [Accessed: 14.01.17].

ADTA (2016) The Knowledge Centre [Online]. *American Dance Therapy Association.* Available from: https://adta.org/faqs/# [Accessed: 14.01.17].

AMTA (2017a) History [Online]. *American Music Therapy Association.* Available from: www.musictherapy.org/about/history/ [Accessed: 14.01.16].

AMTA (2017b) What Is Music Therapy? [Online]. *American Music Therapy Association.* Available from: www.musictherapy.org/about/musictherapy/ [Accessed: 20.01.17].

Antonsen, B., Kvarstein, E., Urnes, Ø., Hummelen, B., Karterud, S. and Wilberg, T. (2017) Favourable Outcome of Long-Term Combined Psychotherapy for Patients with Borderline Personality Disorder: Six-Year Follow-Up of a Randomized Study. *Journal of the Society for Psychotherapy Research*, 27(1), pp. 51–63. Routledge.

Art Therapy Journal (2017) The History of Art Therapy [Online]. Available from: www.arttherapyjournal.org/art-therapy-history.html [Accessed: 15.01.17].

BAAT (2017) About Art Therapy [Online]. *British Association of Art Therapy.* Available from: www.baat.org/About-Art-Therapy [Accessed: 13.01.17].

BADth (2011) Dramatherapy [Online]. *British Association of Dramatherapists.* Available from: http://badth.org.uk/dtherapyy [Accessed: 16.01.17].

BAMT (1998–2017) What Is Music Therapy? [Online]. *British Association of Music Therapy.* Available from: www.bamt.org/music-therapy.html [Accessed: 14.01.17].

BAMT (2017a) History [Online]. *British Association of Music Therapy.* Available from: www.bamt.org/about-british-association-for-music-therapy/history.html   [Accessed: 14.01.16].

BAMT (2017b) BAMT Leaflet – Mental Health [Online]. *British Association of Music Therapy.* Available from: www.bamt.org/british-association-for-music-therapy-resources/bamt-information-leaflets.html [Accessed: 14.01.17].

Bateman, A. and Krawitz, R. (2013) *Borderline Personality Disorder: An Evidence-Based Guide for Generalist Mental Health Professionals.* Kindle edition. Oxford: Oxford University Press.

Benbow, A. and Jackson, J. (2017) 'Remember Me' Dramatherapy with Adults Who Have Autism and Complex Needs and Are Non-Verbal. In Haythorne, D. and Seymour, A. (eds.) *Dramatherapy and Autism.* Abingdon, UK: Routledge.

Bender, D. S., Dolan, R. T., Skodol, A. E., et al. (2001) Treatment Utilization by Patients with Personality Disorders. *American Journal of Psychiatry*, 158, pp. 295–302.

Bolton, W., Lovell, K., Morgan, L. and Wood, H. (2014) *Meeting the Challenge, Making a Difference: Working Effectively to Support People with Personality Disorder in the Community* [Online]. Commissioned by the UK's Department of Health (DH). PDF available from: http://repository.tavistockandportman.ac.uk/864/1/Heather_Wood__MeetingThe Challenge.pdf [Accessed: 01.10.17].

Bunt, L. (2014) *Music Therapy: An Art Beyond Words.* Second edition. New York: Routledge.

Case, C. and Dalley, T. (2014) *The Handbook of Art Therapy.* Third edition. Abingdon, UK: Routledge.

Cassidy, S., Turnbull, S. and Gumley, A. (2014) Exploring Core Processes Facilitating Therapeutic Change in Dramatherapy: A Grounded Theory Analysis of Published Case Studies. *The Arts in Psychotherapy*, 41(4), pp. 353–365.

Christian, J., Wickizer, T. and Burton, K. A. (2016) *A Community-Focused Health and Work Service (HWS)* [Online]. West Conshohocken, PA: Infinity. Available from: http://ssdisolutions.org/book [Accessed: 19.04.17].

CNWL (2013) ICAPT Brochure (The International Centre for Arts Psychotherapies) [Online]. *Central and North West London NHS Foundation Trust.* PDF available from: www.cnwl.nhs.uk/health-professionals/icapt/ [Accessed: 30.12.16].

Colkett, D. (2012) Connecting with the Divine Feminine Ritual Theatre in a Forensic Psychiatric Setting. In Schrader, C. (ed.) *Ritual Theatre: The Power of Dramatic Ritual in Personal Development Groups and Clinical Practice.* London: Jessica Kingsley.

Creek, J. (2010) *The Core Concepts of Occupational Therapy: A Dynamic Framework for Practice.* London: Jessica Kingsley.

DH/Care Pathways Branch/Mental Health Division (2009) Recognising Complexity: Commissioning Guidance for Personality Disorder Services [Online]. PDF available from: http://cipn.org.uk/wp-content/uploads/2017/05/recognising_complexity_june_09.pdf [Accessed: 01.10.17].

Dimeff, L. and Linehan, M. (2001) Dialectical Behaviour Therapy in a Nutshell. *The California Psychologist*, 34, pp. 10–13.

Dokter, D. (2011) Practice-Based Evidence: Dramatherapy and Destructiveness. In Dokter, D., Holloway, P. and Seebohm, H. (eds.) *Dramatherapy and Destructiveness: Creating the Evidence Base, Playing with Thanatos.* Hove, UK: Routledge.

Dutch Association of Dramatherapy (2018) Dramatherapy [Google translate]. Available from: http://dramatherapie.nl/dramatherapie/ [Accessed: 10.03.18].

ECArTE (2017) Home [Online]. *Arts Therapies Education in Europe.* Available from: www.ecarte.info/ [Accessed: 19.01.17].

Edwards, D. (2014) *Art Therapy.* Second edition. In Series: *Creative Therapies Practice.* Los Angeles: SAGE.

Falklof, I. and Haglund, L. (2010) Daily Occupations and Adaptation to Daily Life Described by Women Suffering from Borderline Personality Disorder. *Occupational Therapy in Mental Health*, 26, pp. 354–374.

Feigenbaum, J. (2007) Dialectical Behaviour Therapy: An Increasing Evidence Base. *Journal of Mental Health*, 16(1), pp. 51–68.

Fonagy, P. and Bateman, A. (2007) Mentalizing and Borderline Personality Disorder. *Journal of Mental Health*, 16(1), pp. 83–101.

Fonagy, P. and Bateman, A. (2010) Mentalization-Based Treatment for Borderline Personality Disorder. *World Psychiatry*, pp. 11–15.

Glass, T. A., Mendes de Leon, C., Marrotoli, R. A. and Berkman, L. F. (1999) Population Based Study of Social and Productive Activities as Predictors of Survival amongst Elderly Americans. *British Medical Journal*, 319, pp. 478–483.

Gluck, J. (2014) Mindfulness and Drama Therapy: Insight Improvisation and the Transformation of Anger. In Rappaport, L. (ed.) *Mindfulness and the Arts Therapies: Theory and Practice*. London: Jessica Kingsley.

Grotowski, J. (1995) From the Theatre Company to Art as Vehicle. In Richard, T. (author) *At Work with Grotowski on Physical Actions*. London: Routledge.

Gunderson, J. (2011) Borderline Personality Disorder [Online]. *The New England Journal of Medicine*, 364(21), pp. 2037–2042. Available from: http://search.proquest.com/docview/869106178?accountid=50340 [Accessed: 01.11.16].

Harrison, T. (2000) *Bion, Rickman, Foulkes and the Northfield Experiments: Advancing on a Different Front (Community, Culture and Change)*. In Series: Haigh, R. and Lees, J. (eds.) *Community, Culture and Change*. London: Jessica Kingsley.

HCPC (2013) Standards of Proficiency: Arts Therapists [Online]. *Health Care Professions Council*. Available from: http://hpcuk.org/registrants/standards/download/index.asp?id=399 [Accessed: 23.12.16].

HCPC (2016) Your Duties as a Registrant: Standards of Conduct, Performance and Ethics [Online]. *Health Care Professions Council*. Available from: www.hcpc-uk.org/publications/standards/index.asp?id=38 [Accessed: 23.12.16].

HCPC (2017) Arts Therapists Q & A [Online]. *Health Care Professions Council*. PDF available from: www.hpc-uk.org/assets/documents/10004B66Arts-therapy.pdf [Accessed: 13.01.17].

Holloway, P. and Seebohm, H. (2011) When Worlds Elide: Culture, Dialogue and Identity in Multi-Professional Settings. *Dramatherapy*, 33(1), pp. 4–15.

Jones, L. (2010) The Role of the Occupational Therapist in Treating People with Personality Disorder. In Murphy, N. and McVey, D. (eds.) *Treating Personality Disorder: Creating Robust Services for People with Complex Mental Health Needs*. Abingdon, UK: Routledge.

Jones, P. (2007) *Drama as Therapy Volume 1: Theory, Practice and Research*. Second edition. Kindle edition. Abingdon, UK: Routledge.

Jung, C. (1978) *Man and his Symbols (Picador Version)*. Second edition. London: Pan Books.

Junge, M. (2010) *The Modern History of Art Therapy in the United States*. Springfield, IL: Charles C. Thomas.

Kellogg, S. and Young, J. (2006) Schema Therapy for Borderline Personality Disorder [Online]. *Journal of Clinical Psychology*, 62(4), pp. 445–458. Available from: www.interscience.wiley.com

Kernberg, O., Burnstein, E., Coyne, L., Appelbaum, A., Horwith, L. and Voth, H. (1972) Psychotherapy and Psychoanalysis: Final Report of the Menninger Foundation's Psychotherapy Research Project. *Bulletin of the Menninger Clinic*, 36, pp. 1–275.

Kernberg, O., Frank, E., Yeomans, F., Clarkin, F. and Levy, K. (2008) Transference-Focused Psychotherapy: Overview and Update. *The International Journal of Psychoanalysis* © *Institute of Psychoanalysis*, 89, pp. 601–620.

Koerner, K. (2012) Doing Dialectical Behavior Therapy: A Practical Guide. In Series: Persons, J. B. (ed.) *Guides to Individualised Evidence-Based Treatment.* New York: The Guilford Press.

Law, M., Steinwender, S. and Leclair, L. (1998) Occupation, Health and Well-Being. *Canadian Journal of Occupational Therapy*, 65(2), pp. 81–91.

Lee, S. and Harris, M. (2010) The Development of an Effective Occupational Therapy Assessment and Treatment Pathway for Women with a Diagnosis of Borderline Personality Disorder in an Inpatient Setting: Implementing the Model of Human Occupation. *British Journal of Occupational Therapy*, 73(11), pp. 559–563.

Levine, B. and Land, H. (2015) A Meta-Synthesis of Qualitative Findings about Dance/ Movement Therapy for Individuals with Trauma. *Qualitative Health Research*, 26(3), pp. 330–344.

Levy, K., Clarkin, J., Yeomans, F., Scott, L., Wasserman, R. and Kernberg, O. (2006) The Mechanisms of Change in the Treatment of Borderline Personality Disorder with Transference-Focused Psychotherapy. *Journal of Clinical Psychology*, 62, pp. 481–501.

The Linehan Institute (1996–2016a) What Skills Are Taught in DBT? [Online]. *Behavior Tech: A Linehan Institute Training Company.* Available from: http://behavioraltech.org/ resources/whatisdbt.cfm [Accessed: 11.12.16].

The Linehan Institute (1996–2016b) What Are the Stages of Treatment in DBT? [Online]. *Behavior Tech: A Linehan Institute Training Company.* Available from: http://behavioraltech. org/resources/whatisdbt.cfm [Accessed: 11.12.16].

The Linehan Institute (1996–2016c) The Development of DBT [Online]. *Behavior Tech: A Linehan Institute Training Company.* Available from: http://behavioraltech.org/resources/ whatisdbt.cfm [Accessed: 07.12.16].

Malchiodi, C. (2005) Expressive Therapies History, Theory, and Practice. In Malchiodi, C. (ed.) *Expressive Therapies.* New York: Guilford.

Mosquera, D., Leeds, A. and Gonzalez, A. (2015) Application of EMDR Therapy for Borderline. *Personality Disorder Journal of EMDR Practice and Research*, 8(2), p. 89.

NEA.BPD (2016) For Professionals [Online]. *The National Education Alliance for Borderline Personality Disorder.* Available from: www.borderlinepersonalitydisorder.com/professionals/ [Accessed: 07.10.16].

NHMRC (2013) *Clinical Practice Guideline for the Management of Borderline Personality Disorder* (Full List of Recommendations) [Online]. © Commonwealth of Australia. National Health and Medical Research Council. Melbourne, Australia: National Health and Medical Research Council.

NHS Choices (2017) Treatment, Borderline Personality Disorder [Online]. *NHS Choices.* Available from: www.nhs.uk/Conditions/Borderline-personality-disorder/Pages/ Treatment.aspx [Accessed: 10.07.17].

NHS England (2017) Manual for Prescribed Specialised Services 2017/18 [Online]. PDF available from: www.england.nhs.uk/wp-content/uploads/2017/10/prescribed-specialised-services-manual-2.pdf [Accessed: 23.11.17].

NICE (2009a) *Borderline Personality Disorder: Recognition and Management: Clinical Guideline 78* [Online]. National Institute for Health and Care Excellence. Developed by the National Collaborating Centre for Mental Health. Available from: www.nice.org.uk/guidance/ cg78/chapter/1-Guidance [Accessed: 01.10.17].

NICE (2009b) *Borderline Personality Disorder: Treatment and Management: National Clinical Practice Guideline 78* [Online]. National Institute for Health and Care Excellence. Developed by the National Collaborating Centre for Mental Health. UK: The British Psychological Society and The Royal College of Psychiatrists. [Reproduced with Permission of the Licensor through PLSclear]. PDF available from: www.nice.org.uk/guidance/cg78/ evidence [Accessed: 10.10.17].

NICE (2015) *Personality Disorders: Borderline and Antisocial: Quality Standard 88* [Online]. National Institute for Health and Care Excellence. PDF available from: www.nice.org. uk/guidance/qs88

O'Connell, B. and Dowling, M. (2014) Dialectical Behaviour Therapy (DBT) in the Treatment of Borderline Personality Disorder. *Journal of Psychiatric and Mental Health Nursing*, 21, pp. 518–525.

Odell-Miller, H. (2011) Value of Music Therapy for People with Personality Disorders. *Mental Health Practice*, 14(10), pp. 34–35.

Oxford University Press (2016) Definition of Mindfulness (Number 2) [Online]. Available from: https://en.oxforddictionaries.com/definition/mindfulness [Accessed: 14.12.16].

PDI (2016) Research [Online]. *Personality Disorders Institute*. Available from: www.borderline-disorders.com/borderline-personality-disorder-TFP-research.phpp [Accessed: 03.01.17].

Saint-Exupéry, A. de (1943) [Le Petit prince] *The Little Prince*. Translated by Howard, R. (2009). New York: Houghton Mifflin Harcourt.

Scheiderer, E. M., Wood, P. and Trull, T. (2015) The Comorbidity of Borderline Personality Disorder and Posttraumatic Stress Disorder: Revisiting the Prevalence and Associations in a General Population Sample [Online]. *Borderline Personality Disorder and Emotion Dysregulation*, 2(11). Available from: http://bpded.biomedcentral.com/articles/10.1186/s40479-015-0032-y [Accessed: 20.11.16].

Schrader, C. (2012) *Ritual Theatre: The Power of Dramatic Ritual in Personal Development Groups and Clinical Practice*. London: Jessica Kingsley.

Skodol, A. E., Gunderson, J. G., McGlashan, T. H., et al. (2002) Functional Impairment in Patients with Schizotypal, Borderline, Avoidant or Obsessive-Compulsive Personality Disorder. *American Journal of Psychiatry*, 159(2), pp. 276–283.

Skodol, A. E., Oldham, J. M., Bender, D. S., et al. (2005) Dimensional Representations of DSM-IV Personality Disorders: Relationships to Functional Impairment. *American Journal of Psychiatry*, 162(10), pp. 1919–1925.

Slade, K., Hamilton, L. and Thompson, C. (2015) Psychological Interventions. In Banyard, P., Dillon, G., Norman, C. and Winder, B. (eds.) *Essential Psychology*. Second edition. Kindle edition. London: SAGE.

Sperry, L. (2016) *Handbook of Diagnosis and Treatment of DSM-5 Personality Disorders: Assessment, Case Conceptualization, and Treatment*. Third edition. Kindle edition. New York: Routledge.

Springham, N. and Whitaker, R. (2015) How Do Art Therapists Structure Their Approach to Borderline Personality Disorder? [Online]. *Arts in Psychotherapy*, 43, pp. 31–39. UK: Elsevier.

Rogers, C. (2004) *On Becoming a Person: A Therapist's View on Psychotherapy*. New Edition (initially published in 1967). London: Constable.

Rowan, J. (1990) *Subpersonalities: The People Inside Us*. London: Routledge.

The Schema Therapy Institute (2017) Available from: www.schemainstitute.co.uk/item/training-and-certification.html [Accessed: 09.01.17].

UK Government (1997) *The Professions Supplementary to Medicine (Arts Therapists Board) Order of Council 1997*. The National Archives. Available from: https://www.legislation.gov.uk/uksi/1997/1121/introduction/made [Accessed: 10.03.18].

WFOT (2013) Definitions of Occupational Therapy from Member Organisations [Online]. *World Federation of Occupational Therapists*. Available from: www.wfot.org/Resource Centre/tabid/132/did/608/Default.aspx [Accessed: 24.04.17].

WFOT (2016) Fundamental Beliefs [Online]. *World Federation of Occupational Therapists*. Available from: www.wfot.org/AboutUs/FundamentalBeliefs.aspx [Accessed: 19.04.17].

WLMHT (2017) Cassel Hospital, Inpatient Service [Online]. *West London Mental Health NHS Trust.* Available from: www.wlmht.nhs.uk/cs/cassel-hospital-services/inpatientservice/ [Accessed: 23.10.17].

Zanarini, M. C., Frankenburg, F. R., Hennen, J., Reich, B. and Silk, K. R. (2005) Psychosocial Functioning of Borderline Patients and Axis II Comparison Subjects Followed Prospectively for Six Years. *Journal of Personality Disorders*, 19(1), pp. 9–29.

4

EMBRACE AND CONTAIN THE CHAOS

Dramatherapy for BPD

With gentle words and simple games, I tiptoe closer,
My heart open to the wounds within.
I remain open yet stay rooted within the creative realm,
Clear rituals holding each step of our journey,
Each person blossoms in their own way, in their own time.
So often, a dramatic release is called for,
Energy and noise filling the space.
Playing in a way you may never have played,
Imagining a life, you may never have imagined,
Offering the possibility for change,
Allowing you to see yourselves in a brighter light.

—N. Morris, 2016

NICE released a quality standard (QS88) in 2015 to improve the treatment and care of people with BPD in the UK, advocating flexible, person-centred, psychological therapies. Dramatherapy meets these criteria: offering an empowering process, held within unique structures, with the potential to embrace and contain the emotional chaos often experienced by the client group. Such chaos does not need to be feared, as the philosopher Nietzsche wrote: "I tell you: one must still have chaos in oneself, to give birth to a dancing star" (1885, p. 5). It is perhaps by recognising and accepting our own inner chaos – as well as the chaos that permeates the world around us – that we can work most genuinely with the client group. In this chapter, the rationale for offering dramatherapy to people with BPD will be explored in relation to attachment and trauma. Published research that supports the model, together with approaches used by other dramatherapists working with the client group, will also be presented.

Over the past thirteen years, I have developed and refined a dramatherapy approach for women with BPD, echoed in the foregoing poem. The work takes place within inpatient units, where clients are offered a stimulating and creative space in which to safely explore their inner selves, express themselves freely and interact playfully with others. Encouraging a sense of genuine freedom, especially within a secure setting, is vital to the process. Colkett describes a similar approach with a dramatherapy group for women with BPD in a forensic setting, "choosing interventions moment by moment, to help heal not only the internal emotional disturbance in the present, but possibly past influences, conscious and unconscious beliefs" (2012, p. 267). The approach also resembles the model presented by Jones, in which "*the basic processes are constant* and are utilised in different ways according to specific client need" (2007, l.790–791). Casson, both dramatherapist and psychodramatist, uses a theatrical metaphor to describe the potential of the dramatic process:

> In the theatre of our lives we can feel lost, forget our lines, lose a role, feel frozen, unable to move or change: we may need a prompt, a rehearsal for the next scene or to go back to a previous scene and sort it out. Acting can then enable us to move, to change.
>
> *(2017)*

It seems, however, that genuine change will occur only if an individual allows it to happen. As Nietzsche explains, "the free spirit works out for itself an answer to that riddle of its liberation and concludes by generalizing upon its experience" (2015, l.7484–7485). Levine relates both Freud's idea of 'free association' and Winnicott's concept of 'free play' to a form of chaos, out of which new ideas and feelings can emerge (2005, p. 44). Within the safe boundaries of dramatherapy, a similar process is facilitated, enabling clients to develop a stronger sense of self. As Levine explains, "transitional and liminal states are phases in a process of destructuring and restructuring. Their ultimate purpose lies in the new meanings which emerge out of the ruins of the old" (2005, p. 44).

Dramatherapy: History and definition

Dramatherapy emerged as a profession in the latter part of the twentieth century, having evolved gradually in different parts of the world, influenced by numerous individuals, groups and other modalities (Jones, 2007, l.1591–1592). It is challenging therefore to offer a concise history and, as Malchiodi reflects, drama and other expressive methods have historic links to healing, revealed within medical, anthropological and arts literature (2005, p. 4). Sharing a precise definition of dramatherapy is another challenge, due to its variety of form and application across the world.

Ancient roots

Theatre originated in the ancient world, bringing together poetry, myth, dance, music and religious rituals. In Greek tragedy, Aristotle identified the significance of catharsis. In both medical and ritual literature, it refers to a type of purging or purification. Levine explains that Aristotle used it to describe the process that allowed Athenian audiences to witness the tragic component of humanity in its purest form, helping them to understand and accept the limitations of being human: "We are born, we suffer, and we will die" (2005, p. 56). Rather than eliminate distressing emotions or fears, the cathartic element of Greek tragedy enabled people to connect to these feelings, on a personal, communal and even universal level. Aristotle believed that tragic poiesis – the dramatised imitation of an action – led to catharsis (Levine, 2005, p. 56). These ideas have influenced (and remain highly relevant to) dramatherapy, as do other elements of ancient Greek theatre: a dedicated space in which to contain the creative process, the roles of witness, director, writer and performer, and the inclusion of myth, movement, music, art and ritual.

Shamanism is another ancient practice that has influenced dramatherapy and is considered by some as the ancestor of theatre. Whilst exploring this connection, Pendzik explains that sacred spaces were the original stages: magic circles, altars and defined places in which sacred rituals took place (1988, p. 88). The construct of creating a safe space in which to facilitate the creative, potentially healing process of dramatherapy is core to the approach. As Grainger describes, "The sacred space of ritual encounter becomes the specially contrived therapeutic space of dramatherapy" (2014, l.1996–1997). The ritual aspect should be introduced carefully, however, as individuals will respond differently, depending on personal beliefs, cultures, associations and mental states. Schrader writes, "As dramatherapists we will know the sensitivity and care that is [sic] needed when introducing ritual elements into our work with vulnerable clients, and the profound healing that is possible for them when we find a way of doing this successfully" (2012, p. 35). This is also true when introducing service users to creative techniques and props for the first time. For example when a woman of African descent, struggling with symptoms of schizo-affective disorder, initially encountered theatrical masks in my dramatherapy group, she was terrified, associating them with witchery and black magic. Therapeutic card decks have also provoked distress in a few clients, who feared they were tarot cards and would be used to predict the future.

Theatre meets therapy

Theatre has evolved throughout time in response to the developing world around it, influenced by culture, politics and historic events, as well as talented writers and directors. The theatrical revolution of the twentieth century is pertinent to dramatherapy, during which the healing element of theatre was taken to a new level by pioneering, experimental theatre practitioners, including Brecht in Germany, Brook in England, Stanislavski in Russia, Artaud in France, Grotowski in Poland and Boal in Brazil. Their unique methods and ideas reintroduced the therapeutic potential of theatre and dramatic processes (Jones, 2007, l.953–957), opening a pathway to dramatherapy and continuing to inspire and inform the profession today.

Brecht's social approach to theatre saw drama as a vehicle to transform society, encouraging people to think and enabling them to survive (Roose-Evans, 1989a, p. 67–68). This relates (and remains relevant) to the transformative nature of the individual and group dramatherapy process. Brook's and Grotowski's methods also continue to influence ritual theatre and the ritual approach to dramatherapy (Schrader, 2012, p. 33), whilst Stanislavski's dedication to the psychological development of characters (Drain, 1995, p. 254) informs role embodiment in dramatherapy, where clients are encouraged to understand that within every character (as in themselves) unique impulses and aspects of personality exist. Artaud endeavoured to break down the constrictions of theatre, allowing audience and performer to experience the phenomenon together in new ways. He encouraged improvisation and "in place of the poetry of language, he proposed a poetry of space" (Roose-Evans, 1989b, p. 76), employing art forms such as music, dance, painting and chanting. His approach remains pertinent to current forms of dramatherapy, including the methods I use with the BPD client group. Boal also brought audience and performers together, empowering people through a creative process that transformed spectators into spect*actors* (Boal, 2008, p. xxi). There are many aspects of his work that resonate with the dramatherapy process, such as the notion that true liberation from oppression may be rehearsed through a shared dramatic experience.

Dramatherapy in the twentieth century

From the 1930s, the therapeutic application of drama advanced due to the inspiring work of many individuals in related fields. Hospital Theatre expanded its role beyond simple entertainment and other modalities developed, gaining recognition within health and care settings: drama-in-education, therapeutic theatre, psychodrama and play therapy. Changes were stimulated further in the aftermath of World War II, as mental health problems became more widely recognised due to the emotional and psychological scars imprinted on its soldiers. In 1948, influenced by the post–World War II Veterans Administration Classification, WHO included a new section on mental disorders within its sixth edition of the *ICD*, and in 1952, the APA (American Psychiatric Association) published its first *DSM* (APA, 2017).

There are many significant individuals who either influenced or directly shaped the dramatherapy profession, as well as related modalities and inspiring philosophies. During the 1920s, in revolutionary Russia, Iljine developed therapeutic theatre, whilst Evreinov created theatrotherapy. Meanwhile, Moreno created the Theatre of Spontaneity, and in 1936, he opened the first psychodrama theatre in New York (Jones, 2007, l.1016–1209). Dramatherapy also embraced the concepts of group analytic psychotherapy, Jungian archetypal psychotherapy, Gestalt therapy and systems theory. In 1939, Peter Slade was the first person in the UK to put the words 'drama' and 'therapy' together, during his lecture to the British Medical Association (Jones, 2007, l.818–826). In 1959, he was then the first to publish the two words as one, within his pivotal paper 'Dramatherapy as an Aid to Becoming a Person' for the Guild of Pastoral Psychology (Jennings, 2016, l.438–440). Slade influenced and supported Billy Lindkvist, who played a key role in establishing the Sesame Association for Drama and Movement Therapy (Lindkvist, 2007, l.1527–1533), and inspired Sue Jennings, a founding member of the British Association of Dramatherapy.

Jennings originally developed remedial drama with Gordon Wiseman in the 1960s, renamed dramatherapy in 1970 (Jennings, 2007, l.1559–1574). Jennings continued to pioneer dramatherapy (and play therapy) across the world, establishing and contributing to many training programmes (Jennings, 2012a).

Formal dramatherapy training began in both the UK and North America in the 1970s. By the end of the twentieth century, it was firmly established as a distinct form of psychological treatment within special education and physical and mental health care, across many parts of the world. In Europe, ECaRTE (The European Consortium of Arts Therapies Training and Education) currently has thirty-two member institutions from fourteen countries (ECaRTE, 2017).

The UK Parliament passed an act in 1997 acknowledging dramatherapy (music and art therapy) as a state registered profession under the CPSM (Council for Professions Supplementary to Medicine) (UK Government, 1997). The CPSM was replaced by the HPC (Health Professions Council) in 2002 and renamed the HCPC (Health and Care Professions Council) in 2012 (HCPC, 2017). To work as a dramatherapist in the UK, one must currently complete validated master's-level training, then register with the HCPC and adhere to its regulations.

Defining dramatherapy in the twenty-first century

Dramatherapy continues to expand globally and training is now offered in many parts of the world: South Africa, Canada, the US, Taiwan, Korea, Australia, New Zealand, Israel and much of Europe: the UK, Republic of Ireland, Greece, Cyprus, Norway, the Netherlands, Italy, Romania, Kazakhstan, Switzerland, Austria, Germany and Czech Republic (Jennings, 2012a; Jennings, 2016, l.504–506). It is clearly flexible and far-reaching, able to respond to a variety of cultural, social and political needs.

In North America, NADTA currently describes dramatherapy as

> an active, experiential approach to facilitating change. Through storytelling, projective play, purposeful improvisation, and performance, participants are invited to rehearse desired behaviors, practice being in relationship, expand and find flexibility between life roles, and perform the change they wish to be and see in the world.
>
> *(2017)*

The last part of this definition connects to Gandhi's philosophy and may have been inspired by his words:

> We but mirror the world. All the tendencies present in the outer world are to be found in the world of our body. If we could change ourselves, the tendencies in the world would also change. As a man changes his own nature, so does the attitude of the world change towards him. This is the divine mystery supreme. A wonderful thing it is and the source of our happiness. We need not wait to see what others do.
>
> *(Gandhi, 1999, p. 241)*

In the UK, BADth currently offers the following definition: "Dramatherapy has as its main focus the intentional use of healing aspects of drama and theatre as the therapeutic process. It is a method of working and playing that uses action methods to facilitate creativity, imagination, learning, insight and growth" (2011).

Dramatherapy for people with BPD

I have developed an approach for women with BPD, with simple yet effective rituals, encompassing a free-flowing creative process. The opening and closing rituals help clients to focus on themselves and others in the 'here and now'. They also frame the experiential, central part of the session, making it less daunting. Inspired and guided by the principles of Rogers's person-centred approach, I endeavour to create a dramatherapy space "where unconditional acceptance, regard and approval are present" (Slade et al., 2015, p. 459). As a dramatherapist, I am therefore a guide, opening the door to a range of possibilities, which I trust the client will choose to move through when ready. Grainger describes a similar approach with thought-disordered clients, who were more responsive to a less directive style. He reflects that "allowing scenarios to evolve in their own way, 'at their own speed', frequently produced quite startling examples of insight" (2014, l.216–217).

Interpersonal relationships are fostered within the dramatherapy group and trust is established through a positive therapeutic relationship. Whilst play and projective methods are often used, dramatic techniques change in response to the shifting dynamics and specific needs of the participants. The model I use for one-to-one dramatherapy tends to be influenced by Rowan's subpersonality work (1990) and Jungian archetypes (Jung, 1968), through which clients are encouraged to give voice to their many parts, as a path towards integration of the whole. This relates to the Jungian concept of integrating our internal aspects, including the shadow part, to reach individuation (Stevens, 2001, p. 64, p. 81). More subtly, perhaps, this also underpins many group sessions. I have learnt that offering a safe space to contain the emotional chaos so often experienced helps to alleviate and transform its potential destructiveness: "When you give rise to that which is within you, what you have will save you. If you do not give rise to it, what you do not have will destroy you" (Davies, 2002, verse 70).

Thirteen dramatherapists share their experience

To offer a broader, more varied account of how a dramatherapist might work with the client group, I sent a request for research participants via BADth, LinkedIn and Facebook. Of the twenty individuals who initially responded, thirteen completed questionnaires. After establishing basic details about their work, the research participants were invited to answer a series of reflective questions, exploring their specific experience and approaches:

- How long have you worked with people with BPD/EUPD?
- Describe the setting/settings in which you work with this client group.
- Do you facilitate one-to-one dramatherapy with males and/or females?

- Regarding group dramatherapy, do you facilitate mixed or sole-gender groups, and do the group members have the same or varying diagnoses?
- Describe the approach you use with this client group, including specific psychological influences, dramatherapy models and structures and so forth.
- Outline the significance of clinical supervision with regards to your work with this client group.
- Reflect on the key issues that arise in this work and how easy or difficult you find it to 'let go' at the end of the working day.
- In your own words, how would you describe the client group?
- How do you evaluate your work?
- Please share any further information, thoughts and feelings you have about working with this client group.

Their experiences varied from a seventh-month student placement to over twenty years of professional work. Two had one year's experience, four had between five and fourteen years' and five had between fifteen and twenty years'. Their answers were rich and diverse, covering twenty-one settings, five of them having worked with the client group in more than one place. The variety of settings and clients described by the thirteen participants is a testament to the potential for dramatherapy to support both men and women in this challenging area of mental health:

- Eleven of the settings were inpatient services; five within the NHS, including two forensic hospitals. There was also a private care home, a female prison, a private secure female rehabilitation unit and a private forensic hospital.
- Of the ten outpatient services, eight were in the NHS: one in CAMHS (Child and Adolescent Mental Health Service); three MBT (mentalisation-based therapy) programmes; an eating disorders clinic; and three mental health and learning disability settings. The two outpatient settings (not NHS-based) were a charity substance misuse service and a private practice.
- Of the twenty-one settings, all except one involved adults only.
- Nine of the thirteen dramatherapists had experience in running both group and individual sessions with the client group.
- Eight of them had worked with both men and women with BPD and one had also worked with transgender clients.

The research participants shared a wide variety of techniques, informed by various practitioners and theories. The majority described group dramatherapy as a fluid process, which shifted over time, in response to changing membership and dynamics. Goodwin reflected, "I have noticed that the dramatherapy work needs to be responsive, improvisatory and eclectic to be able to meet the needs of the client" (Goodwin, response to author's questionnaire, 2017).

- Seven revealed the importance of projective techniques involving various props, such as objects, puppets and therapeutic card decks.

- Six described the significance of story work: storytelling, story-making, character and role play.
- Five mentioned the use of play.
- Four wrote about distancing techniques as an aid to manage powerful emotions.
- Four employed non-verbal processes, including art work, music and physical expression.
- Three noted the importance of working within a consistent structure and maintaining clear boundaries.
- Three employed mentalisation techniques (whilst working within MBT services).
- Three made specific reference to Jennings's EPR (Embodiment-Projection-Role) paradigm (2012b).
- Two mentioned the significance of Jones's core processes: dramatic projection, dramatherapeutic empathy and distancing; role playing and personification; interactive audience and witnessing; embodiment: dramatising the body; playing; life-drama connection; and transformation (2007, l.2113–2120).
- The following approaches were crucial to single participants: Gestalt therapy, Jungian concepts, analytic group psychotherapy, psychodynamics and psychoanalysis, the play-drama continuum, developing a secure attachment and using archetypes and mythology.

Relating closely to my own approach, one participant wrote, "For me the life-drama connection is hugely important in terms of patients finding direct relevance, sense and meaning in the work done in the session and experiences in their own relationships to real people" (Goodwin, response to author's questionnaire, 2017).

The healing aspects of drama and theatre are core to the dramatherapy process. Creative techniques that give attention to both body and mind allow people to work through difficult feelings and memories indirectly. This is particularly useful for BPD clients, who are often overwhelmed by their emotions and previous trauma or neglect. In dramatherapy, they are offered an alternative, indirect approach through which to express and process their inner rage and other intense emotions. This helps them to feel contained, which is paramount. As Goodwin shared, "I have found the distancing in dramatherapy to be essential in this work, enabling clients to openly express their feelings through the character or themes of a story or poem" (Goodwin, response to author's questionnaire, 2017). Further observations from the research participants are interspersed through the next few sections (and in Chapter 7).

Dramatherapy for insecure attachment and trauma

Explored in Chapter 2, low self-esteem, a fragile sense of self and negative core beliefs are often experienced by people with BPD due to early attachment difficulties and/or trauma. These are frequently deeply rooted and difficult to change. Gunderson notes that 70% of people with BPD report a history of physical and/or sexual abuse (2011, p. 7). Such abuse often leads to intense shame and self-blame. As Gilmore highlighted, "Most of the women I work with express shame, guilt and deep-rooted feelings of being bad/not good enough" (Gilmore, response to author's questionnaire, 2017). Fonagy and Bateman reveal consistent evidence that during childhood, people with BPD experienced problematic parenting and a challenging family environment, affecting their capacity to make sense of themselves and others (2007, p. 87). Encouraging clients to understand and accept both themselves and others is then key to the dramatherapy process. Often deprived of the opportunity to play freely as children, play is another vital component. As Howe explains, the attachment needs of adults (and children) lacking a secure base "keep over-riding their attempts to be independent, playful, and work-minded" (2011, p. 19). Whilst most clients experience play as a liberating element of dramatherapy, one young woman I worked with found it distressing – a painful reminder of the childhood she never had. It is important, therefore, to introduce play (and all creative interventions) with careful consideration and sensitivity.

Mosquera and colleagues predict that people with BPD will have experienced either insecure or disorganised attachments as children (2014, p. 3), and in Zanarini et al.'s study of BPD, over 80% of the participants revealed they had experienced bi-parental abuse or neglect before the age of 18 (2000, p. 264). The reparative element of the dramatherapy process offers them an alternative experience: a safe and consistent space, in which everyone's thoughts and feelings are heard and validated. Colkett reflected that these clients need the therapist to feel what they feel and desire a good 'mothering' experience: "Most of the healing takes place in the relationship with the therapist" (Colkett, response to author's questionnaire, 2017). This relates to Rogers's person-centred approach to therapy, in which the therapeutic relationship is a key factor (Slade et al., 2015, p. 459).

Dokter notes that self-destructive acts within or between sessions (e.g. substance misuse, self-mutilation and suicide attempts) are particularly frequent among adolescents with BPD, addiction or psychosis (2011, p. 75). She connects these acts to the clients' most troubled inner parts and suggests that an object relations and psychodynamic approach may be helpful: "The integration of the shadow aspect of the personality is an integral part of Jungian individuation" (p. 75). As well as the potential for healing, Dokter reveals that destructiveness may be transmitted between group members and acted out within sessions. This may be counteracted, however, by fostering supportive relationships in the group (2011, pp. 88–90). I have witnessed the phenomenon of 'destructive transmission' among the women I work with – an unfortunate repercussion of their shared communal life. Living together and experiencing group therapy can be intense, with both negative and positive effects.

In relation to understanding early attachment and child development, Jennings has defined the Embodiment-Projection-Role (EPR) paradigm, which can be considered within any therapeutic modality (2012b). It is relevant to people with BPD, whose early development has often been compromised. Jennings's Neuro-Dramatic-Play (NDP) approach – mostly used with children – may also be adapted for adults who have suffered early trauma or neglect. It is a diverse approach, with many influences: attachment theory, neuroscience, play therapy, play, drama, dramatherapy, story-making and story-building, ritual, theatre and performance (2012c).

Jennings identifies three potential causes for the distortion of a child's mind-body development: being over-held and overprotected, being under-held and neglected, or suffering physical and/or sexual abuse. She explains that "children with bodily trauma need extended physical play, to re-build a healthy and confident body" (2012b). Within the dramatherapy groups I facilitate with women with BPD, physical play (using props including balls, ribbon-wands and boom-whackers) plus activities that encourage gentle, physical connection (e.g. group sculpts, large feathers, a bungee ring and play parachute) is regularly used. These techniques allow a safe release of energy and emotion. They are both freeing and reassuring, encouraging trust and connection between self and others.

Separation can cause great anxiety in people with BPD, due to their relationship and attachment difficulties. This may also affect their ability to internalise the therapy experience and therapeutic relationship in between sessions. Inspired by what several of her clients did spontaneously, Brem developed a method that encouraged self-harming patients to express themselves creatively in between sessions, by making or writing something, as an alternative to self-harming. This helped them to remain connected to both process and therapist in between sessions, whilst encouraging them to develop a new coping mechanism: "The creative object can be brought back along to the session like a scar and will be a representation of what has happened when the anxieties were unbearable" (2002, p. 21). Reflecting on attachment and separation issues, Dokter indicates the need for long-term therapy, as individuals need time to develop trusting relationships with both their peers and the therapist "so that grieving can become a part of relating" (2011, p. 88).

As shown in Chapter 2, there are significant links between BPD and post-traumatic stress disorder (PTSD) – connecting to childhood sexual abuse and other trauma (Scheiderer et al., 2015). Malchiodi explains that research within the field of neuroscience and neurodevelopment has shown potential for mind-body techniques, revealing that "art, drama, and play therapies show promise in the amelioration of posttraumatic stress and the expression of traumatic memories" (2005, p. 12). She also describes the reparative potential of expressive therapy in relation to research on early attachment and brain development: "These modalities may be helpful in repairing and reshaping attachment through experiential and sensory means" (Malchiodi, 2005, p. 12).

Reclaiming oneself through ritual theatre and myth

Myths have developed across the world among diverse cultures and in different eras. Campbell describes them as "stories of our search through the ages for truth, for meaning, for significance" (1991, p. 4) and Grainger explores myth, ritual and rites in relation to the emotional health of individuals in any community (2014, l.1818–1821). These elements may be applied within dramatherapy groups, providing members with a shared language and the potential for healing. As Grainger writes, "To present movement, gesture, sounds, objects and words in ritual form is to perform a healing action" (2014, l.1869–1870).

I often use myths in my work, as they offer an effective, yet indirect, window into oneself. Ancient myths continue to inform modern-day reality, and by exploring them in dramatherapy, clients are given the opportunity to discover personal meaning. The metaphoric element of myth work also maintains a comfortable, emotional distance for clients with BPD, allowing them to safely explore their inner depths. May suggests that myth making is crucial to improving mental health, offering "a way of making sense in a senseless world" (1991, p. 15). In dramatherapy groups, I often use Aboriginal Dreamtime stories, myths shared among the Aborigines, to explain how the world was created. These stories are usually unfamiliar to the clients, so they are less likely to provoke negative personal associations, creating a purer dramatic distance. Campbell also encourages us to read the myths of other people's religions, rather than our own, to gain greater insight into ourselves and the world around us (1991, p. 5).

Colkett (also a research participant) records the impact of ritual theatre techniques and myth on women diagnosed with BPD in a medium-secure forensic unit (2012, p. 257). She explains that women who have been sexually and/or physically abused often reject their femininity as an attempt to protect themselves. In contrast, some become over-sensualised. She sought to help her clients come to terms with personal trauma, somehow making it tolerable: "There is no attempt to cure: the opportunity for healing comes from the individual's willingness to engage and explore" (2012, p. 259). Ritual theatre, shamanism and myth provided Colkett with a strong base and she discovered that sharing and then enacting elements of the story of the Hindu goddess Lakshmi enabled her female clients to "release and regenerate their feminine self, allowing them to be soft and powerful, both at the same time" (2012, p. 270).

Colkett notes that her clients had experienced inadequate mothering and nurturing. The themes that arose from the myth then ignited "a female journey into a universal language of feelings and emotions" (2012, p. 267). She reflects that through role work and scene enactments, clients found the courage to embrace and take control of their femininity, perhaps for the first time (p. 270). Empowerment appears central to the process and Colkett explains that the clients who were initially most resistant eventually engaged most productively (p. 257). I have witnessed this within my own practice: reminding clients they are free to make their own choices in the dramatherapy group – and acknowledging that simply arriving and staying the duration take courage – encourages them to attend more regularly and to engage fully when ready. Colkett goes further, often congratulating her patients for having survived the trauma they have experienced (2012, p. 258).

Dramatherapy for men with BPD

Current research suggests that men may be almost as frequently affected by BPD as women, though much less likely to seek help and therefore diagnosis and treatment (NICE, 2009, p. 20). Although women predominate the literature available, Nowinski published specifically about men with BPD in 2014. Whilst there is thought to be little difference between their methods of self-harm and levels of emotional distress, there are distinct differences in their personality traits, co-morbidities and use of treatment (Sansone and Sansone, 2011, p. 16).

Eight of the research participants had worked with men as well as women (though several noted that their referrals remained predominantly female). Whilst acknowledging differences between the male and female response to the drama-therapy process, the participants reflected that many variables would have affected this: personal history, personality, specific symptoms, peer dynamics and transference within the therapeutic relationship.

One participant shared that the sole man in one of her dramatherapy groups was shy and introspective, struggling with severe substance misuse. He did not participate in many of the dramatherapy activities and said very little, although he responded more readily to projective techniques. Another participant shared that many of her male clients with BPD had a significant history of alcohol and drug addiction. This supports the findings of Sansone and Sansone, who report that whilst women with BPD are more likely to present with eating, mood, anxiety and post-traumatic stress disorders, men are more likely to be diagnosed with co-morbid substance use disorders and antisocial personality disorder (2011, p. 1). One participant shared that he felt he could be more direct with his male patients and more oblique with his female patients. He stressed, however, that varying mood and dynamics were the key factors that affected the dramatherapy process with both his male and female clients. Another also reflected that the specific methods used for a male client with BPD were the same as those used for females.

Within prison settings, personality disorders are prevalent and equally diagnosed in men and women. They have been estimated as present in over 50% of the prison and forensic population in the UK, with more men diagnosed with antisocial personality disorder and women with BPD (NHS England and NOMS, 2015). In a forensic set-ting, Seebohm explores the theme of destructiveness from her perspective as a female dramatherapist working with sectioned male clients who had committed serious offences. They had complex pathologies and were diagnosed with either paranoid schizophrenia, schizo-affective disorder or BPD (2011, p. 117). To aid their rehabili-tation, they were referred for either individual or group dramatherapy "to develop insight into both their offending behaviour and their mental illness, as well as to develop capacity for social, reflective and interpersonal skills" (Seebohm, 2011, p. 117).

Seebohm describes a psychodynamic approach in which creative possibility endured, despite the therapeutic relationship and dramatic process often facing attack (2011, p. 117). She reflects that in relation to their personal experiences "the space can become a theatre of war for the patient, both terrorised and terrorising, sometimes leaving the therapist holding the shattered pieces of debris, as in the aftermath of war" (p. 118). This was a highly challenging dynamic and Seebohm endeavoured to work collaboratively with her clients, to find tolerable creative interventions (p. 122). She notes that within "the triangulation with the medium, something can be mediated that was previously intolerable" (p. 129) and it is from this perspective that dramatherapy can perhaps be most effective.

> With the various tools of containment that dramatherapy offers, such as using the mind, body, images, objects and stories, the dramatherapist must be prepared at different times to be cast in all three roles of captor, hostage and bystander, even if these roles are only located in the conscious mind of the therapist. It is only by visiting and playing out these different roles that the actors can be liberated from being perpetually stuck in any one of them.
>
> *(Seebohm, 2011, p. 129)*

Whilst there is little published work on dramatherapy with men with BPD, from the comments shared by the eight research participants, together with Seebohm's reflections, it appears that dramatherapy may be equally effective for both men and women, despite their differences. The approach should then remain flexible and responsive to group and/or individual needs, rather than become gender-specific.

Evaluation and evidence

"Providing a high-quality evidence base is an essential part of ensuring that dramatherapy will continue to be seen as a valuable therapeutic approach and remain funded as part of mental health services" (Cassidy et al., 2014, p. 13). These sentiments are supported by many dramatherapists and are particularly pertinent as service providers across a range of settings are under increasing pressure to justify the therapies they offer with acceptable outcome measures. This is challenging for arts therapists, as Colkett reflects: "How do we measure creativity, spiritual experiences and often intangible healing processes?" (2012, p. 271). She suggests that practice-based evidence may be the answer, through which individuals can describe their subjective experiences. As Dokter notes, however, the current focus on evidence-based practice has created "a situation where the methodology of the randomised control trial (RCT) is privileged as evidence above all others" (2011, p. 36).

NICE is keen to develop evidence-based recommendations for people with BPD and to identify the treatments that help to improve mental state, quality of life, and social and personal functioning, and those that reduce self-harm, use of services and risky behaviours (2009, p. 103). They suggest that all psychological treatments offered should be monitored in relation to these criteria and that RCTs should be undertaken. Unable to assume such a task, I have instead developed a dramatherapy evaluation form, offered to clients at three monthly intervals. I also continue to provide continuous written and verbal feedback, weekly ward-round summaries and CPA reports. The evaluation form has similarities with the CORE GAF (CORE IMS, 2015) and includes the criteria stipulated by NICE (2009). It covers relevant symptoms that reduce within sessions; specific issues that are eased or resolved through the process; and the impact of dramatherapy on an individual's quality of life on the ward. Eighteen questionnaires were completed, two from each of the nine service users on the ward in December 2016 and March 2017. Seven of them attended the group regularly and the remaining two intermittently. Every service user indicated that she would recommend dramatherapy to individuals experiencing similar difficulties. The other results are shown in Figures 4.1, 4.2 and 4.3.

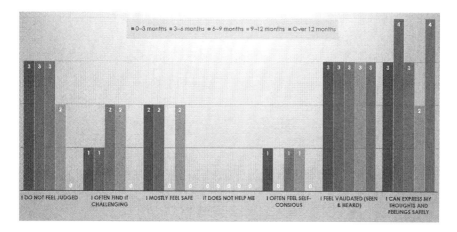

FIGURE 4.1 Clients identify statements most relevant and true of their dramatherapy experience

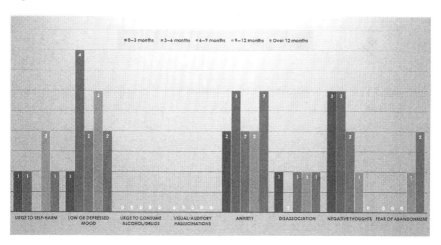

FIGURE 4.2 Clients identify symptoms most likely to decrease in the dramatherapy group

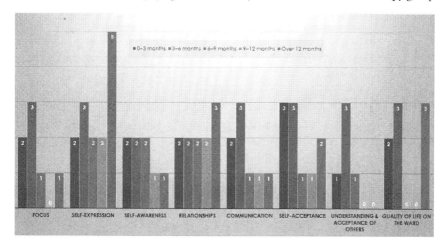

FIGURE 4.3 Clients identify features most likely to improve in the dramatherapy group

The thirteen research participants described a variety of evaluation methods: seven applied two or more, three used a single method and three did not conduct a formalised assessment:

- Four NHS-based participants referred to CORE methods: three used CORE OM (CORE Outcome Measures), which includes thirty-four generic questions across four key areas (well-being, symptoms, functioning and risk). One also used CORE GAF (CORE Goal Attainment Form), on which the client initially identifies up to four major difficulties he or she would like to work on in therapy. On finishing, the client can evaluate the impact of therapy, note areas that require further attention and consider whether he or she would recommend it to others. The fourth of these participants used CORE LD (CORE Learning Difficulties), which includes fourteen questions that help clients with learning difficulties to establish how they have been feeling over the past week (CORE IMS, 2015).
- Five research participants – three within the NHS, one in a charity and one with a private company – used self-evaluation questionnaires, focusing on the client's experience of dramatherapy in relation to their symptoms and functioning.
- One participant working in the NHS described the intervention of a dramatherapy researcher brought in to carry out an extensive evaluation report.
- Single participants described many other methods: HONOS LD (HONOS Learning Difficulties), which evaluates team outcomes rather than specific interventions; EKOS (East Kent Outcome Measure), establishing specific aims, reviewed at intervals and reflected upon in relation to the original aims (similar to the CORE GAF); Outcome Star, an adaptable system for many client groups across numerous settings, supporting people and measuring change; QPR (Question, Persuade and Refer), three steps to help prevent suicide; PROQ3, a John Birtchnell measure, based on relating theory; PEQ, a measure of patient experience following a one-to-one consultation; PROM, patient-reported outcome measures; and audits and focus groups.

Conclusion

Dramatherapy is a dynamic, flexible approach, with the potential to address the complex themes that often arise with the client group: deep-rooted trauma, negative core beliefs, insecure attachment, relationship difficulties and destructiveness towards self and/or others. The creative medium provides a vital third dynamic (within both the therapy process and the therapeutic relationship), helping to contain the overwhelming chaos that can be experienced by both client and therapist. This may then preserve the creativity and the potential for positive transformation. Diverse approaches are employed by dramatherapists, depending on the needs and abilities of their service users. Key tools include: projective methods, distancing, non-verbal techniques, story work (including myth and enactment), play, ritual, Jennings's E-P-R paradigm and N-D-P approach, Jones's core processes and Jungian concepts (including the integration of the shadow and individuation).

Dramatherapy has the potential to help both men and women diagnosed with BPD (and co-morbid disorders) across a wide variety of both NHS and private settings in the UK: forensic hospitals, prisons, adult and adolescent psychiatric inpatient units, outpatient mental health services, MBT- and DBT-centred programmes, substance misuse units and learning disability services. It remains imperative therefore that dramatherapists continue to develop and improve evaluation methods to produce the necessary outcome measures to secure funding and allow this important work to continue.

References

APA (2017) Post–World War II, DSM History [Online]. Available from: https://psychiatry. org/psychiatrists/practice/dsm/history-of-the-dsm?_ga=1.261653774.2023233716.147 8107218 [Accessed: 11.02.17].

BADth (2011) Home, about Dramatherapy [Online]. Available from: http://badth.org.uk/ home [Accessed: 09.02.17].

Boal, A. (2008) *Theatre of the Oppressed (Get Political)*. Second edition. London: Pluto Press.

Brem, A. (2002) The Creative Container between Sessions: Helping Self-Harming Patients to Endure Solitude. *Dramatherapy*, 24(2), pp. 16–22.

Campbell, J. and Moyers, B. (1991) *The Power of Myth*. New York: Anchor Books.

Cassidy, S., Turnbull, S. and Gumley, A. (2014) Exploring Core Processes Facilitating Therapeutic Change in Dramatherapy: A Grounded Theory Analysis of Published Case Studies. *The Arts in Psychotherapy*, 41(4), pp. 353–365.

Casson, J. (2017) Dramatherapy, Dramatherapy and Psychodrama [Online]. Available from: www.creativepsychotherapy.info/dramatherapy-and-psychodrama/ [Accessed: 11.02.17].

Colkett, D. (2012) Connecting with the Divine Feminine: Ritual Theatre in a Forensic Psychiatric Setting. In Schrader, C. (ed.) *Ritual Theatre: The Power of Dramatic Ritual in Personal Development Groups and Clinical Practice*. Kindle edition. London: Jessica Kingsley.

CORE IMS (2015) CORE Measurement Tools [Online]. Available from: www.coreims. co.uk/About_Measurement_CORE_Tools.html [Accessed: 07.04.17].

Davies, S. (translator) (2002) *The Gospel of St Thomas*. Translated for The Nag Hammadi Library, Presented in the Gnostic Society Library. Available from: www.gnosis.org/ naghamm/gosthom-davies.html [Accessed: 01.04.17].

Dokter, D. (2011) Self-Harm in Young People's Psychiatry: Transforming Munch's Scream. In Dokter, D., Holloway, P. and Seebohm, H. (eds.) *Dramatherapy and Destructiveness: Creating the Evidence Base, Playing with Thanatos*. Kindle edition. Hove, UK: Routledge.

Drain, R. (1995) Constantin Stanislavski: From Inner Impulses and Inner Action; Creative Objectives (1916–20). In *Twentieth Century Theatre: A Sourcebook*. New York: Routledge.

ECArTE (2017) Home [Online]. Available from: www.ecarte.info/ [Accessed: 19.01.17].

Fonagy, P. and Bateman, A. (2007) Mentalizing and Borderline Personality Disorder. *Journal of Mental Health*, 16(1), pp. 83–101.

Gandhi, M. (1999) *The Collected Works of Mahatma Gandhi* [Electronic Book, 98 Volumes]. New Delhi: Publications Division Government of India. Available from: http:// gandhiashramsevagram.org/gandhi-literature/collected-works-of-mahatma-gandhi-volume-1-to-98.php

Grainger, R. (2014) *Ritual and Theatre*. Kindle edition. London: Austin Macauley.

Gunderson, J. (2011) *A BPD Brief*. For the NEABPD (National Education Alliance. Borderline Personality Disorder) [Online]. Available from: www.borderlinepersonalitydisorder.com

HCPC (2017) CPSM [Online]. Available from: http://hpc-uk.org/aboutus/cpsm/ [Accessed: 09.02.17].

Howe, D. (2011) *Attachment across the Lifecourse: A Brief Introduction*. Basingstoke, UK: Palgrave Macmillan.

Jennings, S. (2007) Interview with Sue Jennings. In Jones, P. (ed.) *Drama as Therapy Volume 1: Theory, Practice and Research*. Second edition. Kindle edition. Abingdon, UK: Routledge.

Jennings, S. (2012a) International Training, Creative Development [Online]. Available from: www.suejennings.com/international.htmll [Accessed: 01.03.17].

Jennings, S. (2012b) Embodiment-Projection-Role (EPR), Neuro-Dramatic-Play (NDP) and Embodiment-Projection-Role (EPR) [Online]. Available from: www.suejennings.com/eprndp.html [Accessed: 26.03.17].

Jennings, S. (2012c) Neuro-Dramatic-Play (NDP), Neuro-Dramatic-Play (NDP) and Embodiment-Projection-Role (EPR) [Online]. Available from: www.suejennings.com/eprndp.html [Accessed: 26.03.17].

Jennings, S. (2016) Foreword. In Jennings, S. and Holmwood, C. (eds.) *Routledge International Handbook of Dramatherapy* (Routledge International Handbooks). Kindle edition. Abingdon, UK: Taylor and Francis.

Jones, P. (2007) *Drama as Therapy Volume 1: Theory, Practice and Research*. Second edition. Kindle edition. Abingdon, UK: Routledge.

Jung, C. G. (1968) *The Archetypes and the Collective Unconscious*. In Hull, R.F.C. (trans.) *Collected Works of C. G. Jung*. Second edition. Kindle edition. Bollingen Series XX, Volume 9, Part 1. Hove, UK: Taylor & Francis.

Levine, S. K. (2005) The Philosophy of Expressive Arts Therapy: *Poiesis* as a Response to the World. In Paolo, J., Knill, J. P., Ellen, G., Levine, E. G. and Levine, S. K. (eds.) *Principles and Practice of Expressive Arts Therapy: Toward a Therapeutic Aesthetic*. London: Jessica Kingsley.

Lindkvist, M. (2007) Interview with (Marian) Billy Lindkvist. In Jones, P. (ed.) *Drama as Therapy Volume 1: Theory, Practice and Research*. Second edition. Kindle edition. Abingdon, UK: Routledge.

Malchiodi, C. (2005) Expressive Therapies History, Theory, and Practice. In Malchiodi, C. (ed.) *Expressive Therapies*. New York: The Guilford Press.

May, R. (1991) *The Cry for Myth*. London: Norton.

Mosquera, D., Gonzalez, A. and Leeds, A. (2014) Early Experience, Structural Dissociation, and Emotional Dysregulation in Borderline Personality Disorder: The Role of Insecure and Disorganized Attachment. *Borderline Personal Disorder and Emotional Dysregulation*, 1(15).

NADTA (2017) What Is Dramatherapy? [Online]. *North American Drama Therapy Association*. Available from: www.nadta.org/ [Accessed: 23.01.17].

NHS England and NOMS (2015) *Working With Offenders with Personality Disorder: A Practitioners' Guide*. Second edition. Reference 04004. London: NHS England Publications Gateway.

NICE (2009) *Borderline Personality Disorder: Treatment and Management: National Clinical Practice Guideline 78* [Online]. Commissioned by NICE and Developed by the National Collaborating Centre for Mental Health. The British Psychological Society and the Royal College of Psychiatrists. PDF available from: www.nice.org.uk/guidance/cg78/evidence

NICE (2015) Personality Disorders: Borderline and Antisocial – Quality Standard QS88 [Online]. PDF available from: www.nice.org.uk/guidance/qs88

Nietzsche, F. W. (1885) *Thus Spake Zarathustra*. Common, T. (trans.) Paris: Feedbooks.

Nietzsche, F. W. (2015) The Collected Works of Friedrich Wilhelm Nietzsche: The Complete Works. In *Highlights of World Literature*. Kindle edition. n.p.: Pergamon Media.

Nowinski, J. (2014, August) *Hard to Love: Understanding and Overcoming Male Borderline Personality Disorder*. Las Vegas, NV: Central Recovery Press.

Pendzik, S. (1988) Drama Therapy as a Form of Modern Shamanism. *Journal of Transpersonal Psychology*, 20(1), p. 81.

Roose-Evans, J. (1989a) Reinhardt, Piscator and Brecht. In *Experimental Theatre: From Stanislavski to Peter Brook*. Fourth edition. London: Routledge.

Roose-Evans, J. (1989b) The Theatre of Ecstasy – Artaud, Okhlopkov, Savary. In *Experimental Theatre: From Stanislavski to Peter Brook*. Fourth edition. London: Routledge.

Rowan, J. (1990) *Subpersonalities: The People Inside Us*. First edition. London: Routledge.

Sansone, R. A. and Sansone, L. A. (2011, May) Gender Patterns in Borderline Personality Disorder [Online]. *Journal Innovations in Clinical Neuroscience*, 8(5), pp. 16–20.

Scheiderer, E. M., Wood, P. and Trull, T. (2015) The Comorbidity of Borderline Personality Disorder and Posttraumatic Stress Disorder: Revisiting the Prevalence and Associations in a General Population Sample. *Borderline Personality Disorder and Emotion Dysregulation*, 2(11). Available from: http://bpded.biomedcentral.com/articles/10.1186/s40479-015-0032-y [Accessed: 20.11.16].

Schrader, C. (2012) What Is Ritual Theatre? In *Ritual Theatre: The Power of Dramatic Ritual in Personal Development Groups and Clinical Practice*. Kindle edition. London: Jessica Kingsley.

Seebohm, H. (2011) On Bondage and Liberty: The Art of the Possible in Medium-Secure Settings. In Dokter, D., Holloway, P. and Seebohm, H. (eds.) *Dramatherapy and Destructiveness: Creating the Evidence Base, Playing with Thanatos*. Kindle edition. Hove, UK: Routledge.

Slade, K., Hamilton, L., and Thompson, C. (2015) Humanistic Person-Centred Therapy. In Banyard, P., Dillon, G., Norman, C. and Winder, B. (eds.) *Essential Psychology*. Second edition. Kindle edition. London: SAGE.

Stevens, A. (2001) *Jung: A Very Short Introduction*. Second edition. Kindle edition. Oxford: Oxford University Press.

UK Government (1997) *The Professions Supplementary to Medicine (Arts Therapists Board) Order of Council 1997*. The National Archives. Available from: https://www.legislation.gov.uk/uksi/1997/1121/introduction/made [Accessed: 10.03.18].

Zanarini, M., Frankenburg, F., Reich, D., Marino, M., Lewis, R., Williams, A. and Khera, G. (2000) Biparental Failure in the Childhood Experiences of Borderline Patients. *Journal of Personality Disorders*, 14(3), pp. 264–273.

PART 2

Dramatherapy clinical case studies and vignettes

5

BREAKING INNER CHAINS

Dramatherapy on a secure ward for women with BPD

I wish I could find my voice
Of a life where I have a choice
Where I can scream and be heard
Where I can be free like a bird
—*Millie, 2016*

Recommended by the UK's Department of Health (DH), NHS England commissions specialist Tier 4 services, which offer intensive treatment, for adults with severe and complex personality disorder (NHS England, 2017, p. 314). These services are for individuals "whose needs cannot be met by the community services in Tiers 1–3 and who may require residential treatment" (DH/Care Pathways Branch/ Mental Health Division, 2009, p. 4). In 2005, I began working on a Tier 4 secure ward for fifteen women diagnosed with BPD. I was asked to incorporate music as a key feature of the dramatherapy group and the clients responded positively to percussive improvisation and group singing.

One of the first songs I chose to teach the group was 'Blackbird' (Lennon-McCartney, 1968). With a tender melody and metaphoric lyrics, it describes the journey of an injured bird learning to fly – to see and to be free. This seemed to mirror the journey of my clients, all of whom were trying to heal from psychological and physical trauma. Initially, I sang 'Blackbird' to the group, and a few months later, the youngest client (aged 18) showed me the entry she had written in her diary that day. It described how deeply moved she had been by the experience, having never been sung to as a child. In that moment, I understood how significant even the simplest intervention could be. I also learnt that songs could have a profound effect, stirring memories and emotions. As Mannes reflects, "Music, healing, and spirituality have had a connection since the beginning of human history" (2011, p. 203).

During my first month on the ward, a client asked to speak to me after the music-centred dramatherapy group. Rather than speak, however, she dramatically pulled out the stitches from a deep wound, allowing her blood to flow. Symbolically, she had revealed her emotional pain in an immediate, effective, yet maladaptive manner. She was heavily scarred and felt unlovable, anxious that she would never be able to walk down a street without being stared at, judged and misunderstood. As she began to trust me, however, she discovered that she could convey her feelings through music, symbolic words and singing. She did not self-harm in front of me again, and over many months, her mental health improved, and she eventually managed to create a life for herself in the community. Working with this client and witnessing the many steps of her journey gave me insight into the chaotic yet hopeful world of people with severe BPD – also showing me the potential for dramatherapy to support them.

Dramatherapy for women with BPD

In 2009, I began working on another Tier 4 secure ward, accommodating nine women with BPD, many of whom have co-morbid disorders. There are both advantages and disadvantages of working with a group who shares a diagnosis. Mostly, they empathise with one another, offering friendship and support. At times, they also influence (or feel triggered) by each other's behaviour, with detrimental consequences. The service users are encouraged to attend weekly OT (occupational therapy) sessions, DBT (dialectical behavioural therapy) skills and homework groups and have regular one-to-one DBT. The weekly dramatherapy group (and concurrent art and writing–focused dramatherapy group) provides a creative balance to this cognitive, behavioural approach, nurturing the inner child, rather than focusing solely on the adult self: "Whilst DBT offers the patients concrete ideas and coping strategies, dramatherapy allows them to play and to express the unsaid" (Morris, 2014, p. 4). OT plays a significant third role, providing a range of meaningful activities, helping the patients to retain or develop the skills they need for life beyond hospital. Dramatherapy, DBT and OT coexist on the ward in a helpful way for both service users and staff, as evidenced by staff feedback offered later in this chapter.

Whilst many clients enjoy expressing themselves creatively and have natural abilities, others are initially afraid, thinking they lack artistic or dramatic talent and that without them, they will be unable to participate. This often relates to negative past experiences, such as teachers or parents criticising their efforts to sing, create art, write poetry or perform. In both dramatherapy and art and writing–focused dramatherapy sessions, all service users learn that "Creating is a dance with what we can and cannot control and the challenge is to be receptive, ready, and capable of engagement" (McNiff, 2015, pp. 9–10).

Five recurring themes

I have identified five key themes that arise in response to the issues most pertinent to the group, which are developed in dramatherapy (and art and writing–focused dramatherapy) sessions.

Freedom

Freedom is a theme that continuously arises and may be explored from both a philosophical and practical perspective. It is a concept used to describe various qualities or states of being: the power or right to act, speak or think freely; the state of being free (neither imprisoned nor enslaved); and the state of not being affected by something undesirable (Oxford English Dictionary, 2012, p. 287). I facilitate sessions in a relaxed manner, where choice is paramount. Most of the service users are detained under a Mental Health Act section and many have been abused throughout their lives. They feel disempowered by these experiences, so having choice throughout every session motivates them to participate and helps to improve their confidence and self-esteem. Although clients are often desperate to be taken off section and discharged from hospital, this is frequently complicated by their fear of how they will cope in the outside world. Their containment offers a degree of safety. This is illustrated by the following case vignettes.

1. One week, Leona was very upset prior to the art and writing–focused dramatherapy group, having just heard that her best friend had been sectioned. She was tearful and full of mixed emotions, though agreed to attend. In the group, she managed to express her feelings through a piece of free-flowing writing and a symbolic drawing. The creative process allowed her to ventilate and reflect on her feelings. During the sharing ritual (when group members are given the opportunity to show their work to one another) Leona found the courage to read out her piece of writing. It spoke passionately of conflicting emotions: explaining how much she wanted to continue her journey towards recovery, whilst also feeling drawn back towards self-harm and self-destructiveness. She reflected at the end that the process had helped her to make sense of her feelings.

2. Ada was a black woman in her early thirties, with both Asperger's (on the Autistic spectrum) and BPD. Her mother had died from a drug overdose when she and her twin sister were babies and they were adopted by a white family. As a young teenager, she began to struggle with her identity. She endured racial bullying at school and had a difficult relationship with her adoptive parents. Due to the 70% delay in finding families of similar cultural backgrounds for black and minority ethnic children in England, the Children and Families Act 2014 – which amended the Adoption and Children Act 2002 – states that adoption agencies in England should no longer consider ethnicity when placing a child with a family (Gheera and Long, 2014, pp. 8–9). This was many years before Ada was placed with her adoptive family, however. Moreover, it should be noted that a review of research on transracial adoption in the US revealed that "adoption across ethnic boundaries did not in itself produce psychological or behavioural problems in children. However, where a child was adopted across ethnic boundaries, they and their families could face a range of challenges" (Gheera and Long, 2014, p. 9). It is also highlighted that the way adoptive parents deal with this – and their sensitivity to racism – will either help or hinder their child's development.

In her teens, Ada became addicted to Class A drugs and alcohol, which continued into adulthood. She fought with cravings for these substances whilst on the ward and on leave in the community, and struggled to abstain from them. She found dramatherapy both difficult and helpful: during one session, she spoke expressively during the opening ritual (where a large rubber ball, filled with multicoloured beads moving in clear liquid, is passed around the circle – each person encouraged to say how she is feeling). She shared how frustrated she felt with the restricted way of life on the ward, explaining that the constant monitoring was having a negative impact upon her potential relationships with staff and on her mental health. She also said the numerous restrictions were making her feel like a child and she was concerned that her reaction would be rebellious – explaining for example that she had recently absconded from the ward. She said she was trying to control these feelings, however, and did not want to act on them. Ada said that her emotions were building up and without her usual forms of release (alcohol and illicit substances) she was concerned about how they were going to manifest.

After voicing her frustrations and fears, Ada then enjoyed the 'Tension to Relaxation' exercises (using balls, body work and gymnastic ribbon-wands, which encourage a range of motion and creative socialisation). Within the symbolic figure activity, clients were invited to select a wooden, plastic or fabric figurine and to create a home for it. Their figurine was also given the opportunity to speak to the group: Ada chose a grey bendy model and named him Morph. She put him inside a woollen finger puppet, where she explained he was safely enclosed, protected from his environment. His word to the group was 'held'. At the end of the session, Ada shared that although she felt daunted by the idea of dramatherapy, each week she was surprised to find herself enjoying the process.

3. Millie initially found the dramatherapy process uncomfortable and challenging, often describing sessions as 'weird'. She attended every week, however, and as the months progressed, there was a significant shift in her response. Her confidence clearly developed and whilst she continued to find the dramatherapy group unusual, she began to understand and embrace the process. She was also keen to contribute to this book. Some of her poems have been included and Figure 5.1 is a photo of a painting she produced in September 2016, in response to the theme 'Letting go, yet holding on', which connected to the concept of freeing oneself from something (or someone) whilst maintaining a sense of self. She explained that her painting also connected to an idea that had been forming in her mind for several weeks: the dark figure represented Millie and the figure pulling away from it, still partly attached, symbolised the part she was trying to let go of. The dark figure also emanates bright strands of light, to show that despite its darkness, it had the capacity to release positive energy.

Millie used head banging to manage her emotions and felt trapped within a difficult marriage. When discharged from the ward after eleven months, she had a stronger sense of who she was and what she wanted from life. In a recent communication, she shared that she was doing well and that her experience of

FIGURE 5.1 Letting go, yet holding on

dramatherapy had freed her to attend exercise classes (including Zumba) "without being weighed down by embarrassment and shame" and she had begun to interact with people with more confidence.

When the theme of freedom arises, clients are encouraged to consider its meaning in relation to their personal journey towards inner freedom and peace. As well as having freedom of choice in dramatherapy (and art and writing–focused dramatherapy) sessions, service users are free to express their emotions, share their thoughts, speak freely and play freely with their peers. Such 'freedom' takes places within agreed (and necessary) boundaries, however: nobody will speak directly about (or name) a staff member or peer who is not present, everyone will respect one another, regardless of whether they choose to actively participate in the session, and swearing is allowed, so long as all members of the group are comfortable with this and swear words are never directed at specific person. The concept of freedom is explored from different perspectives and is often present within the themes I suggest for the art and writing–focused dramatherapy group. One example of this was 'To be my own puppet master', a theme that followed expressive puppet work in the previous day's dramatherapy group. Millie responded to this theme with the following poem, written in 2016:

> Break your strings,
> Feel your limbs,
> Shake them free,
> Is this me?
>
> Strings within,
> Holding in
> A tangled mess,
> Taking up space.
>
> A joint creation,
> A cast in a play.
> A thing of beauty,
> It can change every day.
>
> Expectations in the wings.
> Look the other way.
> Don't let them in.
>
> Break the strings,
> Write the script,
> Be free to be,
> This is me.
>
> Take centre stage
> With friends and foes.
> Though not in control,
> You can mould.
>
> Choose the story,
> Choose your show.

Hope

Hope: a feeling of expectation and desire for something to happen; a cause or source of hope; to expect and want something to happen; or intend, if possible, to do something (Oxford English Dictionary, 2012, p. 347). The trauma experienced by many clients often thwarts their capacity for hope: they have low expectations, finding it difficult to believe that anything good could happen, and they struggle with trust. Whilst hope is fostered within dramatherapy sessions, it may prove challenging for the therapist to remain hopeful when working with individuals who have suffered significant trauma, brutally self-harm and often feel suicidal. Irving Yalom, professor of psychiatry and pioneer of existential psychotherapy, offers an approach to group therapy with eleven therapeutic factors, the first of which is the "instillation of hope" (Yalom with Leszcz, 2005, p. 4). Viktor Frankl, professor of psychiatry and neurology, Holocaust survivor and founder of logotherapy (a meaning-centred approach to psychotherapy, also known as existential analysis), taught that life's meaning is unique to each of us and can even be found through suffering (2004). His words offer hope to therapist and client alike. This search for hope and meaning is eloquently voiced by client Bella through the following poem, written in 2013:

> Finding a hope, a reason to live.
> A reason to fight, whatever may come,
> The deep dark forest or
> Beautiful sun-filled days.
> Be it a friend who offers a hug,
> To finding a remedy that works for me,
> Accepting the lifebuoy that's offered to me,
> Be it using my mind or taking some pills.
> Accepting my illness and learning to live.
> Looking to the future and believing
> The sun will shine again.
> Knowing that I am held
> And never let go,
> That's when I have my life under control,
> The sickness becomes weak
> And life moves on.

To be seen and heard as a human being, rather than a diagnosis

Challenging stigma and preconceptions (within and outside the self) is a vital part of the process and whilst diagnosis remains relevant (explored in Chapter 2) it should be considered a helpful tool, rather than a means to define a person. Yalom suggests there is too much emphasis on diagnosis and that brief, focused therapy is often offered due to administrative pressures (2002, pp. 3–4). Although logical and efficient, he explains it has very little to do with reality and "represents instead an illusory attempt to legislate scientific precision into being when it is neither possible nor desirable" (2002, p. 4). Yalom advises that focusing on diagnosis can be counterproductive, limiting a therapist's vision. Most importantly, I have learnt that one must approach each client with integrity, empathy and patience. Leona felt passionately about this subject, expressing her thoughts through two long poems, one directed to her doctors (shared at the beginning of Chapter 2) and the other to the public, shown here:

> There's more to me than what you see, and I know exactly what you see.
> You may think you know me through my actions or social media.
> You see the broken girl that's always positive,
> The girl who cuts herself, starves herself and tries to kill herself.
> Have you ever stopped to wonder what's behind the mask?
> Have you ever spent even seconds out of your perfect life to wonder?
> I know you pity me, you see me in hospital without a job and seemingly no prospects.
> But I pity you.
> Because what you don't know
> Is that I am capable of feeling things to such a deep level
> That I question life, death and everything in between.
> You see the pain, but you don't experience the unimaginable highs.
> Don't for one second believe that you know me.
> Because even I don't know the real me.
> I learn new things about myself every day.

Bringing all parts of oneself – including the shadow – into the light

In dramatherapy sessions, clients are encouraged to explore different parts of themselves, improving self-awareness and fostering understanding and acceptance of self and others. This is an initial step towards integrating their internal parts to reach a more balanced self and relates to the Jungian concept of individuation, a process through which an individual strives to "integrate the unconscious into consciousness" (1968, p. 40). Jung explains that "this process follows the natural course of life – a life in which the individual becomes what he always was" (p. 40).

When initiating creative work with clients, McNiff recognises "a pervasive feeling of angst, fear, and hesitation" (2015, p. 119). He encourages them to engage with these emotions, rather than suppress them, suggesting they are an essential source of creativity. He describes them as "the shadow of expression" (p. 119). In relation to Jung's notion of one's hidden darker aspects, McNiff suggests that such feelings need recognition and will eventually complement the lighter aspects (2015, p. 119). People with BPD often experience extreme emotions and a complete split between their light and shadow parts. Such a clear internal divide is revealed in Figure 5.2, a piece created by Chloe.

FIGURE 5.2   Shadow and light

A new way to look at familiar emotions or issues

A new perspective can offer new possibilities, allowing things that felt permanently stuck to shift and transform. This is vital for people with BPD, and dramatherapy invites them to visit memories and explore inner parts, emotions and thoughts, on a creative platform, within the safety of dramatic distance. A variety of interventions may be used – as described in the next section – and through the process, they may be able to view themselves, their memories and others from a different angle. This is revealed through the following case vignettes:

1. Mia was admitted to the ward due to prolonged and severe self-harm via cutting and suicidal ideation. She was in her early twenties, sensitive and kind, with a love of horses and a talent for art. Although the consultant concluded that she had severe depression, rather than BPD, she remained on the ward, as she was benefiting from the containment and therapeutic process. Initially, she felt self-conscious in the dramatherapy group and was able to express herself more freely in the related art and writing–focused dramatherapy group, in which she found moulding Giotto vegetable dough into different forms helpful. As the months progressed, however, she began to feel freer in dramatherapy and came to almost every session. She wrote the following in 2015:

   > I spend most of my life with my guard up, but Nicky's group gives me a safe space to relax my defences. I found the mask work so helpful. I could

take the mask off that I live with every day and show a little more of myself. I also love the art and writing–focused dramatherapy group. I like being given a theme to work with, but also have the freedom to work on whatever I feel I need to express. Sometimes I'm working with very difficult feelings, but I feel safe doing it in this group.

During one art and writing–focused dramatherapy session, I suggested the double theme: 'this is me' and 'creating a personal mantra for the day', in response to what had been expressed in the previous day's dramatherapy group. Mia was one of the four clients present. In response to the double theme, she skilfully drew a hummingbird butterfly during the session, accompanied by a positive mantra about flying freely. During the sharing ritual, she explained that her creative piece had helped to empower her, as she felt she must start doing what she felt was right, rather than what was expected of her. This may have connected to the complicated relationship she had with her parents and sibling, which she begun to work through in family therapy, with the consultant psychiatrist. The creative process supported this work, allowing her the opportunity to consider herself (and her role within the family) from a different perspective.

2. Millie (described earlier) was another of the four clients present in the session that explored the double theme: 'this is me' and 'creating a personal mantra for the day'. In response, she began by painting a woman's face in shades of blue, her hair falling in front of her eyes. She explained that the image symbolised the sadness she was feeling. She then searched for a selection of images (from the Internet) to print out and stick around the image she had painted, in reflection of the mantra she had chosen: 'life is precious'. Through the creative process, it seemed she had wanted to share how she was genuinely feeling, whilst also searching for something to balance out her feelings, offering herself hope. During the closing ritual, Millie's words echoed this. She said it had been good to remember the precious things in life, which she was not always able to see. The creative process had therefore allowed her the opportunity to view things differently.

Six key interventions

I have identified six types of interventions particularly helpful for clients with BPD and included case vignettes to illustrate them.

Releasing tension and repressed emotion via simple, effective methods

The most useful tools have been: balls and bean bags (thrown simultaneously with vigour – towards the centre of the circle – to symbolically let go of something or someone), tuned percussion tubes (also known as boom-whackers, which are hollow plastic tubes, tuned to musical pitches by length, which may be hit upon a variety of surfaces to create different sounds and are used in dramatherapy to create cathartic rhythms – as a group and individually) and a giant parachute (used to physicalise and express feeling states, whilst gaining insight into one another's emotions through mirroring). Expressive movement with colourful, gymnastic ribbon-wands is also freeing and both individual and group feeling sculpts are often powerful.

1. Mary, an Irish woman in her early forties, had suffered extreme abuse through-out her life and struggled with eating disorders and BPD for many years. During her first dramatherapy session, she said she was keen to experience something new. Whilst expressing ourselves individually and interacting as a group with ribbon-wands, she initially chose the yellow ribbon and moved it around deftly, in broad sweeping strokes. She then added the orange, green and red ribbons, to create a Chinese dragon. During the closing ritual, she described the process as absorbing and reflected that whilst working with the ribbon-wand, several had become very tangled (with themselves, or one another's) though we had all managed to unknot ourselves and work through it. She felt this had symbolised the emotional journey of her peers, in working through their relationships with one another and with themselves.

2. Philippa was in her early twenties. She had suffered extreme neglect as a child, and then bullying and abuse as a teenager. She was diagnosed with BPD and struggled with alcohol addiction and self-debasing auditory hallucinations. Dramatherapy became her favourite group. One week, she was feeling very low in mood and shared that she had negative voices constantly in her head. She was tearful and upset about appearing so vulnerable in the group and participated in the activities that followed with less enthusiasm than usual. She expressed herself freely with boom-whackers, however, and explained during the closing ritual that the noise they created had helped to block out the voices.

Symbolic tools and projective methods

Exploring and expressing aspects of the self through a variety of objects and images are a core intervention. Jones describes two main projective approaches: observing the material as a revelation of "emotional conflicts, drives and unconscious motivations" (2007, l.6938) and, from an object relations perspective, viewing it as an indication of "the patterns and constructs which the individual makes with others" (2007, l.6939). The tools in my sessions include trinkets, shells, puppets, masks, figurines, model animals, hats, materials, therapeutic cards decks, emotive paintings and photographs. They can be used within multiple activities: identifying personal strengths and weaknesses; stimulating character work; sharing difficult memories; and gaining insight into self and others. Group landscapes are also created or simply imagined and image making is effective, though primarily used in the art and writing–focused dramatherapy group. These interventions are illustrated through the following case and session vignettes:

1. During one dramatherapy group, Mia (described earlier) shared initially that she was struggling with her mood. In response to the symbolic object and character

activity, she chose to wear a black velvet witch's hat and selected a mini brass cauldron, in which she stood a small wooden mannequin. She described herself as a wicked witch, who she named Witch. In her cauldron, there were many ingredients, to create a man to assist her. When asked if he would have his own mind, she said that yes, he would think for himself. She then revealed that her house was made from skulls and bones, similar to that of Baba Yaga – a witch from Russian folklore. Lastly, she said that Witch just wanted to be left alone.

At the end of the session, Mia said she had particularly enjoyed the character work – and her mood appeared lighter. Schrader describes the story of Baba Yaga (referred to by Mia) as a fairy tale with mythic qualities – in which Baba Yaga is more like an ancient goddess than the witches found in most fairy tales: "She will challenge but she is fair, and if she feels she has met you as an equal, then she will set you free" (2012, p. 117). Jung's complex description of the archetypal anima also connects to the witch and may have linked to Mia's process in this session.

2. Animal models, masks and hand puppets are often used to explore inner aspects and to reflect on group dynamics, encouraging empathy between clients. There are many ways in which to facilitate this. For example in one dramatherapy session, five clients created a landscape comprising different terrains, using materials of varying colours and textures. They chose animals to symbolise themselves and placed them within the scene. They introduced themselves and interaction between the animals developed. The process that unfolded revealed individual emotions, strengths, fears and desires:

> One client felt physically unwell at the start, sharing her concern that an epileptic seizure may be imminent. She chose to stay in the group, however, and chose to be a lion. Whilst interacting with her peers (as a lion), her mood lifted and physical symptoms eased. Another client chose to be a small dog, living in a cave in the mountain, scared of what might be outside. This reflected her difficulty to trust people (both staff and peers) and her ongoing tendency to isolate herself on the ward. It may also have connected to her fear of returning to the community. One client chose to be a crab who wanted to be left alone. She had shared at the start that she was feeling particularly irritable, though found pleasure and relief in being able to express this in a creative manner within the session. Another client, who felt confident to express herself on the ward and in the dramatherapy group, chose to be a female lion cub. She lived in the forest, though enjoyed exploring the entire landscape and interacting with the other animals. The fifth client, who found dramatherapy liberating, though often felt disconnected to her peers whilst on the ward, chose to be a young female polar bear. She lived on a glacier, though enjoyed exploring other parts of the land and meeting the other animals.

3. Sally was in her late teens. She was severely neglected as a baby and exposed to drugs and prostitution from childhood. Although she initially responded well to dramatherapy, she soon began to avoid the group. From our discussions, it seemed the sessions were bringing her lost childhood into focus. When the

story of Peter Pan was introduced for example, one client said that every child knew the story and Sally she admitted she had never heard it. She felt upset by this, alienated from her peers, and left the session. Most of the props used (musical instruments, puppets, animals, figurines etc.) seemed to trigger painful memories. When discussing this with Sally, she said she felt she may benefit from one-to-one dramatherapy, to help her to come to terms with the memories she did not feel ready to confront within a group. Although her request was supported by the MDT, she was soon to begin one-to-one DBT and the team agreed it would be too confusing to have two individual therapists.

Sally felt challenged though less vulnerable in the art and writing–focused dramatherapy group – in which the key props are art and writing materials, and the process less interactive. One week, she created two very different pieces in response to the theme 'facing my fears and phobias' (connecting to the themes explored in the previous day's dramatherapy group): the first explained her fear of self-destruction, asking if she should open the door to face her fears; the second revealed a woman (symbolising herself) directly facing her fears, represented by a roaring tiger (Figure 5.3). During the closing ritual, Sally questioned whether she should continue attending the group, as she wanted to stay well by focusing on happy things and the sessions always made her think too deeply. She was advised that focusing on the positive was an effective coping mechanism, though developing the ability to cope with difficult emotions and deeper thoughts was also essential to her future life in the community, where such feelings may unavoidably surface. Sally listened and, although she understood, she soon stopped attending the group. She also made limited progress in DBT.

FIGURE 5.3   Face your fears

Ritual, story and myth

Explored in Chapter 4, the ritual aspect of dramatherapy connects to ritual practices in ancient cultures, used to celebrate life transitions and community events. Opening and closing rituals then offer a clear container for the group process and allow everyone the opportunity to speak. Story work and myth work are also essential factors of dramatherapy and relate to the Jungian concept of archetypes and the collective unconscious (Jung, 1968; Stevens, 2001a). As Campbell explains, "All over the world and at different times of human history, these archetypes, or elementary ideas, have appeared in different costumes" (1991, p. 61). Traditional stories offer a rich variety of themes, and as Gersie explains, "Every story character is invited to wake up and to grow up" (1997, p. 154). New stories are also created, and familiar ones may be transformed. As well as introducing stories to my clients, they choose stories to share and select key moments to dramatise. As Gersie explains, "We not only make up and live our stories, but need to tell them" (1997, p. 1). Stories may be discussed, characters chosen, tableaux created and, at times, simple lines devised. Schrader emphasises the significance of choice and play within myth work, allowing "numerous possibilities for self-discovery, insight and revelation" (2012, p. 117). Dramatic and aesthetic distancing is also essential, and in her description of ritual theatre work, Schrader explains that through chosen characters, clients have the opportunity to express a myriad of emotions, allowing them "to get close to their pain by being far away from it" (2012, p. 185).

1. Laura had once trained to be a nurse and being a Christian was very important to her. She was in her mid-twenties, mostly suffering from depression and memory problems, due to traumatic life events. She was resistant to most aspects of life on the ward, though made an effort to attend the dramatherapy and art and writing–focused dramatherapy groups. In one dramatherapy session, she initially engaged tentatively, having felt distressed in the morning. She then asserted herself positively in the role of director when devising a moving tableau from her chosen story, 'Noah's Ark'. She showed sensitivity in her casting choices and focused on the following moment: Noah stands alone at the front of the ark, under a clear sky and rainbow. A white dove flies over and offers him a dry stick. It was a poignant moment, signifying hope for the future, after a challenging and dramatic journey. This may have related to Laura's own search for inner peace. She had endured trauma and loss during her training to be a nurse, from which she was struggling to recover. During the closing ritual, she explained that directing her tableau had reminded her of the activities she used to enjoy with her church group – before her mental health had declined. She said she had always preferred to direct rather than perform, an indication perhaps of her desire and need to be in control.

2. Shona was severely neglected as a baby and adopted as a young child. When she turned 19, her mental health seriously declined, and for the past few years, she has remained on section due to life-threatening self-harm. A boyfriend she met on an acute ward wanted her to form a suicide pact and eventually took his

own life. In her mind, she still imagines him encouraging her to end her life and bears unresolved feelings of guilt about his death. Shona had three one-to-one dramatherapy sessions focusing on her attachment to him, during which the archetype card deck proved particularly useful: she chose the saboteur (to symbolise the part of herself that seems to sabotage her progress whenever things are going well); the victim (in connection to the lonely, isolated part of herself); the destroyer (linking again to self-sabotage); and the damsel (connecting to the part of herself who wants to be rescued and loved). Shona was afraid of life beyond hospital and continued to sabotage her progress on the ward. She managed to commit to regular sandtray therapy, however, and regularly attended the dramatherapy group, in which she felt free to express herself and to explore the person she would like to be. Within character work, Tiger Lilly from *Peter Pan* became her favourite role, whom she identifies with freedom.

Sensory work

In both the dramatherapy and art and writing–focused dramatherapy groups, sensory methods are very effective, helping many clients to feel grounded and enabling others to relax and express themselves more freely. They also challenge co-morbid OCD (obsessive-compulsive disorder) symptoms. Brown, Shankar and Smith report that historically, occupational therapists have used sensory integration therapy with children and clients with learning disabilities (2009, p. 14). They explain that recent research has revealed that individuals with BPD may also have features of SPD (sensory processing disorder) "especially in sensory-sensitive and sensory-avoiding domains" (2009, p. 16) and can therefore benefit from a more highly developed approach for adults, sensory processing therapy (2009, p. 14). Brown, Shankar and Smith suggest that a sensory processing method could be "integrated into programmes and inform other modes of therapy including the creative arts psychotherapies" (2009, p. 16), DBT and CBT.

Art and writing–focused dramatherapy sessions run in conjunction with the dramatherapy group, allowing the process to continue, with art and writing as the key tools. Giotto vegetable dough has proved exceptionally useful in this group – an extra pliable form of plasticine used to squeeze and create small models and as a form of 3D paint on cards (applied with fingers rather than a brush). Remarkable images have been created this way:

1. Amy, a service user in her early forties with ASD (autistic spectrum disorder) and BPD, has been on the ward for over two years. Despite her tendency for angry outbursts, she is a kind woman, with an astute memory. During one art and writing–focused dramatherapy session, she struggled to find a way to express herself and Giotto vegetable dough was suggested. She responded positively, squeezing the dough to keep herself calm and grounded. She then created two small balls to symbolise herself: the first was red and bumpy, representing the idea that the devil had got into her head and exploded. The second was smooth and multicoloured, to show how she thought her head should be.

In dramatherapy sessions, a variety of sensory tools are used. Some of the most useful include: balls of various size, weight and texture, large ostrich feathers (which can facilitate self-expression and communication via mirroring and touch) and materials of many colours and textures (used for self-expression, landscape and character work).

2. Jean symbolised her inner desire to bloodlet through a feeling sculpt (a silent pose) with a red velvet cloak draped over her arm. She finds the sensation of velvet against her skin very comforting and often strokes a piece of black velvet during her one-to-one sessions. This also connects to her addiction to bloodletting, as she feels comforted by the flow of warm blood, from deep within her arteries, against her skin.

Play

"It is in playing and only in playing that the individual child or adult is able to be creative and to use the whole personality, and it is only in being creative that the individual discovers the self" (Winnicott, 2005, pp. 72–73). Play also lies at the heart of Bannister's regenerative model of dramatherapy, developed to empower children who have been abused (2003, p. 7). She suggests that the metaphor and symbolism within play can safely contain dangerous or frightening feelings (2003, p. 6). The importance of play in the healthy development of children is well documented (Erikson, 1963; Bowlby and Ainsworth, 1965; Singer and Singer, 1990; Russ, 2004) and will ideally begin between mother and baby through the simple act of mirroring: "When I look I am seen, so I exist. I can now afford to look and see" (Winnicott, 2005, p. 154). This affirming interaction may be replicated in dramatherapy, as the therapist witnesses, mirrors and collaborates with the client. Play between members of a group is also significant, helping to build trust and positive communication. Many of the clients I work with have suffered extreme abuse and neglect as children, so play is exceptionally poignant. Stretching, tensing and relaxing muscles is a helpful place to begin and most enjoy the playful warm-up activities that follow: a variety of movement, ball and vocal games, encouraging focus, dexterity and positive interaction. As tension is released, confidence builds – and clients are able to express a range of emotions safely, without fear of negative repercussions.

1. Bella spent seven months on the ward, before her transfer to a secure rehabilitation unit (Morris, 2014). She was sexually abused throughout her childhood and, as a result, experienced distressing flashbacks, periods of intense paranoia, anxiety and depression, poor self-image and low self-esteem. Her self-harm through cutting was severe and she had been in and out of hospital since her teens. She was also kind and intelligent, with an ironic sense of humour. Metaphor gave Bella a new voice through which to express herself and play allowed her to connect to her inner child and regenerate hope. She particularly enjoyed group games and playing with balloons, balls and glitter. She reflected that it felt

different to anything she remembered from childhood and wondered if she had ever truly played before, or if the intensity of the abuse blocked out any happy memories. Bella had not had therapy as a child and playing within the safety of the dramatherapy space proved to be a great release for her as an adult.

Poetry, song and creative writing

In dramatherapy sessions, emotive poems and song lyrics are often shared and their themes explored. Clients identify key words, sentences or verses with which they connect. As Chavis explains, "When we embrace special words of our choosing to soothe or inspire us, they often function like a companion or a talisman" (2011, p. 11). This process also promotes confidence, as it involves reading out loud, either individually or as a group and encourages self-exploration and choice. On the first BPD ward where I worked, one of the first songs I taught the group was 'Crucify', written by Tori Amos (1992). With strong religious overtones, the powerful lyrics express a desire to be released or rescued from emotional torment and a fractured inner self. Many of the women connected to these words – relating them to their own anger and the fusion they experienced between emotional and physical pain. All of them had severely self-harmed over a significant period (often as an attempt to release intense, unbearable emotion) and the lyrics of the song seemed to encapsulate their needs in a creative, non-harmful manner. It became a favourite song on the ward and the clients would sing it together in the corridors and in the smoking room. As Austin explains, "Within the safety of a song's structure, clients can often access and express intense feelings" (2006, p. 137).

Song writing is another effective process used, wherein each person is invited to contribute a single word, phrase or verse. Together, their words form a group poem, for which I write a melody. Such poetic songs usually express key themes that are relevant to the group at the time. In 2016, 'Freedom Fighters' was the first song to be recorded on the ward and one service user, a gifted musician greatly lacking in confidence, found the courage to play the guitar on the track. This song expressed the group's shared and intense frustration with being on section, in hospital. The process was filled with humour, however, providing a great release. The following lyrics formed the chorus:

> Freedom Fighters, swinging on the door frames,
> Jumping the fence from a trampoline.
> Sectioned patients, section three,
> If we misbehave, they take away our leave

Chavis reflects that words and images "etch paths to self-awareness and help bring about relief from sorrow and confusion" (2011, p. 12). In the art and writing–focused dramatherapy group, creative writing and symbolic art work play a vital role. Clients respond to either the weekly theme or present emotions, expressing themselves through art work, free-flowing writing and poetry. This process inspires several people to write (and draw) in between sessions, providing them with a practical, positive coping mechanism. Chavis also explains that words and images "provide links between our past, present and future and between the people in our lives" (2011, p. 12).

Clarice was in her early twenties. She suffered extreme neglect as a baby. She enjoyed the dramatherapy group, though often avoided the art and writing–focused dramatherapy group – perhaps because she found the process of quiet self-reflection too overwhelming. When she found the courage to attend one week, she wrote a poem to describe how she often hides her emotional pain and inner chaos behind a smile. She was quietly tearful, though responded well to reassurance and support. She then found the courage to read her poem to the group during the sharing ritual, for which she felt proud and relieved.

A detailed case study illustrating the six interventions

Jean is in her early forties. Having suffered extreme abuse and neglect throughout her childhood and teenage years, she came to despise herself deeply, and as an adult, bloodletting became her only solace. Her core belief is that she is bad, a worthless person deserving unhappiness and death. Aside from her difficulties, she remains kind and thoughtful, with a good sense of humour, a love of music, attending gigs and spending time with her sister, niece and friends. She is also a fully qualified first aid instructor, a profession which she hopes to return to when discharged. Her self-care and sleep hygiene are poor, and her BPD diagnosis is further complicated by PTSD (post-traumatic stress disorder), ASD (autistic spectrum disorder), ADHD (attention-deficit hyperactivity disorder), dyslexia and dyspraxia. Jean's history of self-harm includes bloodletting, head banging, biting her forearms and taking life-threatening overdoses. As well as having suicidal ideation and strong urges to self-harm, she struggles with traumatic flashbacks and disassociation, "a complex phenomenon that comprises a host of symptoms and factors, including depersonalization, derealization, time distortion, dissociative flashbacks, and alterations in the perception of the self" (Vermetten and Spiegel, 2014, p. 1).

Jean's family history is complex. Her parents argued a lot and divorced when she was young. As her mother had schizophrenia and struggled with alcoholism, Jean had to live with her father, who remarried. Her father and stepmother then neglected her on both emotional and functional levels. At a young age, she began to inhale solvents and head-bang as an emotional outlet. From the age of 6, she was sexually abused by her maternal uncle (whilst staying with her mother) and, traumatised by the experience, she continues to endure flashbacks and nightmares. He takes shape as a bogeyman, oozing green slime and crawling with spiders. Jean was also bullied throughout her school years and did not learn to read and write until the age of 10. Aged 12, she was sexually exploited by a girl at her secondary school.

Despite the multiple traumas endured, Jean built herself a life in the community. Having left school with minimal qualifications, she returned to education as a young adult and qualified as a first aid instructor. She enjoyed this work and managed to develop some lasting friendships, as well as maintaining a good relationship with her sister and two brothers. When she was 26, her mother died of cancer and in her early thirties, two friends encouraged her to seek justice for the abuse she suffered as child. With their support, she found the courage to report both her uncle and the girl from secondary school. The police investigated both cases and her uncle was arrested. Charges could not be pursued, however, due to the time that had elapsed and insufficient evidence. They interviewed both suspects and her uncle received an official warning. Disheartened by the outcome, Jean's bloodletting escalated to a life-threatening degree and she was admitted to hospital under section. Over the following few years, each time she was discharged, the process repeated itself, and eventually, she was transferred onto the specialist ward where we met.

Initial steps into dramatherapy

Jean was admitted to the ward in October 2015, shortly after having tendon surgery for a wound on her forearm, repeatedly used for bloodletting. She found the new boundaries difficult, struggling to form relationships with both staff and peers, missing staff from her previous hospital. From her first week on the ward, however, Jean appeared relaxed in my presence and made an effort to attend the weekly dramatherapy and art and writing–focused dramatherapy groups. By the end of November, however, she began to avoid them, as her mood plummeted and her urge to bloodlet intensified. In between nursing observations, she managed to bloodlet via the wound on her arm that she had prevented healing. She became anaemic, though refused to take iron supplements, and by late December (a particularly difficult month for her) her physical condition declined so seriously that on Christmas Day, she was transferred to a general hospital for a blood transfusion.

Jean returned to the ward in late December 2016 and remained on one-to-one observations, day and night. Her risk of life-threatening self-harm remained high, which she acted upon by repeatedly trying to choke herself with empty crisp packets and paper. Despite this, our therapeutic relationship continued to develop and whilst her group attendance fluctuated, she remained keen to have informal individual meetings. During these conversations, I began to challenge her negative core beliefs and liaised closely with her one-to-one DBT therapist. Over the following few months, her suicidal ideation and urge to bloodlet remained strong and she gave me several letters expressing suicidal thoughts and intentions, which I shared with the MDT.

In late January 2016, each member of the dramatherapy group created a 'spectogram of self', using small objects (from a large selection) to express aspects of themselves and their lives: Jean chose a tiny blue hippo to symbolise herself and carefully placed it on a small red beanbag, indicating blood. Just behind it, she added a large crystal to represent her friends and family. Beside it, she placed a plastic gun, the trigger pointing towards the hippo. (Her creation is shown in Figure 5.4.) Expressing her preoccupation with bloodletting and suicide, she was encouraged to acknowledge the element of hope she had included, with the crystal symbolising her family and friends. Such delicate strands of light continued to reveal themselves during group sessions.

FIGURE 5.4 Jean's spectogram of self

During our individual meetings, I encouraged Jean to write letters to her former abusers, to express the words she had never been able to say. As Chavis explains, "Directly addressing one's abuser in a letter that is written in a safe and nurturing space can help transform feelings of vulnerability into a sense of self-assurance" (2011, p. 169). Jean engaged deeply with this process, writing powerful letters to her abusive uncle and the girl who had abused her at secondary school. She did not post these letters, or the poem that she wrote to her father in June 2016, though she found writing them cathartic. With courage, she read the following poem to her peers:

> Do you see?
> The child in the playground,
> Skinny girl, dirty girl,
> Wearing NHS glasses,
> The girl they say is thick,
> Stupid and backward?
>
> Do you see?
> The child who's been crushed
> Under the weight of an adult,
> Yes, rape!
> The child forced to do sexual acts
> On another child?

Do you see?
The lack of food, lack of clothes,
Lack of comfort, lack of love,
And a lack of you Dad, yes you!

Do you remember Grandad sayings?
Nowt so blind as those that can't see
Nowt so deaf as those that can't hear
Dad, do you see you?

In June 2016, Jean finally allowed the wound on her arm to heal and agreed to take antipsychotic medication, which helped to reduce the intensity of her flashbacks and suicidal ideation. The OT also initiated an important piece of work, encouraging her to plan and facilitate first aid sessions for her peers, helping her reconnect to her former working self. During an art and writing–focused dramatherapy group in July 2016, a significant shift occurred. She said she wanted to feel something and worked on a dramatic piece that revealed the bogeyman, who continues to haunt her within flashbacks and dreams. She saw something unexpected in her picture during the closing ritual, explaining that it looked as though the bogeyman was being stabbed in the back by former victims, thus protecting the little girl in the foreground. This revealed Jean's growing ability to see beyond what was most apparent, connecting with her unconscious and seeking a new perspective. We later reflected that it could also link to her effort to bring her uncle to justice and that his arrest and official warning may have been enough to deter him from abusing further children.

Jean continued to struggle with the DBT process, and in August 2016, the consultant psychiatrist and MDT agreed that as an alternative, she should begin one-to-one trauma-focused dramatherapy.

One-to-one trauma-focused dramatherapy

Our official one-to-one sessions began in September 2016. Jean's suicidal ideation had decreased significantly, and she was adjusting to the side effects of her new medication. She admitted, however, that she missed bloodletting, as it helped to release strong emotions, stimulated endorphins and satisfied her need for self-punishment. Discussing alternatives, Jean acknowledged her ability to release emotions through the dramatherapy process and said she would like to start exercising to stimulate endorphins. Self-punishment could not be replaced so easily, however, linking to her core belief that she is a bad person or she would not have endured recurrent abuse. The internalised words of her abusers play a significant role here, and during one-to-one sessions, I endeavoured to help her to understand and accept that she is not to blame for the abuse, neglect and bullying she suffered – and that her child self needs love and support, not judgement and punishment. Negative core beliefs are powerful, however, and can be so deeply ingrained that they feel immovable.

Working with adult survivors of child abuse, Appolinari reflects that "Only with long, patient, caring, loving work can they rediscover what they started out as: pure innocent children" (1996, p. 3).

Giving voice to the various aspects of her personality was crucial, as the part Jean named 'Worthless Piece of Shit' had dominated and drowned out the other voices for several years. This relates to the Jungian concept of integrating our internal aspects, including the shadow part, to reach individuation (Stevens, 2001b). Bannister explains that abused children tend to think of themselves as bad and their abusers as good – an overwhelming belief that can lead to dissociation, their personalities fragmenting (2003, p. 4). During her dramatherapy journey, Jean used hand puppets to symbolise and communicate with specific parts of her psyche: the inner child, worthless self, cheeky self, confident self, inner warrior and internal mother. This process is influenced by Rowan, who explains that as we adapt to our life circumstances, different personalities emerge within (1990, p. 7). These sub-personalities may arise from the roles we play, our internal conflicts, fantasy images inspired by heroes or celebrities, the personal unconscious, cultural unconscious and collective unconscious (Rowan, 1990, pp. 21–23). The dramatherapy process that Jean moved through also relates to Jungian concepts, which have informed and influenced subpersonality work (Rowan, 1990, p. 23), particularly the archetypes and the shadow.

Session 1

Jean said she hoped the process would help her to improve her confidence. Her mood was flat and she felt confused at times. We touched on the subject of hurting and anger, which was emotionally painful and triggered her to disassociate.

Session 2

Jean had greater clarity of speech and thought this week (regular anti–side effect medication now helping). She asked for the Pocahontas puppet and chose one for the therapist, which she later named Eddie Harris (a musician). Pocahontas told Eddie that she was scared of the bogeyman, who was trapped inside her mind. We then touched on several deep and significant issues: the loss of impor-tant relationships with former healthcare professionals, which ended suddenly at the last hospital, sexual abuse by her uncle (who appears as the bogeyman) and sexual exploitation by a girl at secondary school. She explained that she had found the courage to make a statement against them six years ago. Whilst there had not been enough evidence to prosecute, the police had been kind and sup-portive, arresting her uncle and telling him they believed Jean and would keep her statement on file. She also spoke of the impact of her mother's schizophrenia, absence and later death (she died at the age of 52, when Jean was 26). Finally, she spoke about the neglect she suffered whilst under the care of her father and stepmother.

Session 3

This week, we explored significant issues. Again, hand puppets were used, and the Pocahontas puppet helped her to give voice to her inner child. A significant part of this process is to encourage her to understand that she is not bad, but that bad things have been done to her. I also wanted to encourage her to learn to mother, rather than punish her inner child. We then discussed the meaning of home and her attachment to her flat. This led to the challenging issue of bloodletting, her reliance on it and the idea of life without it. I reflected that the impact of multiple traumas had become her puppet master in a sense – relating to the theme of the morning's art and writing–focused dramatherapy group. I asked, "Can you imagine life without bloodletting?" Jean answered, "No", and then acknowledged the negative impact that bloodletting could have on her life: losing her flat, remaining under section in hospital, friends and family giving up on her and her physical and mental health continuing to decline. Jean reflected that whatever anyone does to help her, she knows that she is the only one who can truly change her life.

Session 4

Jean shared her fear about meeting new people if she returns to work. I encouraged her to imagine life without bloodletting, supported by the reasons she had found last week. She again gave voice to her inner child through the Pocahontas puppet, quietly expressing deeper fears and emotions. She felt unable to tell her inner child that she was not bad, though instinctively held her to her chest and gently rubbed her back. I spoke softly, encouraging her to comfort her inner child, reflecting that one day she would feel able to tell her that she was not bad. She said, "I deserve everything I get", and appeared exhausted by the process, explaining that she deserved neither love nor hope. We moved into a positive exercise using a therapeutic card deck and she was invited to choose a card for love and a card for hope. I also chose two cards and we gave our love cards to her inner-child puppet and the two hope cards to her adult self. She accepted them but said she had nothing to say at the end of the session. I then asked if Pocahontas wanted to say anything and Jean gave voice to her inner child, with a simple, "Thank you for the hope".

Session 5

Jean engaged deeply. We explored her relationship to addiction and the challenge of letting go of trauma and suffering. She said she would like to write two poems, one on bloodletting, the other about her stepmother. Whilst remembering her child and teenage self, she managed not to disassociate and utilised self-comforting techniques. The two puppets, Pocahontas and Eddie, aided the process.

Aged 4, Jean went to a Church of England primary school, where she was ignored by teachers and children, as her mother (who used to collect her) was Catholic and had mental health problems. She lived with both parents and they argued a lot. Jean described herself as tall and skinny for her age, wearing thick NHS glasses and eyepatches. She did not learn to read or write until she was 10 and was then state-mented (assessed as having special educational needs). She was sent to a special school for Year 6 and part of Year 7, where she was much happier. She was then abruptly moved back to a mainstream secondary school, where the children knew she had come from a special school and again she was bullied. By this time, her parents had divorced and her father remarried. She was neglected and emotionally abused by her father and stepmother, and at age 12, she was sexually exploited by a girl at school. To cope with her distress, she inhaled solvents and head-banged (which she continued as an adult).

Jean questioned whether she had an addictive personality, passed down to her genetically. As well as having schizophrenia, her mother was an alcoholic and her younger brother had been a heroin addict. Her mother said he could not help it, as he was just like her and had an addictive personality. Jean wondered if her addiction to bloodletting and self-harm could also be genetic. We explored this possibility and I shared a concept from Thich Nhat Hanh, suggesting that people may hold onto their suffering, due to its familiarity and fear of the unknown (2012, pp. 217–218). Jean understood this, acknowledging how difficult it was to let go. She then described the sensation of bloodletting as a warm hug that releases the bad. I suggested wrapping herself in a soft red blanket to symbolise the experience and reminded her that bad feelings and suffering at the hands of others did not make her a bad person, but made her feel bad. She disagreed and said she had deserved everything. She then described running away as a young teenager, after which her dad and stepmother did not speak to her for a month.

Session 6

Jean entered the creative process and several issues were explored through discussion and symbolic puppet work. She spoke more about her early solvent abuse and how her addiction and reliance on bloodletting had initially begun accidentally, when blood spurted across the room after accidentally hitting an artery. She then questioned her ability to cope without it once back in the community. Each time she made progress in the past and was discharged from hospital, she soon returned to bloodletting. We discussed what might (or could) be different this time and Jean shared that she continued to struggle to express anger.

Session 7

Jean immersed herself in the creative process this week. She used the Pocahontas puppet to connect to her inner child and self-soothed with the aid of black velvet material and a stress ball. We discussed the idea of giving her anger a voice and developing an inner warrior. With support, Jean completed the acrostic poem she had begun in the morning's art and writing–focused dramatherapy group. It described how she felt about her stepmother and she was encouraged to read it out loud, with energy and conviction. She responded positively to this. During the session, there were moments she appeared exhausted and I reflected that she was working with intense emotions and difficult memories. She is also learning to see she has choices about how to express her inner rage and emotional pain.

Session 8

Jean was keen to attend and made the effort to use the stairs, rather than the lift, despite finding it painful. We discussed her difficulty with motivation on the ward, acknowledging the effort she makes to get up on Mondays and Tuesdays (for dramatherapy and art and writing–focused dramatherapy) compared to the lethargy she experiences the rest of the week. Through reflection, power-thought cards and puppet work, Jean created a personal mantra, as an aid to inspire her to get up each day. Via this process, she found a name for her inner warrior (Sheera) and continued to work with her inner child (Pocahontas).

Session 9

Jean shared her anxieties about her recent assessment with staff from the rehabilitation unit (where I also work). With support, she then identified specific parts of herself (otherwise known as subpersonalities). She described their key qualities, named them, positioned them around her core self (represented by a flower) and selected symbolic objects for them. They included Pocahontas (her inner child, who she is learning to nurture), Worthless (the persistent part that feels bad and cannot let go of past trauma), Sheera (her inner warrior, from whom she feels most distant), Cheeky Jean (the healthy part that tries to see things positively) and In Control (the highly functioning part that feels more confident and in control). Jean would be encouraged to build a better balance between these inner parts and establish a healthy dialogue between them.

Session 10

Jean said she had been finding things difficult and that sleeping was a form of self-preservation. She admitted she had been experiencing many flashbacks and finding therapy challenging. Several times, she closed her eyes and struggled to stay with the process. She appeared most connected to the 'Worthless' part of herself, renamed 'Worthless Piece of Shit', though she comforted her inner child (symbolised by the Pocahontas puppet) throughout the session. When asked to think what her 'In Control' part could say to 'Worthless' to help her, she found the following words: "You're not worthless and you need to concentrate on what you know". Saying these words out loud and with conviction, however, was very challenging.

Session 11

Jean came willingly and although her emotions became quite intense at times – and potentially overwhelming – she responded well to the expressive techniques used to support her. Pocahontas (the inner-child puppet) again provided an important source of comfort. New Year's Eve was a day she remembered her uncle abusing her. She was 6 years old and her mother was asleep at the time. After the rape, Jean climbed back into bed with her mother, who did not notice anything was wrong. She admitted she felt angry with her for not being able to protect her, but then felt very bad about this and wanted to push all the blame back onto herself. As Vermetten and Spiegel explain, "Psychological trauma can have devastating consequences on emotion regulatory capacities and lead to dissociative processes that provide subjective detachment from overwhelming emotional experience during and in the aftermath of trauma" (2014, p. 1). She felt a strong urge to bang her head on the wall, though managed not to do so, agreeing instead to squeeze my hands and shout together. Although she felt embarrassed, it helped to shift her urge to head-bang and stopped her from disassociating. Jean explained that December was a particularly difficult month for her (with memories of both her uncle's abuse and her mother's death). Despite this, she was looking forward to going on leave and spending time with her sister and two of her friends.

Session 12

Jean came willingly and, despite struggling with a low mood and lethargy, engaged deeply in the process. Initially, she shared suicidal thoughts and her fear of deteriorating, with her medication reduced. She then participated fully in a challenging role reversal exercise, for which we created a simple script. Challenging Jean's negative core beliefs remains key to this process, helping her to understand (and more importantly to believe) that she is not bad, but that bad things have happened to her. Towards the end of the session, she admitted that she felt stuck, and throughout the process, she self-soothed by gently hugging her inner-child puppet.

Session 13

Jean expressed ongoing fears about her medication being reduced, concerned that she wouldn't be able to cope with the bogeyman. She said she did not want to feel how she did before. She also spoke about the bullying she had experienced at school and her disappointment in the police investigation six years ago, following the child abuse report she had made. Again, Jean questioned whether her negative core beliefs were in fact true and if she had the strength to change them. Throughout the session, she self-soothed by holding her inner-child puppet. When her emotions appeared to overwhelm her, I guided her back to the present and she chose puppets to symbolise Cheeky Jean, Worthless Jean and Confident Jean (formerly named In Control). She agreed to explore what these different parts might to say each other in a future session and how they may help one another. It was also suggested it may be time to add an internal mother to her set of inner parts, as challenging core beliefs and caring for herself are essential to her recovery.

Session 14

Jean engaged openly and began by sharing some difficult memories: there was a child on her street who used come over regularly, to ask her to come and play at her house. At the other child's house, they would play doctors and the friend always chose to take the role of the doctor, inserting things into Jean's private parts. She also said she had established a sex club in junior school, for which she was reported to the headmaster and felt ashamed. At one stage, she began to disassociate as the material was so distressing. Holding tactile objects (a large piece of black velvet material and her favourite stress ball) helped to reground her, however, and she focused well, despite the challenging nature of the work. She also held her inner-child puppet, and by the end of the session, she appeared energised and a little more positive.

Session 15

Initially, Jean was keen to explain the meaning of the piece she had created in the morning's art and writing–focused dramatherapy group. She shared that it had symbolised her most recent flashback: a memory of when her abusive uncle threatened to cut off her head, boil it and then feed it to the 'Blackies'. We explored this memory, and then reflected on her dramatherapy journey so far, in relation to inner aspects (subpersonalities), symbolic work and challenging negative core beliefs. As well as looking at the past, Jean spoke openly about her fear of moving from the ward to the rehabilitation unit, as it will bring the challenge of forming new relationships.

Session 16

Jean was alert and focused throughout the session. She chose puppets to represent each of her subpersonalities: the Internal Mother (represented by a Shakespeare puppet named Bob), the Inner Child (represented by the Pocahontas puppet), a Worthless Piece of Shit (represented by Jean's least favourite puppet), the Inner Warrior (represented by a soft toy, symbolising Sheera), Cheeky Jean (represented by a smiling Rastafarian type puppet, named Eddie) and Confident Jean (represented by a wizard puppet dressed in blue, Jean's favourite colour). These puppets are shown in Figure 5.5.

Jean chose where to place the Internal Mother, Inner Child and Worthless around her central self and found a few words for each of them to say. Worthless said she still felt like a piece of shit, but was pleased that the therapist cared about her. Jean also spoke about her fear of returning to work in the future and her continued effort not to bloodlet. Her urges continue, prohibited only by a stronger desire not to hurt the people who care about her.

FIGURE 5.5 Jean's subpersonality puppets

Session 17

Jean spoke freely about several things that were troubling her. She had thought about her GP appointment last week and the tests regarding a lump in her breast, but was more preoccupied with other worries. First was the issue of whether her trust will agree to funding the rehabilitation unit and how much longer it will take them to make their decision. She added her concern that if she does not move there, our work together will end. Jean spoke about her future employment opportunities, as her previous line manager (who has remained a good friend) was made redundant.

She also shared that her medication is the best she has ever had, as although her urge to bloodlet remains strong, she continues to resist it, knowing the negative impact it would have on the people who love her. Jean said she could think clearer now, without constant suicidal thoughts, and although flashbacks continue, they are less frequent. Reflecting on her relationship with peers on the ward, she said she felt isolated.

Session 18

Jean came willingly and we explored her feelings about the recent death of a former service user (aged 19) who had been discharged six months earlier. She said she understood how Chloe may have been feeling and spoke of her own battle with suicidal thoughts, previous suicide attempts and urges to self-harm through overdose and bloodletting. Jean did not appear overly anxious about the mammogram and breast biopsy she was having the following day.

She asked if our sessions were going to help her overcome complex PTSD and when the question was reflected back to her, she said she thought they were helping and hoped they would. We then discussed the process so far, beginning with the informal work we began just over a year ago. She had initially written letters and poems to the individuals who had abused and/or neglected her and we explored how this had progressed into our current one-to-one work. Chavis suggests that clients who initially write letters to their abusers should write further letters when able to do so with the essence of an ideal parent figure: "When clients create, develop and affirm their own self-soothing parent voice in their letter-writing, they gain a valuable resource to carry within themselves during times of distress" (2011, p. 169).

Session 19

Jean was keen to attend and apologised for missing the two creative therapy groups this week. She explained she had been feeling very tired and her mood appeared subdued. Whilst we explored this further key themes arose:

1. The sadness she feels about former service user Chloe's death and its impact upon her own internal struggle with life and death.
2. The continued state of 'not knowing' regarding her future placement at the rehabilitation unit.
3. Her feeling of indifference in connection to getting the all-clear following her mammogram.

During the session, attention was given to the concept of strengthening her Internal Mother. This began with an exploration of the archetypal mother and led to Jean sharing some difficult childhood memories. With the emotions that arose, she began to dissociate, though she responded well to self-soothing, sensory techniques and was able to talk through what was happening. Jean said she wanted to disappear, which connects to her tendency to sleep a lot during the day.

Session 20

Jean engaged fully and important issues were discussed, including the mixed feelings she has about the healed wound on her arm and what this continues to represent. Despite the difficult areas touched upon, she remained alert and focused. Whilst speaking about her former professional roles, she became visibly animated and energised, which was encouraging.

Session 21

Initially, Jean admitted that her urge to bloodlet was particularly strong, thinking it may relate to the good news she had received at her hospital appointment last week. She also felt very stressed about her future, with regards to moving to the rehabilitation unit and, more importantly, returning to work. The inner self puppets helped to ground Jean during the session, providing her with comfort when her emotions felt too intense. Worthless, the internal part that believes it deserves punishment, voiced its frustration about losing control and then listened to the Inner Warrior, Internal Mother and Inner Child. Towards the end of the session, Jean chose the words "I do not deserve to be punished, it is others who should be punished". These were written down and she later took them to her room. We also discussed the effort she made to bring her abusive uncle and the girl who had abused her at school to justice. It became clear that Jean's focus must now be on herself, and I encouraged her to see that her survival and happiness would be the best punishment for those who had hurt her.

Session 22

Jean shared her ongoing struggle with the urge to bloodlet and her anxieties about potentially moving to the rehabilitation unit. We also discussed her sleeping issues and the importance of trying to establish a healthier sleep routine, in preparation for the life she wants to rebuild in the community.

Session 23

Jean engaged fully and began by sharing her feelings about the picture card she chose in yesterday's dramatherapy group: it revealed a woman standing in a lake, looking down at her reflection. She said that when she looks at her own reflection, all she sees is a worthless person. We then explored what a person of worth might look like and she described several members of her family, about whom she cares and believes have worth. I reflected that some of the aspects highlighted she also embodied. This led to Jean finding five statements of self-worth to describe herself, in response to the statement 'I am a person of worth because'. She read her statements out loud, though she felt a little uncomfortable and said it did not feel that she was describing herself:

1. I can see good in other people.
2. Without hesitation, I would help other people.
3. I have love in my heart.
4. I am caring.
5. I am determined to achieve whatever I want, and I have worked hard to get this far.

Jean remains closely connected to her negative core beliefs, which reflect the voices of the people who abused and neglected her as a child and teenager. Whilst her pain and anger must be acknowledged, it is equally important that her qualities, strengths and achievements are brought into the light, enabling her to reach a more balanced mental state. At the end of the session, she agreed to put a copy of the positive statements up in her room.

Session 24

Jean was feeling apprehensive and unsafe, as funding for the rehabilitation unit had been granted. We explored her fears and discussed the connection between emotional/mental stress and her desire to bloodlet. I explained that the focus of our work will gradually shift when she moves to the rehabilitation unit: having explored many aspects of her trauma and their connection to her negative core beliefs and coping mechanisms, she has also identified key parts of herself, some of which need further development. The core challenge will be applying what she has learnt and allowing herself to find new ways in which to cope with emotional and mental stress. Key to this is letting go of the past (not forgetting it), allowing her to more fully inhabit the present.

The next few sessions on the ward would focus on helping her to prepare for the transition to the rehabilitation unit, reminding her of the significant progress she had made on the ward over the past twenty months and reinforcing all she has learnt.

Jean's dramatherapy journey in relation to schema therapy

Whilst researching the schema therapy (ST) approach (described in Chapter 3) I recognised a clear similarity with Jean's journey through dramatherapy. ST was developed by Young as a treatment for people with complex and enduring mental health problems, particularly those with personality disorders. It was an adaptation of CT (cognitive therapy) for individuals with "chronic, often lifelong psychological problems; and more deeply entrenched, dysfunctional belief systems" (Kellogg and Young, 2006, p. 446). Young focused on their schemas (also known as core beliefs) and prolonged the treatment, allowing more time to explore childhood experiences and placing more significance on the therapeutic relationship (Kellogg and Young, 2006, p. 446).

Jean developed early maladaptive schema due to childhood trauma that took many forms: parental difficulties and divorce, sexual abuse from an adult male within her family, bullying at school, parental mental health and addiction problems, parental neglect and emotional abuse, and sexual exploitation by another child. Such deep-rooted schema are "enduring and self-defeating patterns that typically begin early in life (. . .) cause negative/dysfunctional thoughts and feelings, and interfere with accomplishing goals and meetings one's needs" (Sperry, 2016, l.780–782). The philosophy at the heart of ST is that all children deserve to have their core needs met, and when this does not happen, developmental problems are likely to emerge (Kellogg and Young, 2006, p. 451). Through dramatherapy, Jean experienced positive reparenting and gradually found the courage to challenge her maladaptive schema and negative core beliefs through gaining a better understanding of her inner aspects (or modes) and allowing them to speak and interact through symbolic puppet work.

Kellogg and Young developed the model further for people with BPD, allowing for their rapidly fluctuating moods, as well as psychological and emotional immaturity (Kellogg and Young, 2006, p. 450). Working with different aspects (modes) of the personality is key to the process. Reminiscent of Jungian archetypes, three groups of internal modes are recognised: child, parent and coping modes (Kellogg and Young, 2006, p. 447). Five central modes are identified within people with BPD: the abandoned and abused child (their central state of being); the angry and impulsive child (the part that knows it has suffered injustice); the detached protector (a regular coping mechanism, emotionally withdrawn, isolative and disconnected); the punitive parent (an internalised experience of parenting); and the healthy adult, which is least present (Kellogg and Young, 2006, pp. 447–449).

Schema therapy helps people to develop their healthy adult mode, which the therapist initially embodies and the client gradually begins to internalise (Kellogg and Young, 2006, p. 449). During Jean's dramatherapy journey, puppets were used to work with key aspects of her personality. The Inner Child and Worthless were initially most present, connecting to each other through pain: whilst the Inner Child craved love and care, Worthless seemed to hold her mental and emotional pain, experienced as self-loathing and externalised through a desire for physical pain and punishment. Cheeky and Confident were Jean's higher-functioning adult parts. Mostly repressed by Worthless, they occasionally resurfaced during her time on the ward, particularly when she ran first aid sessions for her peers or expressed her sense of humour in the dramatherapy group. The Inner Warrior was introduced, helping Jean to draw on her inner strength and courage, followed by the Internal Mother, encouraging her to learn to care for herself.

Schema therapists employ various techniques, also relevant to Jean's dramatherapy journey, through four key strategies:

1. The first and most central is 'limited reparenting', during which the therapist employs strategies to reparent the client, within professional boundaries. One technique is to offer clients a 'transitional object' (Winnicott, 2005, p. 18): I offered Jean a small, soft Superwoman doll, which came to symbolise her Inner Warrior. It became a transitionary object, which she brought to every session. On several occasions, Jean also took pieces of work created in sessions – such as statements, mantras and poems – to put up in her room. Having both the doll and creative pieces in between sessions helped to extend the impact of the process, reminding Jean of the positive work she was doing.

2. The second strategy is 'emotion-focused work', in which experiential techniques are used, including imagery work, dialogues and letter writing. The client's

trauma is carefully explored and the therapist acts as a protective adult. They also have frequent dialogues to fight the internalised punitive parent together, thus reassuring and nurturing the abandoned/abused inner child (Kellogg and Young, 2006, p. 450): very similar methods were used throughout Jean's journey through dramatherapy.

3. The third strategy is 'cognitive restructuring and education', through which the clients' needs and emotions are validated and they learn that it was not their fault that their needs were not met as children and feelings not validated. Their positive qualities are also emphasised "to help to combat the toxic messages of the punitive parent" (Kellogg and Young, 2006, p. 451). Validating their anger is also essential, followed by helping them to manage it in a non-destructive manner. For example positive reinforcement may be used to replace punishment. Such concepts and strategies played a vital role in Jean's dramatherapy journey.

4. The fourth strategy is 'behavioural pattern breaking', through which clients learn to apply what they have learnt in previous sessions to their current life and relationships. Many techniques are used, such as imagery and dialogues, relaxation and assertiveness training, anger management, self-monitoring and goal-setting (Kellogg and Young, 2006, p. 452). Elements of this are relevant to Jean's dramatherapy journey on the ward and would become more applicable and apparent during the next phase of therapy at the rehabilitation unit.

Kellogg and Young outline three treatment phases for people with BPD, suggesting a minimum of two years: bonding and emotional regulation, schema mode change and development of autonomy (2006, p. 452). The first and second phases are most relevant to Jean's process through dramatherapy on the ward, where attention is initially given to the validation of emotions and reparenting, which gradually shifts towards problem solving and, finally, empowering clients to parent themselves (Kellogg and Young, 2006, pp. 452–455). As her dramatherapy journey continues at the rehabilitation unit, Jean will enter a similar process to the third stage of schema therapy, where clients are encouraged to become more independent, with an emphasis on interpersonal relationships and self-identity (Kellogg and Young, 2006, p. 456).

Perspectives from the multidisciplinary team on dramatherapy

I offered a questionnaire to all members of the MDT, seeking their perspectives on the role of dramatherapy on the ward and exploring their unique experience of working with the client group. Seven colleagues responded: the OT (occupational therapist), ward doctor, ward manager, assistant psychologist, a DBT-trained RMN (registered mental health nurse), the consultant psychiatrist and a DBT-trained health care assistant (HCA). They were asked, *What is your understanding or opinion of using dramatherapy as an intervention for this client group?*

The OT, who supported me in the dramatherapy group for two and a half years, wrote:

> Dramatherapy offers a 'fairy tale' world within our unit. Service users have the opportunity to release and express difficult emotions, in a way that they feel safe and nurtured. They have a space within the day to scream, play ball games, act using puppets, imagine themselves in other landscapes, see themselves in different ages and reflect. Dramatherapy allows our service users to connect with their inner selves, explore and imagine a world that it is not just black and white. A world that allows anger, sadness, happiness, guilt and so many other emotions to exist and patients are smoothly and safely encouraged to identify, accept and be. Dramatherapy helps also the team to see other aspects of our clients and so we are able to understand them better and to sympathise with them. Since I started helping Nicky as a co-facilitator in her groups, I feel more skilful working with BPD patients and able to reflect easier on my transference and countertransference.
>
> *(Ntzimani, response to author's questionnaire, 2017)*

The ward doctor, who has worked on the ward for four years, shared her opinion that dramatherapy plays an intrinsic part in the recovery of BPD and has many times complemented the DBT (dialectical behavioural therapy) programme. She noted she had witnessed this first-hand, as well as considering feedback from service users and verbal and written feedback. She explained that our clients often struggle with the shift from feeling daily pain to experiencing a lack of it on the ward, and that therapies such as dramatherapy aid their journey to wellness and wholeness. She reflected that it also helps them to trust and "to understand that these feelings of 'emotional purgatory' are only temporary and part of their healing – allowing for this very necessary adjustment period" (Gour, response to author's questionnaire, 2017).

The ward manager, with six years of experience in the field of BPD, reflected that dramatherapy is particularly beneficial for patients who have difficulty expressing themselves verbally. She noted that she had observed a few patients improving following their involvement in dramatherapy and that it boosts their self-esteem, encourages independence and empowers them (Nojaduka, response to author's questionnaire, 2017).

The psychology assistant, who has worked on the ward for eight years, wrote, "The clients always seem to look forward to dramatherapy. My personal experience is limited but it seems to be a safe place for them to express thoughts and feelings in a creative way" (Johnson, response to author's questionnaire, 2017).

A DBT-trained RMN, who has worked on the ward for a year and a half, described how her initial perception of the group changed after attending a session:

I thought it was just a light, fun group. Quickly I discovered the therapeutic process and just how important this expression of conscious and unconscious emotions is. I observed and heard this from clients. Once for example, the theme was Peter Pan. Initially, I had not imagined this may evoke difficult emotions. However, a client left tearful and shaken, as she had never heard the story of Peter Pan and to her, this represented her lost childhood.

(Abdoun, response to author's questionnaire, 2017)

She also wrote, "Dramatherapy is often the client's favourite group, the therapist is warm and understanding and it provides a creative outlet for feelings and emotions which you sometimes can't verbalise" (Abdoun, response to author's questionnaire, 2017).

The consultant psychiatrist, with thirty years of experience with the client group, wrote:

Words are often not available to the patient to begin to describe complexities in their feelings, thoughts, actions and relationships, all of which can begin to be understood through examination of their interactions with themselves and with others within dramatherapy settings. It is a very useful intervention that stimulates curiosity in the patient about themselves and about their functioning in life. It is a very useful way of engaging a patient in the process of treatment.

(Healy, response to author's questionnaire, 2017)

A DBT-trained HCA, with five years of experience with the client group, described dramatherapy as a group in which our clients can express and try to regulate complex emotions. She has supported in the group several times and reflected that expressing themselves via creative outlets, such as stories, music, poetry and games, may help them to cope with difficult emotions and potentially to learn better distress skills to replace maladaptive behaviours. She also drew parallels between the dramatherapy and DBT process:

DBT teaches clients to sit with their emotions, that emotions are necessary, to be mindful of them and ultimately accept them. From my understanding, techniques in dramatherapy work with clients in all these exact areas and more (. . .) Dramatherapy can also serve as a way to teach clients a form of distraction from their emotions. DBT distress tolerance skills teach them to use various distraction techniques such as writing poetry and listening to (or making) music, which are also used in dramatherapy (. . .) Having clients work together in these groups allows them to share their struggles in a creative way, which can help them validate themselves and their fellow peers. Dramatherapy thus also works on their interpersonal effectiveness skills, which is very important within BPD treatment.

(Bermeo, response to author's questionnaire, 2017)

The client's voice

Listening to the client's voice is paramount to the process, and therapist and client learn from one another. Although questionnaires used to gather data are helpful (and most readily received by institutions) qualitative information adds sincerity and depth. Clients on the ward are regularly invited to describe their experience of dramatherapy in their own words, as well as indicating their response to a series of set questions, focusing on the areas recommended by NICE: mental state and quality of life, social and personal functioning, self-harm and other risky behaviours (2009, p. 103). This chapter will end with the words of clients who were keen to share their feelings about dramatherapy:

> I find dramatherapy relaxing and totally different to how I expected. It always relaxes me and I find it soothing.
>
> *(Shona, 2015)*

> With dramatherapy, it's nice to be able to think and give physical release to our thoughts and give your interpretation of the theme for the session. It's a safe and controlled environment, so at least you know that nothing will happen. It also helps to give some unselfconscious insight into your personality, and your thoughts and reactions in a particular setting with your peers, hopefully giving them a little insight and understanding into what's going on with you. With art and writing–focused dramatherapy, I really like working with my hands and find it very calming. I enjoy the challenge of using the different materials (most of which I have not used before) to see what I can do with them and how the eventual product will emerge.
>
> *(Sadie, 2015)*

> When I join the groups, I feel that it helps to get in touch with my feelings and to be able to express myself in a safe environment.
>
> *(Amy, 2015)*

> When I came into hospital, I'd never done either dramatherapy or art and writing–focused dramatherapy. I felt very low in myself and constantly felt like self-harming, and very often had thoughts of suicide. The first few sessions were a bit daunting, but gradually, I began to feel both sessions were a safe place to express myself; I didn't need to wear the mask I had on the rest of the time. My biggest fear of letting my guard down was that I'd be overwhelmed by my feelings, but instead I found I could feel those things profoundly and deeply when I was in the room, but it wouldn't feel unsafe and those feelings could mostly be left behind at the end of the session.
>
> During my worst patch, I was constantly suicidal, and death was a strong theme in my art work. It was scary, actively expressing my feelings, but helped reduce the intensity of those thoughts, only briefly, but any respite from these thoughts was a welcome breathing space.

I'm also a bit of a perfectionist and quite shy. Art and writing–focused dramatherapy showed me things don't have to be perfect to be meaningful and dramatherapy helped me build confidence in interacting with others.

I'm coming to the end of my stay in hospital and there are so many things that have helped me get to this point, and I would definitely count drama-therapy and art and writing–focused dramatherapy among them. Often, they were the only things I looked forward to in the week, partly because I enjoyed them and partly because they really helped to lift my mood.

(Mia, 2015)

I have been surprised by how much I have been able to engage and benefit. Different themes have opened different doors in my mind and have helped me to access thoughts and feelings that I was unaware were contributing to my behaviour. Using different media to express feelings has allowed me to express difficult emotions more abstractly, then come to accept them and if necessary change them at my own pace. The group has provided me with an opportunity to recognise that we have some shared experiences, which means I feel less alone, but has also allowed me to accept that I am unique and will have my own unique reality, which is valid.

(Millie, 2016)

References

Amos, T. (1992) Crucify. In *Little Earthquakes*, German pressed UK & European issue 12-track CD album. Atlantic Records Label.

Appolinari, C. (1996) Dramatherapy and Personality Disorder: Echoes of Abuse. In Mitchell, S. (ed.) *Dramatherapy: Clinical Studies*. London: Jessica Kingsley.

Austin, D. (2006) Songs of the Self: Vocal Psychotherapy for Adults Traumatised as Children. In Carey, L. (ed.) *Expressive and Creative Arts Methods for Trauma Survivors*. London: Jessica Kingsley.

Bannister, A. (2003) The Effects of Creative Therapies with Children Who Have been Sexu-ally Abused. *Dramatherapy*, 25(1), 2011 [Online].

Bella (Former Service User) (2013) Poem. In Morris, N. (2014) Silenced in Childhood: A Survi-vor of Abuse Finds Her Voice through Group Dramatherapy. *Dramatherapy*, 36(1), pp. 3–17.

Bowlby, J. and Ainsworth, M. (1965) *Child Care and the Growth of Love: Volume 3 of Attachment and Loss*. Second edition. Harmondsworth, UK: Penguin Books.

Brown, S., Shankar, R. and Smith, K. (2009) Borderline Personality Disorder and Sensory Processing Impairment. *Progress in Neurology and Psychiatry*, 13(4), pp. 10–16.

Campbell, J. and Moyers, B. (1991) *The Power of Myth*. Kindle edition. Flowers, B. S. (ed.). New York: Anchor Books (Random House Inc.) Knopf Doubleday.

Chavis, G. G. (2011) *Poetry and Story Therapy: The Healing Power of Creative Expression* (Writ-ing for Therapy or Personal Development). Kindle edition. London: Jessica Kingsley.

DH/Care Pathways Branch/Mental Health Division (2009) *Recognising Complexity: Commis-sioning Guidance for Personality Disorder Services* [Online]. PDF available from: http://cipn. org.uk/wp-content/uploads/2017/05/recognising_complexity_june_09.pdf [Accessed: 23.11.17].

Erikson, E. (1963) *Childhood and Society.* Second edition. New York: Norton.

Frankl, V. (2004) 1984 Postscript. In *Man's Search for Meaning.* Revised edition. London: Rider.

Gersie, A. (1997) *Reflection on Therapeutic Storymaking: The Use of Stories with Groups.* London: Jessica Kingsley.

Gheera, M. and Long, R. (2014) *Inter-Racial Adoption.* Standard Note: SN/SP/6351. Social Policy Section. London: House of Commons Library.

Hanh, T. N. (2012) *Fear: Essential Wisdom for Getting through the Storm.* Kindle edition. London: Rider.

Jones, P. (2007) *Drama as Therapy Volume 1: Theory, Practice and Research.* Second edition. Kindle edition. Abingdon, UK: Routledge.

Jung, C. G. (1968) *Jung, C. G. (1968) the Archetypes and the Collective Unconscious.* Second edition. Kindle edition. Volume 9, Part 1 – Second Edition of Series (2014) Sir Read, H., Fordham, M. and Adler, G. (eds.) *The Collected Works of C. G. Jung.* Translated by R. F. C. Hull. Abingdon, UK: Routledge.

Kellogg, S. and Young, J. (2006) Schema Therapy for Borderline Personality Disorder [Online]. *Journal of Clinical Psychology,* 62(4), pp. 445–458. Wiley Periodicals. Available from: www.interscience.wiley.com

Lennon, J., and McCartney, P. (1968) Blackbird. In *The Beatles* (also known as *The White Album*). Martin, G. (producer) Apple Records Label.

Mannes, E. (2011) *The Power of Music: Pioneering Discoveries in the New Science of Song.* Kindle edition. New York: Bloomsbury.

McNiff, S. (2015) *Imagination in Action: Secrets for Unleashing Creative Expression.* Kindle edition. Boston, MA: Shambhala.

Morris, N. (2014) Silenced in Childhood: A Survivor of Abuse Finds Her Voice through Group Dramatherapy. *Dramatherapy,* 36(1), pp. 3–17.

NHS England (2017) *Manual for Prescribed Specialised Services 2017/18* [Online]. PDF available from: www.england.nhs.uk/wp-content/uploads/2017/10/prescribed-specialised-services-manual-2.pdf [Accessed: 23.11.17].

NICE (2009) *Borderline Personality Disorder: Treatment and Management: National Clinical Practice Guideline 78* [Online]. National Institute for Health and Care Excellence. Developed by the National Collaborating Centre for Mental Health. UK: The British Psychological Society and The Royal College of Psychiatrists. [Reproduced with permission of The Licensor through PLSclear]. PDF available from: www.nice.org.uk/guidance/cg78/evidence [Accessed: 10.10.17].

Oxford English Dictionary (2012) Seventh edition. Waite, M (ed.). Oxford, UK: Oxford University Press.

Rowan, J. (1990) *Subpersonalities: The People Inside Us.* London: Routledge.

Russ, S. W. (2004) *Play in Child Development and Psychotherapy: Toward Empirically Supported Practice.* Mahwah, NJ: Earlbaum.

Schrader, C. (2012) Myth-a-Drama. In *Ritual Theatre: The Power of Dramatic Ritual in Personal Development Groups and Clinical Practice.* Kindle edition. London: Jessica Kingsley.

Singer, D. G. and Singer, J. L. (1990) *The House of Make Believe: Children's Play and the Developing Imagination.* Cambridge, MA: Harvard University Press.

Sperry, L. (2016) *Handbook of Diagnosis and Treatment of DSM-5 Personality Disorders: Assessment, Case Conceptualization, and Treatment.* Third edition. Kindle edition. New York: Taylor & Francis.

Stevens, A. (2001a) Archetypes and the Collective Unconscious. In *Jung a Very Short Introduction.* Kindle edition. Oxford: Oxford University Press.

Stevens, A. (2001b) The Stages of Life. In *Jung a Very Short Introduction.* Kindle edition. Oxford: Oxford University Press.

Vermetten, E. and Spiegel, D. (2014) Trauma and Dissociation: Implications for Borderline Personality Disorder. *Current Psychiatry Reports*, 16, p. 434.

Winnicott, D. W. (2005) *Playing and Reality*. Third edition. In *Routledge Classics*. Abingdon, UK: Routledge.

Yalom, I. D. (2002) *The Gift of Therapy: An Open Letter to a New Generation of Therapists and Their Patients*. Second edition. Kindle edition. London: Hachette Digital, Little Brown Book Group.

Yalom, I. D., with Leszcz, M. (2005) *Theory and Practice of Group Psychotherapy*. Fifth edition. New York: Basic Books.

6

A CRY FOR FREEDOM

Dramatherapy with women in a secure step-down unit

I want to be free now
Was I really so bad?
This is the biggest punishment I've ever had.
I want to be free now
No longer sad
We may need doctors, but we're not mad!
—*N. Morris and service users, 2016*

These words formed the chorus of a song written by a group of women living in a female locked rehabilitation unit. Writing the song together, singing it to staff, family and peers and finally recording it were an empowering process. I began working in this unit in 2009. Stepping down from more secure facilities, most service users have severe and enduring mental health difficulties, predominantly BPD and paranoid schizophrenia. Freedom, choice and acceptance are themes that often arise and dramatherapy provides the women with a space in which to safely voice their frustrations and celebrate their individuality.

Their cry for freedom resonates at different levels. Often voiced as a desire to leave the unit, to be taken off section or released from the mental health system, it also symbolises a deeper wish to be free from the intense emotions, paranoia, frightening hallucinations or flashbacks with which they struggle. A selection of session vignettes, key themes and interventions is shared in this chapter, together with poems and artwork created by service users within sessions, to illustrate the vitality of the work generated. The NICE guidelines for schizophrenia (2014a) are also noted and the issue of stigma and mental health is explored in relation to performance born in the therapy space. Finally, three colleagues from different professions share their thoughts about dramatherapy.

A mixed-diagnosis dramatherapy group

The secure rehabilitation unit supports a maximum of sixteen women with a range of mental health problems. Their length of admission varies widely, depending on individual needs – usually between six and eighteen months. All service users are supported by nursing staff and health care assistants. They are encouraged to attend a variety of groups, including dramatherapy, music-centred dramatherapy and a range of OT groups. They are also assessed for either a DBT (dialectical behavioural therapy) or CBT (cognitive behavioural therapy) recovery pathway. Whilst BPD and paranoid schizophrenia are the most prevalent diagnoses, we also have service users with bipolar disorder and schizo-affective disorder, plus those with co-morbid disorders, such as PTSD (post-traumatic stress disorder), anorexia nervosa and drug and/or alcohol dependency. As well as a shared quest for freedom, finding one's place on the unit (and perhaps in life) is another prevalent theme.

Schizophrenia, schizo-affective disorder and bipolar disorder

> The schizophrenic disorders are characterized in general by fundamental and characteristic distortions of thinking and perception, and affects that are inappropriate or blunted. Clear consciousness and intellectual capacity are usually maintained although certain cognitive deficits may evolve in the course of time. The most important psychopathological phenomena include thought echo; thought insertion or withdrawal; thought broadcasting; delusional perception and delusions of control; influence or passivity; hallucinatory voices commenting or discussing the patient in the third person; thought disorders and negative symptoms.
>
> *(WHO, ICD-10, 2016a)*

The current NICE guideline for managing psychosis and schizophrenia in adults recommends the arts therapies for all service users to help improve negative symptoms (2014a, p. 25). These symptoms refer to the absence of regular human characteristics and specific behaviours that affect their capacity to function in society (Thompson et al., 2015, p. 441). The most common include: poverty of speech, with minimal interaction; flat affect with regards to displaying emotion (often poor eye contact and a monotone voice); lack of energy or interest in life (detaching them further from reality and increasing isolation); withdrawal (through which they focus on their own issues and may be confused by their ideas and fantasies); and catatonia, a silent, motionless state (Thompson et al., 2015, p. 441). In Casson's qualitative study of the impact of dramatherapy and psychodrama on clients who heard voices, 89% reported they found the methods helpful: "Therapy provided people with support that was empowering: enabling them to cope, strengthening them through increasing confidence, raising self-esteem and reducing isolation, thus diminishing the impact or frequency of negative/persecutory voices" (2001, p. 22).

As well as CBT and family therapy, NICE advises that the arts therapies should be considered for all individuals with psychotic disorders, ideally in group format, using a combination of psychotherapeutic techniques and activities that encourage creative expression; it is also noted that therapy can start during an acute phase of their illness (2014a, p. 26). NICE indicates three key aims for an arts therapy group with these clients, which correspond to my approach: (1) helping individuals to experience themselves anew, whilst introducing alternative methods of communication; (2) encouraging self-expression, framed within a positive creative form; and (3) helping them to accept and understand the feelings that surface within sessions, when appropriate (2014a, p. 26).

As well as focusing on negative symptoms, several dramatherapists have described the potential for dramatherapy to help with the positive symptoms of schizophrenia. Grainger for example notes how the aesthetic distance of drama can help with thought disorder (1991) and Casson shares dramatic techniques to help with auditory hallucinations (2001). Positive symptoms are behaviours or thoughts that may appear bizarre in comparison to the individual's usual personality. The most common include: delusions (firm, often complex beliefs, which contradict reality and are most commonly expressed as delusions of persecution, sometimes delusions of grandeur); disorganised thinking and speech (expressed in a rapid, disordered manner, making sense only to the individual); hallucinations (involving all five senses, without external sensory stimulation, most commonly auditory and visual); and inappropriate affect, where emotions are expressed in contrast to the given situation (Thompson et al., 2015, p. 440).

WHO defines schizo-affective disorders as "Episodic disorders in which both affective and schizophrenic symptoms are prominent but which do not justify a diagnosis of either schizophrenia or depressive or manic episodes" (2016b). They describe bipolar as:

> A disorder characterized by two or more episodes in which the patient's mood and activity levels are significantly disturbed, this disturbance consisting on some occasions of an elevation of mood and increased energy and activity (hypomania or mania) and on others of a lowering of mood and decreased energy and activity (depression).
>
> *(WHO, 2016c)*

Whilst several clients experience florid psychotic symptoms within dramatherapy sessions, others struggle to contain suicidal thoughts or the urge to self-harm. There are often complicated dynamics that develop between clients. Their mood, energy and ability to self-reflect also vary immensely. Several years ago, the notion of running two dramatherapy groups was considered: one for the BPD client group, the other for clients with psychosis. Whilst this may have given the sessions a clearer focus and less complex dynamic, it was agreed that the group's potential for uniting the two client groups had greater value. Living together and functioning as a community can be challenging, and having one dramatherapy group, open to all service users, encourages genuine empathy, understanding and positive communication.

As service user Sandra (described later) eloquently wrote in 2016:

> The most important thing that dramatherapy and expressive therapy provide is a relationship of trust with the therapist, with whom I can explore thoughts and feelings I can't release in other ways. The relationship I have formed with the dramatherapist is not only honest and trusting, but also the strongest relationship I have with any staff members. I know that she always has time for me and I believe she genuinely cares. It's more than just a job for her, she makes it her purpose in life to support you, even when words fail you, by showing you other ways to communicate. Her sessions also break down barriers, resolve conflicts and help us all to bond together as a community. We can truly open up about an issue safely in these sessions, amongst each other, or do silly things together without any judgement. We can then learn to trust each other in many ways outside of these groups.

A mother's heartache

Lia was in her mid-twenties and stayed on the unit for ten months. She was diagnosed with paranoid schizophrenia and due to an intense psychotic episode, her baby had been removed from her care and adopted. The Independent Mental Health Task Force reports that "One in five mothers suffers from depression, anxiety or in some cases Psychosis during pregnancy or in the first year after childbirth" (2016, p. 6). During her first few weeks on the unit, Lia was withdrawn and interacted minimally with staff and service users. As she became more comfortable within the environment, however, she began to attend the weekly dramatherapy and music-centred dramatherapy groups, and over the following few months, her mental state and communication skills grew significantly. She became increasingly confident and expressive within these sessions and with the help of CBT and one-to-one therapy, her personal insight also began to develop.

From her first dramatherapy session, she appeared surprisingly at ease with the approach and seemed to derive pleasure from the experience. She soon allowed herself to trust the process, expressing her sense of humour, spirituality, frustrations and desires. She particularly enjoyed character and story work, through which she shared her unique perspective on life. The many characters she created including the following: the Unknown Owl, who lived at the top of a Baobab Tree in Africa; Dayie the Daydreamer, brought to life with a wombat hand puppet; a drunken sailor in the group's improvised voyage at sea; Sloth the sloth, who lived peacefully up a tree and came down only to eat; and Philippa the bag collector (within a magical land created by the group), who was keen for Sainsbury's to start charging for plastic bags and lived in a bag made of concrete, due to the threat of the big bad wolf and his powerful huffing and puffing.

As she started to trust both the process and her peers, Lia began to share her thoughts and feelings more openly, admitting that she enjoyed spending time alone. After a few months, she began to speak tenderly about her baby, explaining that he had been taken away from her and adopted when he was a few weeks old. She said it broke her heart that he was now 1 year old and she would not be allowed to meet him until he turned 18. She desperately wanted to see her son grow up and, towards the end of her admission, focused her energy on fighting for her rights as a mother.

Lia relaxed and had fun in the weekly music-centred dramatherapy groups. Her ability to express herself through song and percussion increased over time and she particularly enjoyed bell ringing. She interacted well with her peers and was enthusiastic to participate in the summer concert, attending extra rehearsals and suggesting new songs for the group to learn. In dramatherapy sessions, Lia consistently voiced her desire to return to the town where she had been living and to regain her independence. She felt trapped on the unit. One week, she selected a therapeutic picture card that revealed the galaxy. She said it represented her perfectly and was the realm that most fascinated her. Another time, she shared that she had a plan with galactic proportions, relating to the stars. She described herself as a very spiritual person, which was sometimes difficult in an overly realistic world.

A service user with BPD

Sandra was in her mid-twenties and her main diagnosis was BPD. She struggled with poor self-esteem, low mood, migraines and continued urges to self-harm. She was a dedicated member of the dramatherapy, art and writing–focused dramatherapy and music-centred dramatherapy groups. Unfortunately, her placement at the unit broke down after eleven months, when she developed psychotic symptoms and became violent towards staff. It was agreed by all parties that she should be transferred to an acute unit. Despite her distress at the time, she left a thank-you card, a detailed dramatherapy feedback form and a signed consent letter to include her story and examples of her work in this book. Included, for instance, is her creative response to the theme David and Goliath (Figure 6.1).

Focusing on dramatherapy, she wrote,

> I sometimes feel silly or uncertain why I am doing certain activities in dramatherapy, but by the end of each session, I come to realise that each activity leads into another and they all give great meaning to each other – leading to a sense of release and a new way of viewing things. Some activities enable you to open up about things in a safe and fun way. Other activities are more contemplative and these are the ones I find most beneficial. Despite initially disliking using therapeutic card decks to express my feelings (having been told they can be used in a dangerous way), using them as prompts became my favourite activity. I really enjoy dramatherapy and find it a very helpful way to open up and express my feelings. It is also good fun.

FIGURE 6.1   David and Goliath

She also offered feedback on the art and writing–focused dramatherapy group, which extends the dramatherapy process, by providing a space for expression though creative writing, art and craft work:

> I have really benefited from art and writing–focused dramatherapy. I love having the chance to be creative, but this group provides more than that. Having a theme to inspire my creativity each week makes the work I produce really meaningful. Working to a theme is also a way to create a completed piece of work that often reflects my current state of mind, feelings, or emotions, rather than just drawing a random picture or painting a box – although I enjoy this too. The work I create in art and writing–focused dramatherapy helps me to communicate with other staff at times too. I also enjoy the creative writing side to art and writing–focused dramatherapy and have been inspired to write so many emotive though provoking and honest poems. These too have helped me in other groups and even in my one-to-one DBT sessions.

Dramatherapy group interventions

Group dramatherapy enables service users with different diagnoses to communicate more openly and to increase their understanding and acceptance of self and others. To illustrate this, I have selected two effective interventions and described how each member of the group responded. In both examples, dramatic projection techniques are used, which Jones describes as core to all areas of dramatherapy practice – enabling clients "to project inner conflicts into dramatic material" (2007, l.3684) and connecting their issues to the therapeutic potential of drama.

An Imaginary Train Journey

In the dramatherapy group, clients are often invited to imagine where they might like to go, if they could transport themselves anywhere in time or place. In the step-down unit, all the service users have been transferred from more acute settings and are working towards moving into the community. They are therefore on a journey – and at times, this is animated through the dramatic process. As Jones explains, "Dramatherapy enables the creation of a symbolic and metaphoric reality that clients can explore" (2007, l.5647). The following session vignette describes how five clients responded to the group's 'Imaginary Train Journey' – an activity through which the group imagined going on a train journey, and one by one, they were invited to stop the train and explore their chosen destination (alone or with their peers) through words and/or simple enactment. This type of activity stimulates the imagination and encourages free association of thoughts and feelings. It also facilitates spontaneous improvisation and positive interaction between clients. Furthermore, it has the potential to enhance self-awareness and empathy towards others:

1. Lia (described earlier) was in her mid-twenties, diagnosed with paranoid schizophrenia. She was a loyal member of the group. She engaged fully throughout this session, her mood positive. She took us to a yellow Lego platform, which led to a "strangely empty mall – not of this world". She described it as a labyrinth and said that we could take whatever we wanted from the shops, as there were no prices or shopkeepers. The world Lia had imagined had no boundaries or figures of authority. This was perhaps the antithesis of the unit (or world) she currently resided in – and the various professionals who had control over her life.

2. Tulip was in her early twenties, diagnosed with schizophrenia and possible brain damage from childhood malaria. She was admitted to the unit just two weeks before attending this session. She arrived a few minutes late, though she was keen to be with us and shared that she looked forward to seeing her mother after the session. At times, she appeared quite childlike. During the 'stamp and release' warm-up, she chose the words "Stop being stubborn and look after your little sister". She then engaged deeply with the group's Imaginary Train Journey:

   > Tulip found a special ticket to heaven and when she reached her destination found her late brother. They embarked on a fantastic journey around the galaxy and did not return until midnight – they were in trouble with God for being so late. She then imagined sneaking back to heaven the following day and, again, travelling around the galaxy with her brother. Tulip named some of the planets and stars they passed, and said they were

aiming to reach Pluto, but could not quite get there, as it was so cold and the wheels of the train froze. Again, they arrived back in heaven at midnight and were in trouble with God. At this point, I interjected, reflecting that it might be difficult to end this journey with her brother and return to earth. Tulip responded wisely, saying that she was ready to say her final goodbye and to get back on the train with the rest of the group. She said that whilst heading back to earth, her special ticket blew away, so she knew she could not return for another visit.

Throughout the process, Tulip's manner was light and joyful, and during the closing ritual, she said how much she had enjoyed being part of the group. She expressed the love she felt for her deceased brother, her desire to see him again and her acceptance that she had to let go. This was a theme that arose for Tulip in future sessions (as described in Chapter 7). She also managed to stay focused and listen to others, which she often found challenging.

3.   Kitty was in her mid-twenties, diagnosed with BPD. She was creative, with a passion and talent for art, drama and singing. On the unit, her urge to self-harm persisted and at times she cut herself severely. Paradoxically, she was self-aware and used the dramatherapy process to its full potential. When she arrived at this session, she appeared subdued in mood and during the stamp and release warm-up, her words were "Do your job!" She then immersed herself in the group's Imaginary Train Journey, transporting us to 1945: we emerged onto a dusty, bustling platform, with rows of small children, sitting with gas masks around their necks. Every child had a number and we each had to take a child to look after. Kitty later explained that her enactment had symbolised her realisation that she had to take care of her own inner child. It seemed that the stamp and release warm-up activity had helped to shift her frustration with staff on the unit and the Imaginary Train Journey had enabled her to acknowledge her desire to be cared for and her fear of becoming independent.

4.   Lola was in her mid-thirties. She had schizo-affective disorder and regularly attended the group. Primarily, it seemed to improve her negative symptoms. During the stamp and release warm-up, her words were "Stand up for your rights", and on the group's Imaginary Train Journey, she took us to a park, where we imagined watching birds fly over a lake, going on the swings, riding a roller coaster and, lastly, each choosing an ice cream. Lola had chosen to focus on positive images and activities, which she found a helpful distraction from her symptoms. This was her usual response to the dramatherapy process: whilst her peers often shared and expressed more personal feelings, thoughts and memories, Lola chose not to (or was unable to).

5.   Amy was in her mid-twenties, diagnosed with BPD and mild ASD (autistic spectrum disorder). She had extreme mood swings and often argued with both staff and peers. She had previously attended dramatherapy sessions on the ward, described in Chapter 5. She was very upset at the start of the session and shared that she had been intimidated by another service user when standing up for

herself. Amy was encouraged to focus on the people in the group and the activities to follow. She gradually calmed down and, with a lot of encouragement, participated a little. During the stamp and release warm-up, her words were "Don't intimidate me!" This helped to channel her anger more positively and she visibly enjoyed the experience. During the Imaginary Train Journey, she then chose to visit a peaceful beach paradise alone. This allowed Amy to express her willingness to participate, as well as sharing her desire and need for personal space.

A Model Animal Community

A week later, the same group created a mini community, using model animals. Animals are regularly used within sessions on the ward (described in Chapter 5) and on this unit. They offer a symbolic means to express both hidden and overt qualities, desires and fears. Characters are developed using animal hand puppets, masks or models. At times, this process of dramatic projection may be less daunting than creating human characters, as the connection to oneself is subtler. Using models – as in this example – provides further dramatic distance, as Secchi explains: "the client does not physically take on roles . . . she is able to project aspects of her role identity into the animals, and to role play through objects" (2007, l.3550). Creating a Model Animal Community with this group helped to facilitate safe and expressive interaction between clients who were learning to live together and support one another, despite experiencing diverse challenges. We began by creating a landscape using different materials to symbolise varying terrains. Each client then chose a model animal to represent herself and placed it within the landscape:

1. Lia was keen to attend and soon to be discharged. She initially shared her frustration that her care coordinator had not yet arranged new accommodation. She then engaged fully, with excellent focus. She described herself as a dreamer and immersed herself in the group's 'Model Animal Community'. She chose to be a blackbird, who was best friends with a fish: the blackbird sat upon the fish, in the middle of the river, which flowed through the landscape. Their plan was to travel together towards the sea. They were excited about their journey and not at all sad to leave their community, though the blackbird told the other animals they were welcome to come too, but would have to find their own path. Whilst Lia had clearly expressed her desire for discharge through the creative structure, it was unclear if she was conscious of having done so. During the closing ritual, she shared that she had enjoyed the group and it had taken her mind off feeling frustrated.

2. Tulip was initially hesitant about coming, disappointed that I had not been able to facilitate a group a couple of days earlier, just after her twenty-first birthday. She decided to attend, however, and her mood soon lifted. She engaged fully and revealed a desire for acceptance and friendship through her participation in the group's Model Animal Community. Tulip chose to be a kangaroo, a mermaid and a lioness with three cubs: the kangaroo was keen to interact with

the other animals in the community, though he was repeatedly rejected when trying to follow them around. I suggested that he approach the mermaid (of whom she was in control). The kangaroo then asked the mermaid for help and she told him to go to the lioness for a magic potion. When he did this, however, the lioness chased him and tried to eat him. He pleaded for his life and she decided to let him live and gave him a magic potion. The kangaroo then drank the potion and Tulip said he could now follow anyone he wanted in the community and would not be rejected. She had clearly expressed her desire to connect to her peers and her defiance when confronted with rejection. During the closing ritual, she said how much she had enjoyed herself.

3. Kitty came willingly and engaged fully. Within the group's Model Animal Community, she chose three animals to symbolise three parts of herself. She later expressed sadness that Lia's animals were swimming out of the community with a smile and no hint of nostalgia. Kitty then decided that her three animals would also go to the river and travel towards the sea, on a current near to the one that Lia's animals had followed. During the closing ritual, she said she had particularly enjoyed the symbolism of the main activity. She usually responded to the dramatherapy process with a greater level of insight and understanding than many of her peers. In this session, she had particularly tried to connect to her peer Lia – communicating that she would miss Lia and hoped that she too would be allowed to move out of the unit soon and into the next stage of her life.

4. Lola arrived a little late, though she was welcomed into the group and engaged fully. She chose to be a puppy in the group's Model Animal Community, who initially played happily by the water's edge, on the opposite side of the river to the other animals. Later in the process, she allowed her puppy to venture around the edge of the river and over to the other side, to play in the woodland. During the closing ritual, Lola shared that she felt happy and pleased to have come. In the Model Animal Community, she had revealed her need for personal space and containment, by placing her puppy on the opposite side to the animals belonging to her peers. With encouragement, she had allowed her puppy to move to the other side, though it continued to play alone. It was not clear if Lola was conscious of what she expressed through her puppy. What was evident is that she found the dramatherapy process useful from a creative and contained perspective, never feeling she had to respond in a certain way or as others did.

5. Amy initially shared that she was feeling "up and down" and wanted only to watch. During the closing ritual, she said that she had not enjoyed watching her peers interact through the Model Animal Community, as this type of activity would not occur in the "real community" and this was supposed to be a rehabilitation unit. I explained that through the exercise, her peers had expressed their thoughts and feelings in a safe way and had interacted with one other – both important skills to practise for life in the community. Amy did not appear to absorb or accept this explanation, however, so I simply congratulated her for remaining respectful of the other service users, despite disliking the process.

Therapeutic performance

Performing work conceived in the dramatherapy group was a concept that emerged in 2013. The journey began with the unit's first Christmas concert, during which the service users performed a song they had written in the dramatherapy group, titled 'Accept Me'. Its theme was stigma in mental health, suggested by service user Emily (described later in this section). It was the first song created within a session that was heard outside the therapy space.

> Treat me like a human being,
> I'm an equal you're not seeing,
> Look beyond the label, see under the mask,
> Trapped and lost, everything comes at a cost
> Don't reject me, just accept me, stigma sucks!
> *(Morris and the Singing Swans, 2014a)*

Following the first Christmas concert on the unit, service user Emily and her peers asked to create their first performance piece to show to staff, other residents and guests, during Mental Health Awareness Week 2015 (Mental Health Foundation, 2017, pp. 40–41). In dramatherapy sessions, they were then guided to shape tableaus and scripts, inspired by stories of stigma in the wider community, experienced by three individuals. They named their piece *Stigma*. This process relates to the process of 'self-revelatory performance' – defined by Emunah as "a form of drama therapy and theatre in which a performer creates an original theatrical piece out of the raw material of current life issues" (2015, p. 71). Poetry and pictures were also created by service users to use as a backdrop for the performance. Emunah explains that whilst issues shared through self-revelatory performance may relate to past experiences and ongoing themes, "the focus is on how these issues impact the performer's present life" (2015, p. 72). After a month of preparation, *Stigma* was performed before a highly appreciative audience of staff, visitors and service users. The performers felt proud of their achievement. Emunah explains that self-revelatory performance is primarily a healing process: from devising and writing the piece through to rehearsing and finally sharing it with an audience. It allows the performers to feel "a powerful combination of accomplishment, acceptance and connection" (2015, p. 81).

Singing Swans

Performing *Stigma* was a momentous occasion that led to a shared desire to perform again, culminating in our first summer concert. For this occasion, the service users wrote a new song titled 'We're Only Human'. Colleagues and management were particularly impressed by our two original songs and agreed to my proposed visit to a small recording studio to record them. I provided the instrumentals and three clients and I sang the lyrics. The group named themselves 'the Singing Swans', and for the CD cover, they chose an image of a duckling looking at its reflection in a large mirror and seeing a swan. Unfortunately, several clients were unable to attend the trip, due to risk factors assessed on the day. They all received a copy of the CD, however, and everyone agreed that the songs should be shared on YouTube, to encourage members of the public to listen to their words.

> Together, we stand as a wall
> You can knock us, but we can't fall
> Why do you have to be so rude?
> We're only human
>
> Enhance the spirituality
> Freedom and individuality
> Gain perspective of who you are,
> We're only human
> *(Morris and the Singing*
> *Swans, 2014b)*

The journey from the therapy space into live performance and finally a recording studio had a positive and unique impact on the clients involved: Emily, Laura, Lesley, Kara and Jenna.

1. Emily was in her late twenties, diagnosed with BPD and type 2 diabetes. She had very low self-esteem, struggled with self-care and had a history of drug and alcohol problems. From the age of 3, her father had sexually abused her, and in her teens, she gave birth to their child. Despite the trauma of her pregnancy, she loved her daughter deeply and her motivation for recovery was to improve their relationship and to play an active part in her life. In dramatherapy and music-centred dramatherapy groups, a hidden confidence and humour slowly emerged, and Emily initiated the creation of the song 'Accept Me' and the performance of *Stigma* for Mental Health Awareness week. Enjoying the performance and the summer concert, she was then one of the three clients who fully participated in the Singing Swans project. A year later, she wrote a powerful poem about her suicidal thoughts, which she read during the summer performance.

   Having responded positively to the dramatherapy group process during her first three months on the unit, Emily was offered a series of individual sessions with a third-year student on placement. She had thirty sessions in total, during which the student, Caroline Baker, applied Rowan's theory of subpersonalities (1990) to enable Emily to identify and find relationships between the different parts of herself – as I had done with client Jean (described in Chapter 5). Before moving into embodied work, they worked with miniature figures and objects (Baker, 2015). Emily spent two years in the unit, struggling at times with severe mood fluctuations and ongoing urges to use alcohol and drugs. After a long and challenging journey, she was finally discharged and taken off section. She has since developed a more positive relationship with her teenage daughter and is living and employed in the community.

2. Laura was in her early twenties, diagnosed with BPD, and had a forensic history. She struggled to cope with murderous thoughts and overwhelming guilt much of the time, though felt safe and free to express herself within the dramatherapy and music-centred dramatherapy group sessions. She began to write lyrical, uplifting poetry and was very pleased when her words were chosen for the chorus of 'We're Only Human'. Laura managed to overcome her anxiety about performing and took part in the summer concert. She was also keen to visit the recording studio, though sadly she relapsed quite seriously before the event and was transferred to an acute setting. During her relapse, she stopped attending groups, though she found comfort in playing a small xylophone from the music box. This was given to her as a parting gift, to remind her of the positive steps she had taken in our sessions.

3. Lesley was in her late thirties, diagnosed with medication-resistant schizophrenia, struggling with intense mood swings and paranoia. She felt angry and frustrated when not allowed to attend the trip to the recording studio, though she found solace in receiving a copy of the CD. On the unit, she enjoyed singing the chorus of 'Accept Me' in communal areas and asked me to write a melody for an emotional poem she had written. In a single one-to-one session, she cried as I sang it to her.

4. Nina was in her early twenties, diagnosed with BPD and mild learning difficulties. Her mood and confidence fluctuated a great deal, though they improved significantly during her time on the unit. She consistently attended the weekly dramatherapy, art and writing–focused dramatherapy and music-centred dramatherapy groups, though she became highly anxious and paranoid on the concert and recording dates. She was pleased to have a copy of the Singing Swans CD, however, and keen for her friends and family to listen to the songs on YouTube. Kara received consistent support from the OT assistant and eventually experienced a positive discharge. She is now employed and enjoying her life in the community. She has since visited the unit – invited to give a talk to the service users.

5. Jenna was in her mid-thirties, diagnosed with anorexia nervosa and BPD. She was emotionally neglected and physically abused throughout her childhood. She attended only a few dramatherapy sessions. Whilst responsive to the process, she was extremely guarded and found the group experience too overwhelming. Art was the creative medium she most enjoyed and she worked on many pieces in her bedroom. Although she never attended the music-centred dramatherapy group, she viewed the visit to the recording studio as a unique opportunity. Initially, she came as an observer, though she felt inspired to join us in the studio and sang on one of the tracks. This achievement meant a great deal to Jenna, and although she continued to avoid the creative therapy groups, she was keen to embark upon five valuable sessions of bereavement-focused

individual dramatherapy (described in Chapter 7). Two years later, Jenna wrote the following words in an art and writing–focused dramatherapy session, used to form the chorus of a group song:

> I did not mean to shout and cry
> You saw the side that I tried to hide
> Emotions flow as I find my voice
> Just want to know that I have a choice

Moving songs and drama out of the therapy space and into performance had a positive impact on most of the clients and provided them with a clear goal. The visit to the recording studio then offered an empowering experience for the three clients able to attend and the Singing Swans CD was a tangible reward for every client who had been part of the process. They all felt very proud of their achievement and it gave them a voice that reached beyond the unit.

Self-revelatory performance

Emily's desire to perform before her peers and staff had also encouraged me to facilitate something I had not thought possible. Summer and winter performances became regular events at the unit. They often include original group songs, together with poetry and prose written by individuals. Some clients have used these performances to share how it feels to live with their mental health conditions – which again relates to Emunah's model of self-revelatory performance (2015).

1. Karen was a young woman in her late teens, originally thought to have Emerging EUPD, and then diagnosed with bipolar disorder. During her fourteen months on the unit, she regularly attended all three creative therapy groups: dramatherapy, music-centred dramatherapy and art and writing–focused dramatherapy. After nine months, she decided to work on a project for the winter concert, through which she could share how it felt to have bipolar disorder. She was keen for her parents to witness this and invited them to attend. The performance then contributed to the "carer-focused education and support programme" advised by NICE (2014b, p. 16), offered in the form of the Carers Forum at the unit. Karen asked me to paint her face with a design and colours to express her experience of veering between manic and depressive episodes. She then asked me to photograph her. The large poster she created for the concert featured a description of bipolar disorder, an emotional, original poem and the photographs taken. On the day of the performance, she was enthusiastic to participate, though nervous about her self-revelatory piece. After singing confidently with her peers, however, she found the courage to share her poster and felt immensely proud of her accomplishment. As Emunah explains, "The experience of acceptance is the reward for the risks taken in revealing personal matters" (2015, p. 81).

2. Rena was a young woman with schizo-affective disorder. She enjoyed the creative therapy sessions, though her attendance fluctuated with her mood. She had a complex relationship with her twin sister, who also had mental health problems. She loved to sing and enjoyed recording an original song with her peers, for which she had contributed lyrics, as well as performing in the unit's concerts. During one performance, she agreed to read out a poem she had written in the art and writing–focused dramatherapy group. It described how her hallucinations helped her to cope with loneliness. The process of writing, sharing and then performing her poem before an audience helped to transform her isolation into a shared experience: "There is no undoing nor fixing, and possibly not even any clear resolution, but there can well be a discovery of how to live with, learn from and construct out of our experience" (Emunah, 2015, p. 75).

> I scream into the darkness,
> Filling my room with the sound.
> I know no one can hear me,
> No one is really around.
> Feeling my body with my fingers,
> Pinching the fat on my chin,
> I can feel my chest tighten,
> Feel my anger erupt within.
> The creatures and voices tell me I'm not alone.
> I believe them – they let me know it.
> Listening to them day after day
> Hurts just a tiny little bit,
> 'Coz I know I'm not 'normal'
> Whatever that's supposed to mean.

Colleagues reflect on dramatherapy

I offered a questionnaire to all members of the MDT, hoping to obtain different perspectives on the role of dramatherapy on the unit and to explore their unique experience of working with the BPD client group. Three colleagues responded: the social worker, ward manager and occupational therapist. They were asked, *What is your understanding or opinion of using dramatherapy as an intervention for this client group?*

1. The manager – with nine years of experience with the BPD client group – described dramatherapy as an essential intervention as part of the treatment for service users with BPD. She also suggested that:

> Dramatherapy is an important intervention before the service user starts the process of mindfulness. They must first learn to express their inner self and it is often difficult for some service users to express themselves using spoken words. The art of self-expression and use of dramatherapy as an escapism is essential.

(Howell, response to author's questionnaire, 2017)

2. The occupational therapist – with eighteen months of experience with the BPD client group – described dramatherapy as a powerful intervention that allows service users to take on different roles and to share views and feelings that may not surface elsewhere. She also wrote:

> With regards to BPD, I feel that it does work, and working with the group for a year, I have been able to see that they are enjoying the arts as a tool to express themselves, understand emotions and feel they will be accepted as they are in role play.
>
> *(Vara, response to author's questionnaire, 2017)*

3. The social worker – with two years of experience with the BPD client group – wrote:

> In my opinion, using dramatherapy is vital in the recovery of service users with BPD. Some of our service users have had to deal with unimaginable abuse and trauma and have had their childhoods stolen from them. Dramatherapy enables service users to get in touch with their inner child and allows them to express themselves naturally, without thinking about being 'mature and adult' by voices telling them 'to stop acting like a child'.
>
> *(Gyasiaddo, response to author's questionnaire, 2017)*

References

Baker, C. (2015) *'Through the "Looking" Glass': An Investigation into 'Being Seen'; within a Private Mental Health Setting*. Unpublished MA Dissertation: Roehampton University, London.

Casson, J. (2001) Dramatherapy, Psychodrama and Voices [Online]. *Dramatherapy*, 23(2), pp. 22–25.

Emunah, R. (2015) Self-Revelatory Performance: A Form of Drama Therapy and Theatre. *Drama Therapy Review*, 1(1), pp. 71–85.

Grainger, R. (1991) Message and Meta-Message: The Relational Truth of Dramatherapy of Dramatherapy. *Dramatherapy*, 13(2), pp. 12–14.

Independent Mental Health Taskforce (2016) *The Five-Year Forward View for Mental Health for the NHS in England* [Online]. Stevens, S. (commissioner) for NHS England. Independent Mental Health Task Force. Available from: www.england.nhs.uk/mentalhealth/taskforce/ [Accessed: 03.17.17].

Jones, P. (2007) *Drama as Therapy Volume 1: Theory, Practice and Research*. Second edition. Kindle edition. Abingdon, UK: Routledge.

Mental Health Foundation UK (2017) *A New Way Forward: A World with Good Mental Health for all* [Online]. Available from: www.mentalhealth.org.uk/publication-download/new-way-forward [Accessed: 17.06.17].

Morris and Service Users (2016) *We're Not Mad* (No Recording Available).

Morris and the Singing Swans (2014a) *Accept Me*. Available to listen to at: www.nickymorrisdramatherapy.com/

Morris and the Singing Swans (2014b) *We're Only Human*. Available to listen to at: www.nickymorrisdramatherapy.com/

NICE (2014a) *Clinical Guideline CG178: Psychosis and Schizophrenia in Adults: Prevention and Management* [Online]. In NICE Guidelines. Available from: www.nice.org.uk/guidance/cg178 [Accessed: 21.06.17].

NICE (2014b) *Clinical Guideline CG185: Bipolar Disorder: Assessment and Management* [Online]. In NICE Guidelines. Available from: www.nice.org.uk/guidance/cg185 [Accessed: 09.12.17].

Rowan, J. (1990) *Subpersonalities: The People Inside Us.* London: Routledge.

Secchi, N. (2007) Dramatherapy: Projective Techniques. In Jones, P. (author) *Drama as Therapy, Volume 1: Theory, Practice and Research.* Second edition. Kindle edition. Abingdon, UK: Routledge.

Thompson, C., Slade, K. and Hamilton, L. (2015) Negative Symptoms, in Schizophrenia Spectrum, within Psychopathology: Theories and Causes. In Banyard, P., Dillon, G., Norman, C. and Winder, B. (ed.) *Essential Psychology.* Second edition. Kindle edition. London, UK: SAGE.

WHO–World Health Organisation (2016a) F20 Schizophrenia. *ICD-10 Online Version: 2016.* Available from: http://apps.who.int/classifications/icd10/browse/2016/en#/F20 [Accessed: 22.06.17].

WHO–World Health Organisation (2016b) F25 Schizoaffective Disorders. *ICD-10 Online Version: 2016.* Available from: http://apps.who.int/classifications/icd10/browse/2016/ en#/F25 [Accessed: 22.06.17].

WHO–World Health Organisation (2016c) F31 Bipolar Affective Disorders. *ICD-10 Online Version: 2016.* Available from: http://apps.who.int/classifications/icd10/browse/2016/ en#/F31 [Accessed: 22.06.17].

7

DANCING BETWEEN LIFE AND DEATH

This chapter introduces grief as an enduring theme, arising on both conscious and unconscious levels. Case and session vignettes are used to highlight the potential for dramatherapy to support clients struggling to cope with issues around death: those struggling with suicidal thoughts, others who have survived suicide attempts and several with friends or family members who have committed suicide or died from natural causes. As Yalom explains, whilst self-awareness makes us human, it also reveals our mortality: "Our existence is forever shadowed by the knowledge that we will grow, blossom, and, inevitably, diminish and die" (2008, p. 1). Clients often feel overwhelmed by their emotions, as expressed in Figure 7.1. Many express

FIGURE 7.1 Filled with sadness

an ambivalence towards life, fluctuating between the desire to live and a yearning for death. The emotional pain they experience, whether in response to their past or present, may also have a considerable impact on those working with them. This is explored in relation to personal practice and research, including the feedback from ten colleagues and thirteen dramatherapists. The complexity of the therapeutic relationship is also considered in relation to attachment and rejection, hope and futility, transference and countertransference. Finally, regular clinical supervision is stressed as a crucial process.

Dramatherapy and grief

I frequently remind clients that whilst dramatherapy sessions are often fun and uplifting, the creative process can safely contain all emotions and memories. Grief is a theme that naturally arises, and whilst an essential part of life, it can have a profound effect on people, "leading to a breakdown in our personal sense of meaning and an experience of existential crisis" (Holloway, 2011, p. 157). Several clients have been referred for one-to-one bereavement-focused dramatherapy sessions. Gersie, a renowned dramatherapist and expert on story work in education and therapy, describes the complex emotions, even terror, experienced when losing a loved one. She notes the impossibility of preparing for its impact, suggesting that "Death is the great expected unexpected. It is the anticipated yet unknown journey" (Gersie, 1991, p. 30). Using stories to support people through bereavement, Gersie explains how stories were formed and have been shared since ancient times, to help us to understand and accept the reality of death (1991, p. 55). Many of the service users I work with have explored the theme of loss within the dramatherapy group – finding personal meaning through story and metaphor. This is highlighted through the following two case vignettes.

Losing a brother

Tulip (mentioned in Chapter 6) was in her early twenties, diagnosed with schizophrenia and possible brain damage from childhood malaria. During several dramatherapy group sessions, she shared thoughts and feelings about her late brother, who took care of her as a child. One week, a symbolic animal exercise was introduced, in which each client chose from a large selection of animal models to express themselves: Tulip chose a small lion cub and a lion, who was the cub's older brother. She created a story which began with the two animals having fun together and setting out on adventure. On their journey, they found a dark, magical tree, which could talk and had large wings. Scared, they ran away from the tree and found themselves in a meadow full of beautiful flowers. When the older brother turned around, however, the young cub had disappeared, having returned to the magical tree. Tulip wore a black velvet cloak to symbolise the tree, and although she wanted to carry on with her story, she understood that she had to stop, as others had not yet spoken.

When asked how she thought the characters in her story related to her internal self, she was unsure. I reflected that the young cub reminded me of Tulip and her need to be looked after and that the older lion seemed to represent her late brother, whom she had spoken about in previous sessions. I also suggested that the frightening tree may represent her illness and the difficult symptoms she experiences. Tulip understood and said she agreed with the analysis. During the closing ritual, she expressed how much she had enjoyed the animal work.

A father's suicide

Jenna (mentioned in Chapter 6) was in her mid-thirties, diagnosed with anorexia nervosa and BPD. She had been emotionally neglected and physically abused throughout her childhood. Whilst highly responsive to dramatherapy, she found the group process too overwhelming and could not tolerate the shared experience. She then requested one-to-one dramatherapy sessions, to help her to understand her father's suicide. The MDT agreed and Jenna was offered five sessions.

Session 1

It was an emotional hour and her tears began to flow the moment she was offered a heart stone (as our opening ritual) inscribed with the word peace. Jenna shared that peace was her desire and identified guilt as the feeling with which she continuously struggles. The guilt was connected to her father's suicide. Encouraged to use imagery, she said it was "a heavy weight that envelops my entire body". She then described in detail the day she was told of his suicide and the impact this had on her life. Alongside the guilt, she revealed sorrow, compassion, regret and bewilderment. Jenna wanted to understand why her father had decided to take his own life two years ago and wished she could have helped him. She felt tormented by the image of him deceased, hanging, his belt around his neck.

She was invited to select two symbolic figures, one for her, the other for her father. She chose a soft white polar bear for herself, explaining that as the biggest, it represented the weight of her guilt. For her father, she chose a small, featureless wooden mannequin. She handled it gently and tearfully explained she had chosen it because it had no face. I suggested that Jenna may rediscover his missing features over the following weeks. Holding the heart stone at the end of the session, she said it felt strange to have cried so much, as she had thought her tear ducts had dried up.

Session 2

Jenna began by sharing her struggle to be herself on the step-down unit (the secure female rehabilitation service described in Chapter 6) due to the unpredictability of her peers. She tearfully spoke about her father's suicide and said that within this space, she felt she could be herself and did not have to suppress her feelings. She returned to the question of why her father had taken his own life and I suggested that it may prove unanswerable, which might be painful to accept. She agreed, acknowledging that neither knowing nor understanding why he did it was the most painful aspect. In the early stage of her grief, she had imagined taking her own life in the same manner as her father, so she could understand how he had felt that day, then join him in death and ask why he had done it. She said she would never willingly take her own life, however, having felt the devastating impact it has on those left behind. She spoke of a friend on a previous ward who had committed suicide, which increased her fear of getting close to her peers on the step-down unit. Jenna said she had a large family, with whom she was no longer in contact. They had been very unsupportive during her years in hospital and she no longer felt the need to be who they wanted. She then questioned whether her father had been selfish to commit suicide. She was reassured and encouraged to accept her anger. She felt relieved, explaining she had never given herself permission for this.

Session 3

This week, Jenna had significant back pain and shared that she found her many physical problems (resulting from years of anorexia) frustrating. When handed the heart stone, she tearfully began to speak about her father and again reflected that for so long, she had felt unable to cry, yet in these sessions her tears flowed. Looking at the faceless figure of the small wooden mannequin, symbolising her father, she was invited to choose cards from several therapeutic decks to explore different dimensions of her father and their relationship. She used *The Answer Is Simple* deck (Choquette, 2009) and significant themes arose: as a child and teenager, Jenna had suffered emotional neglect and physical abuse from her mother. She had not been allowed to be herself and remained in constant fear of saying or doing the wrong thing – which seemed to mirror her fear of being herself on the step-down unit. Several other questions surfaced: Why do I feel so guilty about not helping a father who never even hugged me? Why can't I be angry with him for neither visiting nor contacting me during my two-year admission at the previous hospital? As she asked these questions, I felt angry, indicating a strong countertransference of emotions. Jenna said she wanted to feel angry, though feared her anger may be uncontrollable if released and she would then become like her parents. I reflected that anger can implode, if not safely released, which her eating disorder revealed. She understood and agreed. At the end, I suggested that she write a letter to each of her parents, expressing what she needed to say.

Session 4

Jenna brought a letter she had written to her father. She read it aloud, tears flowing freely, sharing afterwards that it felt like she was really speaking to him. She then read out a letter she had written to him when first hearing of his suicide – and similarities between the two letters were acknowledged. Jenna had many questions for her father. She asked why he had taken his life and whether could she have done anything to help him. She also referred to her childhood, asking if he had known about the hell she had endured with her mother, when he no longer lived with them. She was reminded that releasing her emotions and voicing her questions, whilst learning to accept they will remain answerable, could help her to move closer to the peace she craves. She found this a positive yet painful process.

Session 5

Jenna initially described her recent struggle with food. She believed it was a reaction to her mother's birthday and a fellow service user's overdose. She also reflected that our sessions had increased her sensitivity. She felt certain, however, that whilst the process had been emotional and challenging, it had been the right time for it and would ultimately help her. She then shared the booklet from her father's cremation ceremony, keen to show me his photograph. I reflected that the faceless wooden mannequin, symbolising him in previous sessions, may no longer be needed. Jenna was tearful, yet smiling, acknowledging how similar she looked to him in one of the photos. She was the only child to have inherited his auburn hair and it was suggested that she internalise this image, to balance with the one that tormented her – a lonely man, hanging lifeless from his belt. She was encouraged to preserve the booklet somehow, as it appeared quite worn and was clearly important to her. She said she would like to, as it was the only thing she owned relating to her dad.

To close her brief journey through one-to-one (bereavement-focused) drama-therapy, Jenna worked with six 'Inner Child' cards (Myss, 2003) and said of her father, "he's in the arms of the angels now". She shared that she no longer felt she had to grieve alone, having spoken so freely about her bereavement in our sessions. As Gersie explains, despite our personal beliefs, we all need "To find a way of expressing our loss, which will lead to the healing of our pain" (1991, p. 19). Jenna chose two of the cards to symbolise this transition: the first showed a child sitting alone on a planet among other empty stars. The second showed an adult and a child flying together, hand in hand. We laughed, seeing that the child had short red hair like Jenna and the adult had long dark hair like mine. Finally, she acknowledged she had questions that would never be answered, and although her guilt remained, she felt a little closer to the peace she desired.

Self-harm, suicide and lost souls

The UK's Department of Health reports "high rates of self-harm resulting in over 200,000 hospital attendances per year in England" (DH, 2017, p. 19). In their latest booklet on self-harm, the Mental Health Foundation describes it as "any behaviour where someone causes harm to themselves, usually as a way to help cope with difficult or distressing thoughts and feelings" (2016, p. 6). It notes it often involves cutting, burning or nonlethal overdoses, which may provide temporary relief from distress, only to be followed by guilt and shame, leading to an enduring cycle of self-harm (pp. 6–7). The Mental Health Foundation also challenges several myths about self-harm, describing it as neither an attention-seeking behaviour nor enjoyable and stressing that it affects males as well as females (2016, pp. 12–13). The doctor on the specialist secure ward for women with BPD described the disorder as a complex group of emotional injuries to an individual's sense of self. She then explained the role of self-harm in our patients' lives:

> They tend to resist helpful intervention, especially if it interferes with their need to 'change the channel' on what they are feeling, during episodes of distress. Their familiar lifelong agency envelopes them like an 'old blanket' and it oddly comforts. Even when acting out self destructively, catalysing excruciating pain beyond that with which they're already struggling, they have at least 'orchestrated change' and there is a sense of relief and power in this.
>
> *(Gour, response to author's questionnaire, 2016)*

Whilst self-harm does not relate directly to suicide, it might become a long-term coping strategy for those who engage with it when they are young. This may increase their potential for future suicide attempts (McManus et al., 2016, p. 14). Therefore, self-harm and suicidal thoughts must always be taken seriously, as they may indicate a future suicide attempt, or accidental death. Holloway also reflects that when acute mental health symptoms resolve, clients may become more vulnerable to suicide – as witnessed in a one-to-one dramatherapy client, whose "hopefulness was very quickly followed by a distressing anxiety that such optimism might prove to be misplaced, or cruelly snatched away" (2011, p. 157). The DH published a strategy for reducing and preventing suicides across England in 2012. Reviewed annually, it released its third progress report in 2017 and defined self-harm, including suicide attempts, as the "single biggest indicator of suicide risk" (p. 19). Whilst the suicide rate is relatively low in young people, extra precaution is needed, as between 10% and 20% are believed to self-harm (Mental Health Foundation, 2016, p. 8).

WHO estimated over 800,000 suicide deaths worldwide in 2012 (2016, p. 36) and the rate of suicide in England is said to have increased since 2007, with an average of thirteen deaths per year (Hunt, 2017, p. 4). Suicide is "the biggest killer of men under 50 as well as a leading cause of death in young people and new mothers" (Hunt, 2017, p. 4). It has been estimated that 10% of people diagnosed with BPD commit suicide (Gunderson, 2011, p. 3), with 60% to 70% attempting suicide within their lifetime (Oldham, 2006, p. 20). Oldham also reveals that personality disorders are thought to be present in over 30% of individuals who die by suicide, 40% of those who make suicide attempts and 50% of psychiatric outpatients who die by suicide (2006, p. 20). Millions of people are affected by suicide, as Hunt explains: "The death of someone by suicide has a devastating effect on families, friends, workplaces, schools and communities" (2017, p. 4). The Independent Mental Health Task Force for NHS England describes inequalities and fragmented services commissioned between CCGs (clinical commissioning groups), local authorities and the NHS, which must be addressed regarding suicide prevention (2016, p. 23). The following year, Appleby (chair of the UK's National Suicide Prevention Strategy Advisory Group) wrote, "We know that in mental health services, key components of suicide prevention are safer wards, early follow-up on hospital discharge and crisis resolution home treatment teams" (2017, p. 6).

Over the past twelve years, one young woman took her life whilst a patient on the secure ward and several clients have committed suicide following their discharge from both the ward and step-down unit. Most were living in the community at the time, though two were in secure hospitals. Whilst many service users have coped well in the community after discharge and created meaningful lives, good support (from both a family and professional perspective) is essential – and perhaps an acceptance that recovery will be an ongoing journey. One may become somewhat desensitised when continuously confronted with suicidal ideation and self-harm – and it is imperative to remember the individuals who have died. There is much to learn from these experiences and the following vignettes memorialise four service users who lost their battle with life. The first three also demonstrate how dramatherapy group rituals helped to support their peers with grief in the aftermath of their deaths – a vital process described in depth by Schrader (2012, p. 91).

Kit

Kit was a reserved, gentle woman, aged 20. She always wore a hoodie with the hood up, helping her to feel safe. She attended the dramatherapy group every week and found comfort in holding the monkey puppet from the collection of props. Throughout her childhood, Kit was sexually abused, first by her father, and then by her stepfather. The abuse had not stopped, which she disclosed to staff on the ward in the weeks before her death. She then tried to find the courage to tell her mother and report the abuse to the police. It was Christmas time and she gave me a card, thanking me for the dramatherapy group and accepting her just as she was.

A couple of weeks later, whilst out on leave, Kit swallowed several razor blades broken into a sandwich. She suffered severe internal injuries and bled to death on a general hospital ward. Shortly before heading to the ward to run a group the following day, I was told of her death. I was deeply shocked and upset, and then anxious that the patients would not want to see me. I thought the last thing they needed was a dramatherapy session. A supportive colleague (the OT on the step-down unit at that time) told me I must be strong, as the patients would need the group more than ever. She was right. Using our sharing ritual ball and a deck of therapeutic picture cards titled *Cope* (Lukyanova, 2002) the patients and I expressed how we felt about our shared loss. A few weeks later, a new client in the group, who had not known Kit, chose the monkey hand puppet to express herself. Bella, who had been close to Kit, found this incredibly difficult. When she moved to the step-down unit, I gave her the puppet in memory of Kit, which brought her great comfort.

Lorna

Lorna was in her early twenties. She was a soldier in the British Army, where she had faced abuse and then struggled with the birth of her daughter. Her mental health had rapidly declined, which led to her admission on the secure ward for women with BPD. Unfortunately, this placement broke down when her behaviour escalated into violence. She was transferred to an acute ward, though she remained in contact with her peers. When her mental state stabilised, her CPN (community psychiatric nurse) applied for funding to allow her to return to our ward. Lorna told her peers that she was looking forward to rejoining them. Whilst awaiting funding, however, tragically she hung herself on the acute ward and died. Her death came as a shock to both service users and staff on our ward. In a dramatherapy group a few days later, Abi chose the orange butterfly hand puppet to symbolise Lorna, as orange was her favourite colour and she was now free to fly like a butterfly. Each patient then chose an animal to place around the butterfly and expressed her feelings about Lorna.

Chloe

Six months after her discharge from our ward, Chloe relapsed and was admitted to an acute ward, where she tied a ligature that proved fatal. She was just 20 years old. She had spent most of her teenage years in hospital and initially came to our ward with a diagnosis of BPD. She suffered from persistent psychotic symptoms, however, and her diagnosis was altered. She also had a history of anorexia and ongoing OCD. Chloe had many highs and lows on the ward. About four months before her discharge, the MDT agreed that she could have a short course of one-to-one (bereavement-focused) dramatherapy.

Session 1

Chloe was keen to attend and responded positively, speaking openly about her best friend, Sarah, who had died in a road traffic accident at the age of 16. She described her fear of losing members of her family and her desire to protect them with OCD rituals. At the end, she said she felt inspired to work on reducing these rituals and we agreed to meet for three further sessions.

Session 2

Chloe again responded positively. This week, she spoke openly about Jane, the founder of her dance school, who recently died. We reflected on how this loss may also connect to a loss of her childhood and early teens. She looked close to tears at times, though she said she was unable to cry, which she thought might be due to medication. She also acknowledged the anger she felt at having lost her late teens to mental illness, having been in hospital from the age of 15. Finally, we spoke about accepting the painful reality that death is part of life and remains out of our control.

Session 3

Chloe and I met for our third session and agreed to meet for a final session next week. She described the positive progress she was making in all areas of her mental health and we again discussed the challenge of accepting the parts of life that are out of our control and those of which we can try to take control. We also read the story of the Shoshone butterfly legend (Wilson, 2009), together reflecting on the grieving journey. As Grainger reflects, "Imaginative stories give us a picture of death and life as co-existing – death in life, life in death" (2014, p. 142).

Session 4

Chloe came for her final session and said how well she had been feeling for several weeks and that she felt ready for discharge. She shared her frustration about life on the ward, stressing how upsetting she finds the rude behaviour of certain service users towards staff. She then engaged fully in the six-part story-making structure (6PSM), a projective method inspired by Gersie's teachings and further developed by Lahad (Lahad, 2013, p. 47). It is used in relation to the assessment and treatment of many clients engaging in dramatherapy, and Dent-Brown describes its significance for people with personality disorders: "diagnosis merely helps the doctor (or therapist) to orient themselves in the field; it is the story that enables them to start to help the patient" (1999, p. 10). Furthermore, Dent-Brown and Wang have identified pessimism and failure as frequent components of the six-part stories created by individuals with BPD (2004, p. 12). The 6PSM may also be used to support Lahad's BASIC Ph model of assessing and then fostering an individual's personal strengths, coping strategies and resilience (Lahad and Leykin, 2013, pp. 16–20). In Chloe's case, we discussed the symbolism of the story she had created, and then summarised her journey through the four sessions. She said at the end, it had felt like a positive and helpful experience.

Chloe was a dedicated and enthusiastic member of the dramatherapy group, and before her discharge, she said she would be pleased for examples of her work to be included in this book and signed a consent letter. She was often playful in dramatherapy sessions and formed close relationships with several of her peers on the ward. Her death had a huge impact on them and on all the staff who had worked with her. Shortly after she died, I facilitated a dramatherapy group that most clients attended. The group chose to symbolise Chloe with a purple boom-whacker, as purple was her favourite colour and she had always enjoyed using the boom-whackers to express her inner rage and frustration. The following paragraph describes each client's response to this session.

Ella was deeply distressed, though made the effort to attend. She had been close to Chloe and accepted the support offered by her peers. Jean shared her sadness and some humorous memories. Rina described herself as feeling numb in response to the news. She had been close to Chloe and said at the end, she had been unsure whether to come, though was glad to have done so. She also reflected that her peers were a very special group of people. Rebecca agreed with Rina and offered support to others, particularly Ella. She later noted the mood of the group had lightened as the session had progressed. Mia offered support to her peers and Clarice admitted that she wanted to help everyone, though was unsure what to say. She later reflected that the group had provided a positive way to connect to one another. It was Millie's final session and although she engaged well, her mood was understandably subdued. She expressed sadness about Chloe's death and offered support to the peers she knew had been close to her. She also admitted that the tragedy had increased her anxiety about her impending discharge.

Jane

Jane was in her late twenties. She was admitted to the secure ward after giving birth to a baby son on a similar ward, where she had spent most of her pregnancy. The baby was immediately removed from her care and adopted, due to the instability of her mental state. On our ward, she revealed herself to be a kind and creative woman, who had suffered abuse and neglect throughout her life. Jane enjoyed the drama-therapy and expressive therapy groups, voicing her feelings and sharing her passion to be reunited with her son when he turned 18.

Her self-harm continued, however, and due to her high risk of accidental (or intentional) suicide, she was transferred to an acute unit. A few months later, the MDT was told that she had hung herself whilst in hospital and tragically died. "One in five mothers suffers from depression, anxiety or in some cases psychosis during pregnancy or in the first year after childbirth. Suicide is the second leading cause of maternal death, after cardiovascular disease" (Independent Mental Health Task Force, 2016, p. 6). Jane had experienced the additional trauma of enduring her pregnancy on a secure mental health ward and having her baby removed from her care and adopted immediately after his birth. Figure 7.2 shows a model she made

FIGURE 7.2 Pregnant

from Giotto modelling dough, symbolising herself during her pregnancy on the first ward.

Sadly, several other young women died following their discharge from hospital, and whilst some of their deaths may have resulted from intentional suicide, others might have been accidental, resulting from self-harm that took them to a point of no return.

Emotional impact on staff

A questionnaire was offered to all members of the multidisciplinary teams in the two settings described in Chapters 5 and 6, of which ten colleagues completed it. Simultaneously, a small-scale survey of BADth members was conducted, through their newsletter and social media platforms. Thirteen dramatherapists working in the field of BPD then completed a similar questionnaire. The twenty-three research participants were asked, *How easy or difficult do you find it to 'let go' at the end of the working day?*

Many participants acknowledged how challenging it could be and one drama-therapist wrote, "People with borderline traits try to pull me into their world and dramas, so it takes a lot of effort to let go". Several also described helpful techniques, including physical activity, mindfulness, personal therapy, speaking with colleagues and, most crucially, regular clinical supervision.

> In reply to the question, *What are the key issues that arise in your work with this client group?*, self-harm, ambivalence towards recovery and emotional projections were the issues that dominated. These are explained in more depth ahead.

Suicide and self-harm

Yalom describes the suicide of a patient as one of the two most devastating experiences for a therapist. He reflects that if working with deeply disturbed clients, it remains a continuous threat and "Even the most mature and seasoned therapist will be tormented by shock, sadness, guilt, feelings of incompetence, and anger at the patient" (2002, p. 257). In the questionnaires completed by ten colleagues across two specialist units, one shared her response to the suicide of a former patient in relation to letting go at the end of the working day:

> In the past month, I have lost my first BPD client to suicide and have been having a bit more difficulty letting go. Such news is never wanted by mental health workers. I have been feeling the exact same feelings of grief expected from a friend or co-worker's death. I hadn't thought about how much of an actual strong relationship I had formed with this ex client whom I worked closely with for almost one year. In the last month specifically, I've learned how much impact our clients can have on our own lives, how they have a big

way of touching our lives. I've also found there is not much advice on how a therapist grieves the loss of a client. I've had thoughts whether it's appropriate to even cry, to attend the funeral and whom to talk to about my feelings related to the death.

(Bermeo, response to author's questionnaire, 2017)

Most clients with BPD harm themselves, often severely. As well as cutting, burning and nonlethal overdoses, this regularly includes digesting dangerous liquids or objects, tying ligatures and inserting objects into the vagina. Self-harm emerged as a dominant feature in several questionnaires. One dramatherapist wrote, "Severe self-harm or intent to kill oneself – this would always have an effect on me, particularly if the patient attempted to self-harm on the unit after informing staff that everything was okay". Another wrote, "I have worked with lots of clients who self-harm by sticking sharp objects into their vaginas", the thought of which she found particularly difficult to let go of at the end of the day. The OT on the specialist secure ward for women with BPD wrote:

Working with BPD patients is like a roller coaster and it does affect you. You might feel okay and not affected when a patient discloses that she has inserted a blade into her vagina or when you have to restrain in order to stop a patient from cutting themselves. It is the mentality of a good soldier: I'm strong and nothing affects me. But actually, it does and you need space and time to realise what just happened. I do value my team's support, my partner's love and my breaks from work. You need 'oxygen' to keep going, but sometimes I forget to breathe.

(Ntzimani, response to author's questionnaire, 2017)

Emotional projections and ambivalence

The dynamics that develop between client and therapist can be complex and at times challenging to manage. As Seebohm, a dramatherapist working in a forensic setting, suggests, "It is through the transference and countertransference that we have with our clients that we are brought face to face with both the client's destructiveness as well as our own" (2011, p. 127). Emotional projections are often experienced in dramatherapy sessions with the BPD client group; thus an understanding of transference and countertransference (as defined within the psychodynamic approach) will help to enhance the process. As a dramatherapist, I am influenced by the psychodynamic model and clinical supervision provides a helpful space to reflect and learn from these phenomena.

In simple terms, transference refers to the feelings that clients have about their therapist – emotions thought to connect to their past and present relationships, offering the therapist some insight into their internal world (Slade et al., 2015, p. 457) and countertransference describes the feelings experienced by the therapist towards their client – emotions thought to originate from the client and considered a type of unconscious communication (Slade et al., 2015, p. 257). These processes can be further complicated in dramatherapy, where the dramatherapist takes a more active role in the process (than in psychodynamic psychotherapy), stepping into sub-roles, such as director and actor (Jenkyns, 1996, p. 50). Both the dramatherapist and their client/clients may therefore be more open to emotional projections. In one-to-one dramatherapy, I have worked with this phenomenon directly, whilst in groups, I focus on the dynamics between the clients, encouraging them to support one another and to develop their understanding and acceptance of self and other.

In the twenty-three questionnaires, most participants described the challenge of working with the emotions projected onto them by the clients. One dramatherapist described them as "disturbing, violent, manipulative and destructive". Another highlighted her clients' need to continuously challenge boundaries and their difficulty in returning to a baseline emotion. One participant described her anxiety rising in response to highly expressed emotions around aggression, envy, hostility, rivalry and scapegoating – challenging her own experiences, beliefs, fears and fantasies. Feelings of inadequacy may also surface and can at times be a shared experience between therapist and client, as one dramatherapist shared:

> Most of the women I work with express shame, guilt and deep-rooted feelings of being bad/not good enough. Perhaps the most difficult feeling to untangle for me is that of not being a good enough therapist – I think this work, in essence, is re-parenting – and that somebody else would do a much better job. This feels more like reality and taps into my own doubts, which are harder to shake than feelings of rage, which are more alien to me.

Another participant described the impact of being rejected or the dramatherapy material being dismissed. One reflected, "I find they often challenge you as much as they can, to see if they can trust you. Sometimes they put all their efforts into demonstrating that they can't trust you. I find in them a general search for 'fusion'. It is like they want to come back to an original 'heaven' where no boundaries, no words and no explanations are needed". This may relate to the client's desire to be loved unconditionally and held, as if back in the womb.

The doctor on the specialist ward for women with BPD eloquently described the client group's ambivalence towards recovery:

> They have a natural, significant ambivalence about getting truly well, as it represents a crisis of identity. I have found their resistance palpable, as a trained clinician: Their dysfunctional identity feels familiar to them – it's far more comforting and easier to maintain than exploring a healthy and wholesome new one. They alternate between seductive and abusive, with a Jekyll and Hyde type temperament. I would describe it as an all good/all bad reflex, which is central to borderline pathology.
>
> *(Gour, response to author's questionnaire, 2016)*

Dr Preeti Gour reflects on suicide

How does one prevent suicide? Having worked for five years in a PD service, I have been able to review clinical cases resulting in suicide following discharge. It has been emotional and intense to say the least. Most would speculate and say the simple way to prevent a fatality would be restricting access to lethal means. However, having worked intensively with this high-risk client group, I have learnt that a combination of preventative methods helps. I refer to these as interventions: pharmacology, psychosocial and psychotherapy, such as dramatherapy.

Many books, journals and more recently websites emphasise the need to identify interventions with proven efficacy for preventing death by suicide: one such intervention used on our unit was conducted by the dramatherapist on a weekly basis with client Jean, whose case is described in Chapter 5. Suicide is complex, it has many facets and no one cause can be identified. There are individual and contextual factors to consider: individual factors include mental disorders, such as BPD, genetic predisposition and psychological vulnerabilities. Contextual contributions include abuse, socioeconomic suppression and family influences; exposure to suicidal behaviours; and, most importantly, lack of support at the point of crisis. In my experience on the ward, the MDT has focused on prevention, married with a range of initiatives, such as dramatherapy.

Focusing on suicide prevention, we utilise universal interventions: reduction of access to potential ligatures and ligature points; limiting contraband, education via DBT and OT, and promoting awareness through family therapy and the carers group. Selective interventions then focus on those with a heightened risk: individuals who express suicidal ideations but do not act on them and those with co-morbidities, such as EUPD and eating disorders, physical health problems, such as chronic pain disorder, and substance misuse. Specific planning is essential to address and support these service users. For those who have not been able to engage (e.g. in DBT) a bespoke plan would be formulated, catering for their needs. Finally, there are clients who indicate more evident or immediate signs of suicide risk: often those recently admitted to the ward, or individuals who have prematurely discharged themselves from services. This category I believe has less engagement holistically, minimal support networks and poor community input.

So what can be done? How effective can we become at prevention of suicide? Self-harm is recognised as a major risk factor for suicide, so it makes sense to reduce self-harm, which would ultimately reduce suicide. Self-harm is also worthy of attention in its own right. Patients who receive interventions, such as DBT, complemented by dramatherapy have shown decreased levels of self-harm compared to patients who have prematurely disengaged with no interventions. There is an onus on those such as myself working in the field of BPD to continue to monitor and evaluate our activities. I conclude no single intervention is the cure. We have to draw on broader disciplines and use a range of methods, whether it is DBT, dramatherapy or OT, to triangulate and strengthen the recovery plan. I am confident the gap of what is known and unknown in terms of the effectiveness of particular approaches to prevent self-harm and suicide will decrease in years to come.

The role of clinical supervision

NICE stipulates that all mental health professionals providing therapy for people with BPD should have regular access to both supervision and staff support (2009, p. 14). When working with the client group, Kellogg and Young also stress the importance of supervision, explaining that therapists must be fully aware of their own issues and beliefs, enabling them "to understand and control their counter-transferential reactions" (2006, p. 457). Whilst it is incredibly rewarding to work in this field, strong emotions will inevitably stir within both client and therapist. The therapist needs space to reflect on whatever feelings emerge, enabling him or her to understand the transference and countertransference of emotions and to maintain professional boundaries. This process is enhanced by the support of a professional supervisor, who can offer a necessary external perspective.

Ten of the thirteen dramatherapists who completed the questionnaire acknowledged the role of supervision in helping them to cope with this issue. One shared, "I was impacted by the level of emotional projection and I relied on clinical supervision to help understand what was happening. The objectivity of the supervisor seems to be important in separating and identifying overwhelming feelings" (2017). Another wrote, "Supervision supports me to differentiate my own feelings from the transference and counter-transference, spot any splitting and get off the drama triangle" (2017). Karpman, a psychiatrist practising Transactional Analysis (TA), developed the concept of the 'drama triangle' in 1968 (Weinhold and Weinhold, 2017, p. 9) to explore the dysfunctional dynamic that often evolves in families and other social groups – moving between the roles of persecutor, rescuer and victim. Seebohm has identified an alternative triad of roles in her dramatherapy work with forensic clients: captor, hostage and bystander (described in Chapter 4). She suggests these roles may be projected onto the dramatherapist at different times, and by inhabiting different roles, clients (referred to as actors) "can be liberated from being perpetually stuck in any one of them" (2011, p. 129). This could relate to any role (or roles) that a client may feel trapped in, such as the shamed abuse victim, or angry, unlovable child, identified in my work with women with BPD.

Of the ten colleagues who completed questionnaires, nine described supervision as vital in helping them to manage issues with: transference and countertransference; adoration and rejection; overwhelming emotions relating to clients' emotional and physical pain; isolation, confusion and frustration. The social worker on the step-down unit wrote the following:

> Clinical supervision is vital! The client group is very challenging and can often reject intervention by opposing the professional or poking holes in the intervention, which can be demoralising or even embarrassing for the unsuspecting professional. Clients who are not yet skilled in managing their emotions can appear to explode externally with emotions, negative or positive such as anger or affection. Professionals need to be aware of how to manage varying emotions such as anger and affection that may cross boundaries, such as inappropriate touching, in a way that validates and minimises rejection to

the client. These are things that we learn during or after an event has happened and therefore clinical supervision is vital for reflective practice and learning.

(Gyasiaddo, response to author's questionnaire, 2017)

One research participant noted that a supervisor must understand the complexities of the client group to "assist the therapist in untangling projections and attending to their self-care" (Gyasiaddo, response to author's questionnaire, 2017). Jones describes dramatherapy supervision as 'emergent' – continuously developing and adapting to support a variety of approaches and specific needs – reflecting the diversity and creativity of the field of dramatherapy (2008, p. 13). Researching the connection between the personal and professional challenges encountered by psychotherapists, Adams highlights their recognition of supervision, reflecting "we need supervisors to ensure that we do not lose sight of ourselves, and therefore lose sight of our patients" (2014, p. 111).

Conclusion

In Zografou's account of working with clients with addictions, she describes a dramatherapy process that allowed "Destructive tendencies, nihilism, hostility and despondency (to) engage in battle with hope, imagination, desire and optimism" (2011, p. 108). Working with such destructive forces – whether internalised or externalised by clients – is emotionally demanding. It is therefore imperative to take care of one's own mental and physical health. This certainly relates to the BPD client group and should include regular clinical supervision, from a qualified dramatherapy (or arts therapy) supervisor, with a thorough understanding of the client group. This will enable the dramatherapist to genuinely support his or her clients and to manage the various tensions, dynamics and existential challenges that may arise.

References

Adams, M. (2014) *The Myth of the Untroubled Therapist: Private Life, Professional Practice.* London: Routledge.

Appleby, L. (2017) Foreword. In *Preventing Suicide in England: Third Progress Report on the Cross-Government Outcomes Strategy to Save Lives* [Online]. Published by the DH (UK's Department of Health) on behalf of HM Government. Available from: www.gov.uk/government/publications/suicide-prevention-third-annual-report [Accessed: 24.12.17].

Choquette, S. (2009) *The Answer Is Simple: Oracle Card* (62-card deck and guide book). Carlsbad, CA: Hay House.

Dent-Brown, K. (1999) The Six-Part Story Method (6PSM) as an Aid in the Assessment of Personality Disorder. *Dramatherapy*, 21(2), pp. 10–14.

Dent-Brown, K. and Wang, W. (2004) Pessimism and Failure in 6-Part Stories: Indicators of Borderline Personality Disorder? *The Arts in Psychotherapy*, 31(5), pp. 321–333.

DH (2012) *Preventing Suicide in England: A Cross-Government Outcomes Strategy to Save Lives Suicide Prevention Strategy* [Online]. Published by the DH on behalf of HM Government. Available from: www.gov.uk/government/publications/suicide-prevention-strategy-for-england [Accessed: 03.07.17].

DH–UK Department of Health (2017) *Preventing Suicide in England: Third Progress Report on the Cross-Government Outcomes Strategy to Save Lives* [Online]. Published by the DH on behalf of HM Government. Available from: www.gov.uk/government/publications/suicide-prevention-third-annual-report [Accessed: 03.07.17].

Gersie, A. (1991) *Storymaking in Bereavement: Dragons Fight in the Meadow.* London: Jessica Kingsley.

Grainger, R. (2014) *Theatre and Encounter: The Psychology of the Dramatic Relationship.* Bloomington, IN: Trafford.

Gunderson, J. (2011) *A BPD Brief* [Online]. Revised edition. NEA.BPD (National Education Alliance. Borderline Personality Disorder). Available from: www.borderlinepersonalitydisorder.com

Holloway, P. (2011) Surviving Suicide: The Book of Life and Death. In Dokter, D., Holloway, P. and Seebohm, H. (eds.) *Dramatherapy and Destructiveness: Creating the Evidence Base, Playing with Thanatos.* Kindle edition. Hove, UK: Routledge.

Hunt, J. (2017) Ministerial Foreword. In *Preventing Suicide in England: Third Progress Report on the Cross-Government Outcomes Strategy to Save Lives* [Online]. Published by the DH on behalf of HM Government. Available from: www.gov.uk/government/publications/suicide-prevention-strategy-for-england [Accessed: 03.07.17].

Independent Mental Health Taskforce (2016) *The Five-Year Forward View for Mental Health for the NHS in England* [Online]. Published by the Independent Mental Health Task Force, commissioned by Stevens, S. on behalf of NHS England. Available from: www.england.nhs.uk/mentalhealth/taskforce/ [Accessed: 03.17.17].

Jenkyns, M. (1996) *The Play's the Thing: Exploring Text in Drama and Therapy.* London: Routledge.

Jones, P. (2008) The State of the Art of Supervision: Review and Research. In Dokter, D. and Jones, P. (eds.) *Supervision of Dramatherapy.* In Schaverein, J. (series ed.) Supervision in the Arts Therapies. Abingdon, UK: Routledge.

Kellogg, S. and Young, J. (2006) Schema Therapy for Borderline Personality Disorder. *Journal of Clinical Psychology*, 62(4), pp. 445–458. Wiley Periodicals. Available from: www.interscience.wiley.com

Lahad, M. (2013) Six-Part Story Revisited: Seven Levels of Assessment Drawn from the 6PSM. In Lahad, M., Shacham, M. and Ayalon, O. (eds.) *The "BASIC Ph" Model of Coping and Resiliency: Theory, Research and Cross-Cultural Application.* London: Jessica Kingsley.

Lahad, M. and Leykin, D. (2013) Introduction: The Integrative Model of Resiliency: The BASIC Ph Model, or What Do We Know about Survival? In Lahad, M., Shacham, M. and Ayalon, O. (eds.) *The "BASIC Ph" Model of Coping and Resiliency: Theory, Research and Cross-Cultural Application.* London: Jessica Kingsley.

Lukyanova, M. (Artist) (2002) *Cope* (a Therapeutic Picture Card Deck). Avalon, O. and Egetmeyer, M. (writers). OH Publishing. Available from: http://oh-cards.com/index.php?article_id=64&clang=1 [Accessed: 27.06.17].

McManus, S., Bebbington, P., Jenkins, R. and Brugha T. (eds.) (2016) *Mental Health and Wellbeing in England: Adult Psychiatric Morbidity Survey 2014.* Leeds: NHS Digital.

Mental Health Foundation (2016) *The Truth about Self-Harm* (an information booklet) [Online]. Mental Health Foundation, UK. Available from: www.mentalhealth.org.uk/search/?query=self+harm&op=Search [Accessed: 01.07.17].

Myss, C. (2003) *Archetype Cards: A 78-Card Deck and Guidebook.* Carlsbad, CA: Hay House.

NICE (National Institute for Health and Care Excellence) (2009) *Borderline Personality Disorder: Recognition and Management: Clinical Guideline 78.* Developed by the National Collaborating Centre for Mental Health. Available from: www.nice.org.uk/guidance/cg78/chapter/1-Guidance

Oldham, J. M. (2006) Treatment in Psychiatry: Borderline Personality Disorder and Suicidality [Online]. *Am J Psychiatry,* 163(1), pp. 20–26. Available from: http://dx.doi.org/10.1176/appi.ajp.163.1.20 [Accessed: 10.11.16].

Schrader, C. (2012) 'We Don't Need Therapy, We Have Ritual': An Overview of the Work of Malidoma Somé and a Personal Experience of a Dagara Grief Ritual. In Schrader, S. (ed.) *Ritual Theatre: The Power of Dramatic Ritual in Personal Development Groups and Clinical Practice.* Kindle edition. London: Jessica Kingsley.

Seebohm, H. (2011) On Bondage and Liberty: The Art of the Possible in Medium-Secure Settings. In Dokter, D., Holloway, P. and Seebohm, H. (eds.) *Dramatherapy and Destructiveness: Creating the Evidence Base, Playing with Thanatos.* Kindle edition. Hove, UK: Routledge.

Slade, K., Hamilton, L. and Thompson, C. (2015) Definition and Goal. In Banyard, P., Dillon, G., Norman, C. and Winder, B. (eds.) *Essential Psychology.* Second edition. Kindle edition. London: SAGE.

Weinhold, B. and Weinhold, J. (2017) *How to Break Free of the Drama Triangle and Victim Consciousness.* Colorado Springs, CO: CICRCL Press.

WHO (2016) *World Health Statistics 2016: Monitoring Health for the SDGs, Sustainable Development Goals* [Online]. WHO Library Cataloguing-in-Publication Data. Available from: www.who.int/gho/publications/world_health_statistics/2016/en/ [Accessed: 15.07.17].

Wilson, R. (2009) *The Shoshone Butterfly Legend.* Available from: www.ya-native.com/Culture_GreatBasin/Shoshone/theshoshonebutterflylegend.html [Accessed: 23.12.17]

Yalom, I. (2002) *The Gift of Therapy: An Open Letter to a New Generation of Therapists and Their Patients.* Second edition. Kindle edition. London: Hachette Digital, Little Brown Book Group.

Yalom, I. (2008) *Staring at the Sun: Overcoming the Dread of Death.* Kindle edition. London: Hachette Digital, Little Brown Book Group.

Zografou, L. (2011) Dramatherapy and Addiction: Learning to Live with Destructiveness. In Dokter, D., Holloway, P. and Seebohm, H. (eds.) *Dramatherapy and Destructiveness: Creating the Evidence Base, Playing with Thanatos.* Kindle edition. Hove, UK: Routledge.

8

HOPE, COURAGE AND CREATIVITY

> To finish this war and find my peace,
> I must look back at battles won.
> What weapons did help me win?
> Was it the key that locked me in?
> Was it people's belief in me?
> Was it the strength from all close by?
> Or money spent on self-help books?
> Or hours sat in therapy?
>
> —Bella, 2014

As the opening verse demonstrates, there are many things that can support the recovery of individuals with BPD, though each must pursue his or her own journey to discover what genuinely helps. The first hurdle may be finding the courage to leave the familiarity of emotional and physical suffering, which could throw people into a temporary state of loss and confusion, their identity having fused with their pain. In this final chapter, the suggestion is that with belief, hope and courage, individuals can find new meaning in their lives, the antithesis of the ambivalence between life and death described in Chapter 7. On their therapeutic journey, the creative energy of dramatherapy has the potential to empower and nurture them, through individual or supportive group therapy.

Belief and hope

Belief is significant to both therapist and client. Whilst the therapist endeavours to hold onto hope, the client's ambivalence between life and death may threaten its survival. As shared in the opening chapter, Carey (a journalist with the *New*

York Times) reflects "the enduring stigma of mental illness teaches people with such a diagnosis to think of themselves as victims, snuffing out the one thing that can motivate them to find treatment: hope" (2011, p. 1). These themes connect to the spiritual dimension of dramatherapy. Grainger (dramatherapy pioneer, researcher, priest and professional actor) describes the significance of faith, love and spirituality in several of his works. Through group workshops for example, he describes the potential for "the spirituality of personal sharing and encounter, and the spirituality of inspired imagination" (2002, p. 4). Many people with BPD have suffered excruciating trauma, and whilst Yalom describes the 'instillation of hope' as the first of eleven elements vital to successful therapy (Yalom with Leszcz, 2005, l.314–315), this may prove to be therapists' greatest challenge. However, if they can sustain their belief that healing and change are genuinely possible, the client is then given the opportunity to believe it too. As Pitruzzella suggests, "Whatever the dramatherapist's religious or spiritual beliefs might be, what they cannot miss is a trust in men and women as creative beings, owning the talent to regenerate themselves" (2004, p. 128). Belief and hope then interconnect, one allowing the other to exist, as shown in the second verse of Bella's poem, written in 2014:

> The strongest weapon I have gained
> Is what all good soldiers need . . . a belief in myself
> Determination in wanting victory,
> And knowing
> That when wounds are painfully sore
> And it seems no one is near,
> Someone somewhere really does care
> And will use their shield to keep me safe
> While exhaustion reigns
> Then strength returns
> To fight each battle, till none are left
> Then victory of my war is here
> Then peace and calm return once more

"The instillation and maintenance of hope is crucial in any psychotherapy. Not only is hope required to keep the client in therapy so that other therapeutic factors may take effect, but faith in a treatment mode can in itself be therapeutically effective" (Yalom with Leszcz, 2005, l.379–380). Belief is then relevant in a wider perspective, relating to both the client's and therapist's belief in themselves, the therapeutic approach and in one another. Schrader highlights the potential for dramatherapy rituals to heal and transform, "bringing hope to those who have given up hope" (2012, p. 92). Reflecting on her dramatherapy work within addiction services, however, Zografou warns that "Faith and hope are the first casualties of destructive resistance if it is only seen as a foe and not as a disguised friend" (2011, p. 115). To remain hopeful with BPD clients, patience and flexibility are also essential, as the OT on the secure ward explained:

> Working with this client group can be an emotional and physical challenge for the therapist. You are called to bring a balance in their lives, where building independence will not make them feel abandoned and self-harming behaviours will be addressed in a way they feel neither punished nor encouraged. (. . .) You have to be flexible and patient, expecting the worse and the best at the same time.
>
> *(Ntzimani, response to author's questionnaire, 2017)*

Courage and meaning

Thich Nhat Hanh (Zen master, Buddhist monk and author) reflects that people often focus on the past: "We feel more comfortable making our home there, even if it holds a lot of suffering" (2012, l.217–218). Unconsciously, we remain tied to our infant selves, their fears and desires. These need to be released, to allow our adult selves to develop (Hanh, 2012, l.223–227). This concept relates to dramatherapy, through which many parts of the self, including the inner child, may be liberated. Johnson – a Jungian analyst and lecturer – also describes the importance of embracing our internal shadow, to avoid projecting it onto others and falsely separating dark from light (1993, l.227–229). This concept is particularly relevant to BPD clients, who often feel split and unconsciously project their feelings onto others. Johnson stresses the significance of engaging in ceremonial or symbolic creativity, to express the shadow and avoid the brutality that will otherwise surface (1993, l.226). Dramatherapy offers such a process, and Holloway, Seebohm and Dokter have researched its potential within the realm of destructiveness – either internalised or externalised by clients. They describe the unique way it can contain destructive thoughts and desires, allowing people to enact, narrate and reflect upon the experience (2011, p. 20).

Levine relates Freud's idea of free association and Winnicott's concept of free play to a form of chaos, out of which new ideas and feelings will surface (2005, p. 43). Jennings describes a similarly free and creative phase of the dramatherapy process, in which drama is "both the container of the chaos and the means to explore it" (1987, p. 15). This free-flowing space is held in between opening and closing rituals – mirroring the 'destructuring and restructuring' period defined by Levine, where new meanings may "emerge out of the ruins of the old" (2005, p. 44). This potentially transforming process enables clients to develop a stronger, renewed sense of self. Grainger describes this as "the re-discovery of our own power to be another self and yet still be ourselves" (2012, p. 226). To release the grip of the past and fully inhabit the present, however, requires immense courage and effort, particularly if an individual has endured a trauma, such as child abuse:

> You suffered greatly. You were fragile and vulnerable. You were likely afraid all the time. You didn't know how to protect yourself. Perhaps in your mind you continue to be abused again and again, even though you are an adult now. You are no longer that child who was fragile and vulnerable, with no means of defence. Yet you continue to experience the suffering of the child, because you always revisit those memories even though they are painful.
>
> *(Hanh, 2012)*

Confronting the past and learning to accept it cannot be altered may be a painful process. Despite this, Miller – renowned childhood researcher, psychotherapist and author – suggests, "We become free by transforming ourselves from unaware victims of the past, to responsible individuals of the present" (1997, p. 2). Frankl, an innovative neurologist and psychiatrist who survived the Holocaust, shared his belief that life's meaning is unique to each of us, and can even be found through suffering (2004). Hanh also proposes that by grounding ourselves in the present "we can look at the past in a different way and transform its suffering" (2012, l.210–211). Each of these concepts relates to the transformative, creative process of dramatherapy. Inspired by Buddhist philosophy, Gammage (dramatherapist, play therapist and psychotherapist) proposes that "our psychological and spiritual selves are intrinsically united, as are our physical, social, emotional, sexual and intellectual selves" (2017, p. 16). To illuminate the idea of embracing one's own suffering to allow genuine growth, Hanh recounts the story of Mara and the Buddha: here, the Buddha is compared to a beautiful flower and Mara to the garbage that becomes compost and nourishes the flower. For any person suffering, Mara then represents his or her emotional or physical pain:

> When you are there for yourself, there is an energy that embraces you, embraces your pain, embraces your suffering, your fear, your despair. It also embraces the good, positive qualities within you. The capacity of being joyful again, of being happy again, of being loving and tolerant – these qualities are within us, and they need to be embraced in order to grow; these are flowers. And the fear, despair, and sorrow in us need to be embraced in order to become compost. They will nourish the flowers.
>
> *(Hanh, 2013)*

Survivors

Hanh reflects, "The only way to ease our fear and be truly happy is to acknowledge our fear and look deeply at its source" (2012, l.55). For people with BPD, however, confronting their deepest fears may be overwhelming and potentially traumatic. Any therapeutic work must therefore be managed with extreme sensitivity and patience. With dramatic distance and ritual, dramatherapy offers safety and containment. In Chapter 7, several case vignettes were shared, describing clients who tragically lost their battle with life. There are others who have come close to death, however, though they somehow found the courage to move away from the edge and back onto the path towards life, as highlighted in the following two vignettes.

Vignette 1

Laura had two admissions on the secure ward for women with BPD. She was intelligent and kind, with a history of anorexia and life-threatening self-harm. She came close to death on several occasions whilst on the ward and in the community. During her second admission, she found the expressive therapy group particularly helpful, taking her creative pieces to individual DBT sessions for further exploration. Figure 8.1 is a model she fashioned from Giotto vegetable dough, expressing her enduring desire to become a mother.

Laura found dramatherapy challenging, due to the many props used and her ongoing OCD symptoms. Despite various practical attempts to support her with this, such as cleaning the props with disinfectant spray each week, the most effective approach was to allow Laura to engage at her own pace, in a manner that suited her. Whilst choosing not to make physical contact with anything or anyone, she responded well to other elements of the process, particularly verbal symbolism, story and poetry. Following her final discharge, she found a way to thrive in the

FIGURE 8.1   Baby in a basket

community. She returned to her own home and now works closely with universities, teaching students about mental health issues from a survivor's perspective.

Vignette 2

Jean, whose case study was shared in detail in Chapter 5, survived several suicide attempts before her admission to the secure ward for women with BPD. There, she came close to death within the first few months. With the aid of antipsychotic medication, a kind, yet firm approach from the MDT, the OT's endeavour to reconnect Jean to her former working self and her poignant journey through one-to-one dramatherapy, she began to confront her inner demons and tentatively accepted that she was worthy of care. Her journey now continues on the step-down unit, where she will hopefully consider the possibility of creating a new life, free from self-punishment.

Pendzik explains that whilst a shaman travels to the underworld to find and then dramatise the source of a person's torment, the dramatherapist journeys alongside their clients into their unconscious, where together they meet and release inner monsters with dramatic techniques (1988, p. 85). These are the manifestations of traumatic memories (neglect, abuse and loss), the cause of self-hatred and low self-esteem. Throughout this book, many case and session vignettes have revealed the potential for dramatherapy to transform these monsters. The doctor on the DBT-centred secure ward described the centrality of emotional development work in helping clients to relinquish PD traits and, more importantly, to heal: "If we solely provide a treatment which does not cater for emotional growth, the service user resumes faulty, entrenched behaviours and recreates trauma over again. Dramatherapy is pivotal in supporting the emotional development work" (Gour, response to author's questionnaire, 2016).

To conclude, I have written a poem for the survivors of BPD, those who have battled their inner demons and, despite coming close to either a spiritual or physical death, have found the strength to continue their journey through life:

Survivors

Hope has been vanquished,
She no longer feels alive,
Will she journey to the other side?
Or find meaning and survive?
She bravely confronts her demons,
Releasing their powerful grip.
With self-belief and courage,
She climbs aboard her ship.
She sails through the darkness,
Creativity burning through,
With hope she discovers meaning,
She bathes in light anew.

FIGURE 8.2 Hope (drawn for this book by a former service user, 2017)

References

Bella (Former Service User) (2014) *Poem* – verses 1 and 2.

Carey, B. (2011) Expert on Mental Illness Reveals Her Own Fight [Online]. *The New York Times*. Available from: www.nytimes.com/2011/06/23/health/23lives.html?_r=0 [Accessed: 07.12.16].

Frankl, V. (2004) 1984 Postscript. In *Man's Search for Meaning*. Revised edition. London: Rider.

Gammage, D. (2017) *Playful Awakening: Releasing the Gift of Play on Your Life*. London: Jessica Kingsley.

Grainger, R. (2003) *Group Spirituality: A Workshop Approach*. Hove, UK: Brunner-Routledge.

Grainger, R. (2012) Ritual Theatre and Existential Change. In Schrader, C. (ed.) *Ritual Theatre: The Power of Dramatic Ritual in Personal Development Groups and Clinical Practice*. Kindle edition. London: Jessica Kingsley.

Hanh, T. N. (2012) *Fear: Essential Wisdom for Getting through the Storm*. Kindle edition. London: Ebury Digital.

Hanh, T. N. (2013) Mara and the Buddha: Embracing our Suffering [Online]. Transcript of a talk given in August 1996. Plum Village website. Available from: https://plumvillage.org/transcriptions/mara-and-the-buddha-embracing-our-suffering/ [Accessed: 22.05.17].

Holloway, P., Seebohm, H. and Dokter, D. (2011) Understandings of Destructiveness. In Dokter, D., Holloway, P. and Seebohm, H. (eds.) *Dramatherapy and Destructiveness: Creating the Evidence Base, Playing with Thanatos*. Kindle edition. Hove, UK: Routledge.

Jennings, S. (1987) *Dramatherapy: Theory and Practice 1*. Abingdon, UK: Routledge.

Johnson, R. A. (1993) *Owning Your Own Shadow: Understanding the Dark Side of the Psyche*. Kindle edition. EPub edition. New York: HarperCollins.

Levine, S. K. (2005) The Philosophy of Expressive Arts Therapy: Poiesis as a Response to the World. In Knill, P. J., Levine, E. G. and Stephen Levine, S. K. (authors) *Principles and Practice of Expressive Arts Therapy: Toward a Therapeutic Aesthetic*. London: Jessica Kingsley.

Miller, A. (1997) *The Drama of Being a Child: The Search for the True Self.* New edition, revised and updated. English translation. New York: Basic Books.

Pendzik, S. (1988) Drama Therapy as a Form of Modern Shamanism. *Journal of Transpersonal Psychology*, 20(1), p. 81.

Pitruzzella, S. (2004) *Introduction to Dramatherapy: Person and Threshold.* Abingdon, UK: Brunner-Routledge.

Schrader, C. (2012) 'We Don't Need Therapy, We Have Ritual': An Overview of the Work of Malidoma Somé and a Personal Experience of a Dagara Grief Ritual. In Schrader, S. (ed.) *Ritual Theatre: The Power of Dramatic Ritual in Personal Development Groups and Clinical Practice.* Kindle edition. London: Jessica Kingsley.

Yalom, D., with Leszcz, M. (2005) *The Theory and Practice of Group Psychotherapy.* Fifth edition. New York: Basic Books.

Zografou, L. (2011) Dramatherapy and Addiction: Learning to Live with Destructiveness. In Dokter, D., Holloway, P. and Seebohm, H. (eds.) *Dramatherapy and Destructiveness: Creating the Evidence Base, Playing with Thanatos.* Kindle edition. Hove, UK: Routledge.

ABBREVIATIONS

ACAT	Association of Cognitive Analytic Therapy (UK)
ADMP	Association of Dance Movement Psychotherapy (UK)
AMTA	American Music Therapy Association
APA	American Psychiatric Association
APD	Antisocial personality disorder
ASD	Autistic spectrum disorder
BAAT	British Association of Art Therapy
BADth	British Association of Dramatherapy
BAMT	British Association of Music Therapy
BPD	Borderline personality disorder
CAT	Cognitive analytic therapy
CBASP	Cognitive behaviour analysis system of psychotherapy
CBT	Cognitive behavioural therapy
CCGs	Clinical commissioning groups (UK)
CMHT	Community mental health team
CNWL	Central and North West London NHS Foundation Trust (UK)
CPA	Care Programme Approach
CPSM	Council for Professions Supplementary to Medicine (UK)
CRT	Crisis resolution team
CT	Cognitive therapy
DBT	Dialectical behavioural therapy
DH	Department of Health (UK) (renamed DHSC [Department of Health & Social Care] in January 2018)
DMP	Dance movement psychotherapist
DMT	Dance movement therapist
EDMR	Eye movement desensitisation and reprocessing
EUPD	Emotionally unstable personality disorder

HCPC	Health and Care Professions Council (UK)
HHS	US Department of Health and Human Services
ICAPT	The International Centre for Arts Psychotherapies (UK based)
ISST	The International Society of Schema Therapy
MACT	Manual assisted cognitive therapy
MBT	Mentalisation-based therapy
MBCT	Mindfulness-based cognitive therapy
MDT	Multidisciplinary team
NAMI	National Alliance on Mental Illness (USA)
NEA.BPD	National Education Alliance for Borderline Personality Disorder (USA)
NIH	National Institutes of Health (US medical research agency)
NICE	National Institute for Health and Care Excellence (UK)
NIMH	National Institute of Mental Health (US mental health research agency)
NHMRC	National Health and Medical Research Centre, for the Australian government
NHS	National Health Service (UK)
OT	Occupational therapy/occupational therapist
PD	Personality disorder
PDI	Personality Disorders Institute (US)
PTSD	Post-traumatic stress disorder
RCT	Randomised controlled trial
ST	Schema therapy
TC	Therapeutic community
UKCP	UK Council for Psychotherapy
WHO	World Health Organization

INDEX